Chinese

Practical Cookery

Chinese

p

This is a Parragon Publishing Book
First printed in 2000

Parragon Publishing
Queen Street House
4 Queen Street
Bath BA1 1HE, UK

ISBN: 0-75254-183-8

Printed in Indonesia

NOTE

Unless otherwise stated,
milk is assumed to be whole, eggs are large,
and pepper is freshly ground black pepper.

Recipes using uncooked eggs should be
avoided by infants, the elderly, pregnant women, and anyone
suffering from an illness

Contents

Introduction   10

Soups

Poultry

Meat

Fish & Seafood

Noodles

Rice

Introduction

The abundance of Chinese restaurants testify to the fact that Chinese cuisine is hugely popular in the West. This book will show you how to recreate authentic Chinese dishes in your own home. Along with the more famous Cantonese and Szechuan specialties, there are also less familiar, but equally delicious, recipes from other regions.

There can be few places in the world nowadays that are unfamiliar with Chinese cuisine. It first became known in the West with the arrival of Chinese workers in the United States during the gold-rush years and today there are Chinese restaurants from San Francisco to Helsinki and from Sydney to Edinburgh. Home-cooked Chinese food is a more recent phenomenon – at least, in the Western kitchen – but, once the ingredients and the wok became easily available and people realized how quick and easy it is to prepare, it soon became popular.

Besides being delicious, which is undoubtedly its most attractive characteristic, Chinese food is both healthy and economic.Carbohydrates, such as rice, which release energy slowly and are recommended by nutritionists as an important part of a healthy diet, are served at every meal. Vegetables, too, play a starring role and they are cooked in ways, such as stir-frying and steaming, which preserve most of their vitamins

and minerals. With a few exceptions, high-cholesterol, high-fat ingredients, such as dairy products and red meat, are either absent altogether or included sparingly.

To a considerable extent, the distinctive flavors of Chinese food resulted from the need to be economical. Bulky but bland foods, such as noodles, were served in relatively large amounts to satisfy the appetite. Expensive ingredients, such as meat and fish, could be used in only small quantities, so they had to be prepared in ways that made the

most of them – combined with herbs, spices and other flavorings. As a result, Chinese cuisine probably has the largest repertoire of any in the world. Fuel was scarce, so fast food was a necessity, resulting in the art of stir-frying in which ingredients are tossed in a round-bottomed, cast-iron wok over high heat to cook quickly. This preserves the flavor, color, texture, and nutrients. Steaming, also a favorite Chinese cooking technique, similarly results in flavorsome, attractive, and nutritious dishes. Bamboo baskets are stacked one above another over a single heat source, thus saving fuel.

A desire for balance and harmony has permeated all aspects of Chinese life since the days of Confucius and this applies to food as well as everything else. Spicy dishes are complemented by sweet-and-sour ones; dry-cooked dishes are balanced with those bathed in sauce, meat is matched with seafood. Dishes are chosen to complement each other in texture, flavor, and color and it is not considered correct to serve more than one dish with the same main ingredient or to cook them using the same technique. Consciously or unconsciously, Chinese cooks, from the housewife to the professional chef, all work to this ancient Taoist principle of Yin and Yang in which balance and contrast are the key. Mealtimes, too, are a time of harmony, when the family – often three generations – gather and share a selection of different dishes, as well as their daily news.

Regional Cooking

China is a huge country and the terrain and climate vary dramatically from one region to another. The crops grown and the livestock raised are equally diverse, giving rise to distinctive regional culinary traditions.

The North

Beijing has been the capital of China for about 1,000 years and, as befits such an important city, its culinary tradition is venerable. The emperor's chief chef was a highly respected figure whose responsibilities included maintaining the health of the Imperial family through a careful balance of herbs, spices, and other ingredients, not simply creating appetizing dishes. Each newly appointed chef considered it a matter of honor to outdo his predecessors and there was also much rivalry with visiting chefs who accompanied dignitaries from other provinces when they came to Beijing. As a result, Beijing cuisine, which still tends to be called Peking in culinary circles, is varied and elegant. It has also been influenced by the Moslem culinary traditions of Central Asia through a number of Tartar invasions. Sesame seeds and the oil and paste made from them, which now feature in the cooking of all regions of China, were originally introduced by the Tartars. The popularity of lamb, rather than pork, unique to the Northern provinces, is probably also a result of Moslem influences. Outside the city, the cooking is simpler and lacks the light-handed touch that is characteristic of Beijing. Sauces and dips tend to be strongly flavored and leeks, onions and garlic are popular vegetables. Mongolian or chrysanthemum firepot dishes – a kind of stock-based fondue – are a speciality.

Wheat, rather than rice, is the staple ingredient in Northern Chinese cuisine and it is used to make noodles, dumplings, crepes, and steamed buns. The climate can be very harsh, but produce in this region includes pak choi, onions, grapes, and peaches. Freshwater fish, especially carp, are popular in the area around the Huang Ho River and shrimp and other seafood are abundant in the coastal regions. Drying, smoking, and pickling are typical preserving techniques.

The South

The first Chinese emigrants came from Kwangtung in the nineteenth century, so this is probably the best-known style of Chinese cuisine in the West. The capital of the province, Canton, was the first major trading port in the country, so it was open to many foreign influences. However,

Regional Cooking

probably the most important influence, from the culinary point of view, was internal. In 1644 the Ming dynasty was overthrown and the Imperial household, together with its retinue of chefs, fled to Canton from Beijing. This has resulted in a style of cooking that is renowned for its variety, sophistication, and excellence.

Steaming is a characteristic technique in Southern China and small fish, little bundles of meat or patties and, above all, dumplings, are often cooked this way. Dim sum, which literally means "to please the heart" are a Cantonese speciality. These small, steamed, filled dumplings are as popular in the West as they are in China, but there they are never served as an appetizer. Rather, they are eaten as snacks at teahouses in the morning or afternoon. In fact, an alternative way of saying you are "going to a dim sum restaurant" is "going out for morning tea".

Char siu roasting is another Cantonese technique. No kind of roasting is common in Chinese homes, which often do not have ovens, but this method is popular in restaurants. Meat is seasoned and marinated well and then roasted at a very high temperature for a short time. This results in the marinade becoming encrusted on the meat in a crisp outer layer, while the inside remains succulent and juicy. Only very tender cuts of meat, particularly pork, can be prepared in this way.

Agricultural produce in this semi-tropical region is abundant and varied. Vegetables are often simply stir-fried and served plain or just with oyster sauce. They may also be combined with meat or fish. Spinach, pak choi, and dried mushrooms feature widely. Fresh fruit, frequently served on its own as a dessert, may also be combined with meat or fish in sweet-and-sour dishes. Fish and seafood, particularly abalone, crab, lobster, shrimp, and scallops, are plentiful. They are usually stir-fried or steamed, often flavored with ginger, and cooking meat with fish is typically Cantonese. Generally, food is not highly spiced, as the Cantonese prefer to enjoy the natural flavors of the ingredients. Light soy sauce is a popular flavoring and other typical sauces include hoisin, oyster, black bean, and plum.

The East

The delta of the Yangtse River makes this one of the most fertile regions in China. The abundant produce includes broccoli, scallion), sweet potatoes, pak choi, soy beans, tea, wheat, rice, corn, and nuts, and the region is well known for its superb vegetarian dishes, noodles, and dumplings. Freshwater fish are found in the many streams and lakes, especially in Kiangsu, which also has a long tradition of deep-sea fishing.

The provinces that comprise this region each have a particular style of cooking, but all are characterized by their richness. The vast cosmopolitan city of Shanghai has assimilated many influences from both other parts of China and abroad. Its cuisine is unusual in that it features dairy products and uses lavish quantities of lard. Shanghai dishes are typically rich, sweet, and beautifully presented. The school of cooking in the surrounding area is known as Kiangche, the name being an amalgamation of the two provinces of Kiangsu and Chekiang. Duck, ham, and fish dishes are specialties, often prepared with piquant spices.

This region produces the best rice wine in the country. It is one of the most prosperous parts of China and has a long gourmet tradition. In Fukien to the South, the cuisine is less sophisticated, relying mainly on fish and a wealth of fresh produce. It is strongly influenced by neighboring Kwangtung.

The West

Surrounded by mountains, Szechuan has a mild, humid climate and rich fertile soil. Its cuisine is most noted for its robust, richly colored dishes flavored with hot spices, such as chilies and Szechuan peppercorns. Strongly flavored ingredients, such as garlic, ginger, onions, leeks, and sesame seed paste are typical and hot pickles are a specialty.

Food preservation techniques, for which Western China is famous, include smoking, drying, salting, and pickling. Yunnan, to the South of Szechuan, produces superb cured, smoked raw ham.

Szechuan cooking is traditionally described as having seven kinds of flavors – sweet, salty, sour, bitter, fragrant, sesame, and hot – based respectively on honey or sugar, soy sauce, vinegar, onions or leeks, garlic or ginger, sesame seeds. and, finally, chilies. Methods of cooking are varied, ranging from dry-frying with very little oil and no additional liquid to cooking in a clear, well-flavored broth, which is then reduced to make a thick, rich sauce. Deep-fried, paper-wrapped bundles of marinated meat or fish are an extremely popular Szechuan speciality.

Basic Recipes

Chinese Stock

This basic stock is used in Chinese cooking not only as the basis for soup-making, but also whenever liquid is required instead of plain water.

MAKES 2½ QUARTS

1 lb 10 oz chicken pieces

1 lb 10 oz pork spare ribs

3¾ quarts cold water

3-4 pieces gingerroot, crushed

3-4 scallions, each tied into a knot

3-4 tbsp Chinese rice wine or dry sherry

1 Trim off any excess fat from the chicken and spareribs; chop them into large pieces.

2 Place the chicken and pork in a large pan with the water; add the ginger and scallion knots.

3 Bring to a boil and skim off the scum. Reduce the heat and simmer uncovered for at least 2-3 hours.

4 Strain the stock, discarding the chicken, pork, ginger, and scallions; add the wine and return to the boil. Simmer for 2-3 minutes.

5 Refrigerate the stock when cool; it will keep to 4-5 days. Alternatively, it can be frozen in small containers and be defrosted as required.

Fresh Chicken Stock

MAKES 1¾ QUARTS

2 lb 4 oz chicken, skinned

2 celery sticks

1 onion

2 carrots

1 garlic clove

few sprigs of fresh parsley

2½ quarts water

salt and pepper

1 Put all the ingredients into a large saucepan.

2 Bring to the boil. Skim away surface scum using a large flat spoon. Reduce the heat to a gentle simmer, partially cover, and cook for 2 hours. Allow to cool.

3 Line a strainer with clean cheesecloth and place over a large jug or bowl. Pour the stock through the strainer. The cooked chicken can be used in another recipe. Discard the other solids. Cover the stock and chill.

4 Skim away any fat that forms before using. Store in the refrigerator for 3-4 days, until required, or freeze in small batches.

Fresh Vegetable Stock

This can be kept chilled for up to three days or frozen for up to three months. Salt is not added when cooking the stock: it is better to season it according to the dish in which it its to be used.

MAKES ABOUT 1½ QUARTS

9 oz shallots

1 large carrot, diced

1 celery stalk, chopped

½ fennel bulb

1 garlic clove

1 bay leaf

a few fresh parsley and tarragon sprigs

2 quarts water

pepper

1 Put all the ingredients in a large saucepan and bring to a boil.

2 Skim off the surface scum with a flat spoon and reduce to a gentle simmer. Partially cover and cook for 45 minutes. Leave to cool.

3 Line a strainer with clean cheesecloth and put over a large measuring jug or bowl. Pour the stock through the strainer. Discard the herbs and vegetables.

4 Cover and store in small quantities in the refrigerator for up to 3 days.

Fresh Lamb Stock

MAKES 1¾ QUARTS

2 lb 4 oz bones from a cooked joint or raw
   chopped lamb bones

2 onions, studded with 6 cloves, or sliced or
chopped coarsely

2 carrots, sliced

1 leek, sliced

1-2 celery stalks, sliced

1 Bouquet Garni

about 2 quarts water

1 Chop or break up the bones and place in a large saucepan with the other ingredients.

2 Bring to a boil and remove any scum from the surface with a perforated spoon. Cover and simmer gently for 3-4 hours. Strain the stock and leave to cool.

3 Remove any fat from the surface and chill. If stored for more than 24 hours the stock must be boiled every day, cooled quickly, and chilled again. The stock may be frozen for up to 2 months; place in a large plastic bag and seal, leaving at least 1 inch headspace to allow for expansion.

Fresh Fish Stock

MAKES 1¾ QUARTS

1 head of a cod or salmon, plus the
   trimmings, skin, and bones or just the
   trimmings, skin, and bones

1-2 onions, sliced

1 carrot, sliced

1-2 celery sticks, sliced

good squeeze of lemon juice

1 Bouquet Garni or 2 fresh or dried bay
   leaves

1 Wash the fish head and trimmings and place in a saucepan. Cover with water and bring to a boil.

2 Remove any scum with a perforated spoon, then add the remaining ingredients. Cover and simmer for about 30 minutes.

3 Strain and cool. Store in ther refrigerator and use within 2 days.

Ccornstarch Paste

Ccornstarch paste is made by mixing 1 part cornstarch with about 1½ parts cold water. Stir until smooth. The paste is used to thicken sauces.

Plain rice

Use long-grain rice or patna rice, or better still, try fragrant Thai rice

SERVES 4

1¼ long-grain rice

about 1 cup cold water

pinch of salt

½ tsp oil (optional)

1 Wash and rinse the rice just once. Place the rice in a saucepan and add enough water so that there is no more than ³/₄ inch of water above the surface of the rice.

2 Bring to boil, add salt and oil (if using), and stir to prevent the rice sticking to the bottom of the pan.

3 Reduce the heat to very, very low, cover, and cook for 15-20 minutes.

4 Remove from the heat and let stand, covered, for 10 minutes or so. Fluff up the rice with a fork or spoon before serving.

Fresh Coconut Milk

To make it from fresh grated coconut, place about 9 oz grated coconut in a bowl, pour over about 1 pint of boiling water to just cover and leave to stand for 1 hour. Strain through cheesecloth, squeezing hard to extract as much thick milk as possible. If you require coconut cream, leave to stand then skim the cream from the surface for use. Unsweetened shredded coconut can also be used in the same quantities.

How to Use This Book

Each recipe contains a wealth of useful information, including a breakdown of nutritional quantities, preparation, and cooking times, and level of difficulty. All of this information is explained in detail below.

The nutritional information provided for each recipe is per serving or per portion. Optional ingredients, variations or serving suggestions have not been included in the calculations.

The number of chef's hats represents the difficulty of each recipe, ranging from easy (1 chef's hat) to difficult (5 chef's hats).

This amount of time represents the preparation of ingredients, including cooling, chilling, and soaking times.

This represents the cooking time.

The ingredients for each recipe are listed in the order they are used.

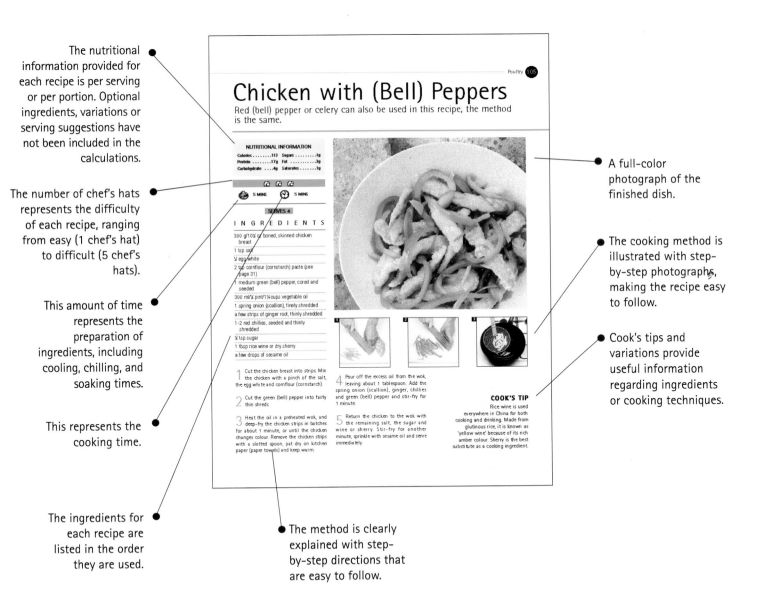

A full-color photograph of the finished dish.

The cooking method is illustrated with step-by-step photographs, making the recipe easy to follow.

Cook's tips and variations provide useful information regarding ingredients or cooking techniques.

The method is clearly explained with step-by-step directions that are easy to follow.

Content of the sample recipe page:

Poultry 105

Chicken with (Bell) Peppers

Red (bell) pepper or celery can also be used in this recipe, the method is the same.

NUTRITIONAL INFORMATION

Calories . . . . 113 Sugars 1g
Protein . . . . 17g Fat 3g
Carbohydrate . . . . 4g Saturates 1g

5 MINS 5 MINS

SERVES 4

INGREDIENTS

300 g/10½ oz boned, skinned chicken breast

1 tsp salt

¼ egg white

2 tsp cornflour (cornstarch) paste (see page 31)

1 medium green (bell) pepper, cored and seeded

300 ml/½ pint/1¼ cups vegetable oil

1 spring onion (scallion), finely shredded

a few strips of ginger root, thinly shredded

1-2 red chillies, seeded and thinly shredded

½ tsp sugar

1 tbsp rice wine or dry sherry

a few drops of sesame oil

1 Cut the chicken breast into strips. Mix the chicken with a pinch of the salt, the egg white and cornflour (cornstarch).

2 Cut the green (bell) pepper into fairly thin shreds.

3 Heat the oil in a preheated wok, and deep-fry the chicken strips in batches for about 1 minute, or until the chicken changes colour. Remove the chicken strips with a slotted spoon, pat dry on kitchen paper (paper towels) and keep warm.

4 Pour off the excess oil from the wok, leaving about 1 tablespoon. Add the spring onion (scallion), ginger, chillies and green (bell) pepper and stir-fry for 1 minute.

5 Return the chicken to the wok with the remaining salt, the sugar and wine or sherry. Stir-fry for another minute, sprinkle with sesame oil and serve immediately.

COOK'S TIP

Rice wine is used everywhere in China for both cooking and drinking. Made from glutinous rice, it is known as 'yellow wine' because of its rich amber colour. Sherry is the best substitute as a cooking ingredient.

Soups

Soup is an integral part of the Chinese meal, but is rarely served as an appetizer as it is in the Western world. Instead, soup is usually served between courses to clear the palate and act as a beverage throughout the meal. The soup is usually presented in a large tureen in the middle of the table for people to help themselves as the meal

progresses. The soups in this chapter combine a range of flavors and textures. There are thicker soups, thin clear consommés, and those which are served with wontons, dumplings, noodles, or rice in them. Ideally the soup should be made with fresh stock, but if this is unavailable, use a bouillon cube and reduce the amount of seasonings, otherwise the soup may be too salty. It is always worth making your own Chinese Stock (see page 14) if you have time.

Corn & Lentil Soup

This pale-colored soup is made with corn and green lentils, and is similar in style to the traditional crab and corn soup.

NUTRITIONAL INFORMATION

Calories 171   Sugars 9g
Protein . . . . .5g   Fat 2g
Carbohydrate . . .30g   Saturates 0.3g

 5 MINS   30 MINS

SERVES 4

INGREDIENTS

2 tbsp green lentils

4 cups vegetable stock

½ inch piece gingerroot, chopped finely

2 tsp soy sauce

1 tsp sugar

1 tbsp cornstarch

3 tbsp dry sherry

11½ oz can corn kernels

1 egg white

1 tsp sesame oil

salt and pepper

TO GARNISH

scallion, cut into strips

red chili, cut into strips

1 Wash the lentils in a strainer. Place in a saucepan with the stock, gingerroot, soy sauce, and sugar. Bring to a boil and boil rapidly, uncovered, for 10 minutes. Skim off any froth on the surface. Reduce the heat, cover, and simmer for 15 minutes.

2 Mix the cornstarch with the sherry in a small bowl. Add the corn with the liquid from the can and cornstarch mixture to the saucepan. Simmer for 2 minutes.

3 Whisk the egg white lightly with the sesame oil. Pour the egg mixture into the soup in a thin stream, remove from the heat, and stir. The egg white will form white strands. Season with salt and pepper to taste.

4 Pour into 4 warm soup bowls and garnish with strips of scallion and red chili. Serve the soup immediately.

COOK'S TIP

To save time use a 15 oz can of green lentils instead of dried ones. Place the lentils and corn in a large saucepan with the stock and flavorings, bring to a boil, and simmer for 2 minutes. Continue the recipe from step 2 as above.

Seafood & Bean Curd Soup

Use shrimp, squid, or scallops, or a combination of all three, in this healthy and tasty soup.

NUTRITIONAL INFORMATION

Calories 97	Sugars 0g	
Protein 17g	Fat 2g	
Carbohydrate 3g	Saturates 0.4g	

 3½ HOURS    10 MINS

SERVES 4

I N G R E D I E N T S

9 oz seafood: peeled shrimp, squid, scallops, and so on, defrosted if frozen

½ egg white, lightly beaten

1 tbsp cornstarch paste (see page 15)

1 cake bean curd

3 cups Chinese Stock (see page 14)

1 tbsp light soy sauce

salt and pepper

fresh cilantro leaves, to garnish (optional)

1 Small shrimp can be left whole; larger ones should be cut into smaller pieces; cut the squid and scallops into small pieces.

2 If raw, mix the shrimp and scallops with the egg white and cornstarch paste to prevent them becoming tough when they are cooked. Cut the cake of bean curd into about 24 small cubes.

3 Bring the stock to a rolling boil. Add the bean curd and soy sauce, bring back to a boil, and simmer for 1 minute.

4 Stir in the seafood, raw pieces first, cooked ones last. Bring back to a boil and simmer for just 1 minute.

5 Adjust the seasoning to taste and serve, garnished with cilantro leaves, if liked.

COOK'S TIP

Bean curd is made from puréed yellow soya beans, which are very high in protein. Although almost tasteless, bean curd absorbs the flavors of other ingredients. It is widely available in grocery stores, Oriental stores, and health-food stores.

Spinach & Bean Curd Soup

This is a very colorful and delicious soup. If spinach is not in season, watercress or lettuce can be used instead.

NUTRITIONAL INFORMATION

Calories 33   Sugar 1g
Protein ....4g   Fat 2g
Carbohydrate ....1g   Saturates 0.2g

 3½ HOURS   10 MINS

SERVES 4

INGREDIENTS

1 cake bean curd

4½ oz spinach leaves without stems

3 cups Chinese Stock or water

1 tbsp light soy sauce

salt and pepper

1 Using a sharp knife, cut the bean curd into small pieces about ¼ inch thick.

2 Wash the spinach leaves thoroughly under cold running water and drain thoroughly.

3 Cut the spinach leaves into small pieces or shreds, discarding any discolored leaves and tough stems. (If possible, use fresh young spinach leaves, which have not yet developed tough ribs. Otherwise, it is important to cut out all the ribs and stems for this soup.) Set aside the spinach until required.

4 In a heated wok or large skillet, bring the Chinese stock or water to a rolling boil.

5 Add the bean curd cubes and light soy sauce, bring back to a boil, and simmer for about 2 minutes over medium heat.

6 Add the shredded spinach leaves and simmer for 1 more minute, stirring gently. Skim the surface of the soup to make it clear, adjust the seasoning to taste.

7 Transfer the spinach and bean curd soup to a warm soup tureen or individual serving bowls and serve with chopsticks, to pick up the pieces of food and a broad, shallow spoon for drinking the soup.

COOK'S TIP

Soup is an integral part of a Chinese meal; it is usually presented in a large bowl placed in the middle of the table and consumed as the meal progresses. It serves as a refresher between different dishes and as a beverage throughout the meal.

Chinese Cabbage Soup

This is a piquant soup, which is slightly sweet-and-sour in flavor. It can be served as a hearty meal or appetizer.

NUTRITIONAL INFORMATION

Calories 65	Sugars 7g
Protein 3g	Fat 0.5g
Carbohydrate 11g	Saturates 0.1g

5 MINS   30 MINS

SERVES 4

INGREDIENTS

1 lb pak choi

2½ cups vegetable stock

1 tbsp rice wine vinegar

1 tbsp light soy sauce

1 tbsp superfine sugar

1 tbsp dry sherry

1 fresh red chili, thinly sliced

1 tbsp cornstarch

2 tbsp water

1 Wash the pak choi thoroughly under cold running water, rinse and drain. Pat dry on paper towels.

2 Trim the stems of the pak choi and shred the leaves.

3 Heat the vegetable stock in a large saucepan. Add the pak choi and cook for 10–15 minutes.

4 Mix together the rice wine vinegar, soy sauce, superfine sugar, and sherry in a small bowl. Add this mixture to the stock, together with the sliced chili.

5 Bring to a boil, lower the heat and cook for 2–3 minutes.

6 Blend the cornstarch with the water to form a smooth paste.

7 Gradually stir the cornstarch mixture into the soup. Cook, stirring constantly, until it thickens. Cook for 4–5 minutes longer.

8 Ladle the Chinese cabbage soup into individual warm serving bowls and serve immediately.

COOKS TIP

Pak choi, also known as bok choi or spoon cabbage, has long, white leaf stems and fleshy, spoon-shaped, shiny green leaves. There are a number of varieties available, which differ mainly in size rather than flavor.

Hot & Sour Soup

This well-known soup from Peking is unusual in that it is thickened. The hot flavor is achieved by the addition of plenty of black pepper.

NUTRITIONAL INFORMATION

Calories 124   Sugars 1g
Protein . . . . .5g   Fat 8g
Carbohydrate . . . .8g   Saturates 1g

3½ HOURS   25 MINS

SERVES 4

I N G R E D I E N T S

2 tbsp cornstarch

4 tbsp water

2 tbsp light soy sauce

3 tbsp rice wine vinegar

½ tsp ground black pepper

1 small fresh red chili, finely chopped

1 egg

2 tbsp vegetable oil

1 onion, chopped

3¾ cups chicken or beef consommé

1 open-cap mushroom, sliced

1¾ oz skinless chicken breast, cut into very thin strips

1 tsp sesame oil

1 In a mixing bowl, blend the cornstarch with the water to form a smooth paste.

2 Add the soy sauce, rice wine vinegar, and black pepper.

3 Finely chop the red chili and add to the ingredients in the bowl; mix well.

4 Break the egg into a separate bowl and beat well. Set aside while you cook the other ingredients.

5 Heat the oil in a heated wok and fry the onion for 1–2 minutes until soft.

6 Stir in the consommé, mushroom, and chicken and bring to a boil. Cook for about 15 minutes or until the chicken is tender.

7 Gradually pour the cornstarch mixture into the soup and cook, stirring constantly, until it thickens.

8 As you are stirring, gradually drizzle the egg into the soup, to create threads of egg.

9 Pour the hot-and-sour soup into a warm tureen or individual serving bowls, sprinkle with the sesame oil, and serve immediately.

Vegetarian Hot & Sour Soup

This popular soup is easy to make and very filling. It can be eaten as a meal on its own or served as an appetizer before a light menu.

NUTRITIONAL INFORMATION

Calories 61   Sugars 1g
Protein . . . . .5g   Fat 2g
Carbohydrate . . . .8g   Saturates 0.2g

30 MINS   10 MINS

SERVES 4

I N G R E D I E N T S

4 Chinese dried mushrooms
  (if unavailable, use open-cap
  mushrooms)

4½ oz firm bean curd

1 cup canned bamboo shoots

2½ cups vegetable stock or water

⅓ cup peas

1 tbsp dark soy sauce

2 tbsp white-wine vinegar

2 tbsp cornstarch

salt and pepper

sesame oil, to serve

1 Place the Chinese dried mushrooms in a small bowl and cover with warm water. Leave to soak for 20–25 minutes.

2 Drain the mushrooms, squeeze out the excess water, and reserve. Remove the tough centers and cut the mushrooms into thin shreds. Shred the bean curd and bamboo shoots.

3 Bring the stock or water to a boil in a large saucepan. Add the mushrooms, bean curd, bamboo shoots, and peas. Simmer for 2 minutes.

4 Mix together the soy sauce, vinegar, and cornstarch with 2 tablespoons of the reserved mushroom liquid.

5 Stir the soy sauce and cornstarch mixture into the soup with the remaining mushroom liquid. Bring to a boil and season with salt and plenty of pepper. Simmer for 2 minutes.

6 Serve in warm bowls with a few drops of sesame oil sprinkled over the top of each.

COOK'S TIP

If you use open-cup mushrooms instead of dried mushrooms, add an extra ⅔ cup vegetable stock or water to the soup, as these mushrooms do not need soaking.

Lettuce & Bean Curd Soup

This is a delicate, clear soup of shredded lettuce and small chunks of bean curd with sliced carrot and scallion.

NUTRITIONAL INFORMATION

Calories	113	Sugars	.........2g
Protein	.........5g	Fat	...........8g
Carbohydrate	....3g	Saturates	.......1g

 5 MINS   15 MINS

SERVES 4

I N G R E D I E N T S

7 oz bean curd

2 tbsp vegetable oil

1 carrot, sliced thinly

½ inch piece gingerroot, cut into thin shreds

3 scallions, sliced diagonally

5 cups vegetable stock

2 tbsp soy sauce

2 tbsp dry sherry

1 tsp sugar

1½ cups romaine lettuce, shredded

salt and pepper

1 Using a sharp knife, cut the bean curd into small cubes.

2 Heat the vegetable oil in a heated wok or large saucepan, add the bean curd, and stir-fry until browned. Remove with a perforated spoon and drain on paper towels.

3 Add the carrot, gingerroot and scallions to the wok or saucepan and stir-fry for 2 minutes.

4 Add the vegetable stock, soy sauce, sherry and sugar. Stir well to mix all the ingredients. Bring to a boil and simmer for 1 minute.

5 Add the romaine lettuce to the wok or saucepan and stir until it has just wilted.

6 Return the bean curd to the pan to reheat. Season with salt and pepper to taste and serve the soup immediately in warm bowls.

COOK'S TIP

For a pretty effect, score grooves along the length of the carrot with a sharp knife before slicing. This will create a flower effect as the carrot is sliced. Or try slicing the carrot on the diagonal to make longer slices.

Noodle & Mushroom Soup

This soup is very quickly and easily put together, and is cooked so each ingredient can still be tasted in the finished dish.

NUTRITIONAL INFORMATION

Calories	74	Sugars	.........1g
Protein	........13g	Fat	...........3g
Carbohydrate	....9g	Saturates	.....0.4g

   4 HOURS 10 MINS

SERVES 4

I N G R E D I E N T S

¼ cup dried Chinese mushrooms or 1⅓ cups field or crimini mushrooms

4 cups hot fresh vegetable stock (page 14)

4½ oz thread egg noodles

2 tsp sunflower oil

3 garlic cloves, crushed

1 inch piece gingerroot, shredded finely

½ tsp mushroom ketchup

1 tsp light soy sauce

2 cups bean sprouts

cilantro leaves, to garnish

  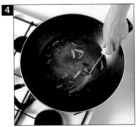

1 Soak the dried Chinese mushrooms, if using, for at least 30 minutes in 1¼ cups of the hot vegetable stock. Remove the stems and discard, then slice the mushrooms. Reserve the stock.

2 Cook the noodles for 2–3 minutes in boiling water. Drain, rinse, and set aside until required.

3 Heat the oil over a high heat in a heated wok or large, heavy skillet. Add the garlic, ginger, and mushrooms. Stir over a high heat for 2 minutes.

4 Add the remaining vegetable stock with the reserved stock and bring to a boil. Add the mushroom catsup and soy sauce and mix well.

5 Stir in the bean sprouts and cook until tender. Serve over the noodles, garnished with cilantro leaves.

COOK'S TIP

Dried mushrooms are highly fragrant and add a special flavor to Chinese dishes. There are many different varieties, but shiitake are considered the best. Although not cheap, a small amount will go a long way and they will keep indefinitely in an airtight jar.

Mushroom Noodle Soup

A light, refreshing clear soup of mushrooms, cucumber, and small pieces of rice noodles, flavored with soy sauce and a touch of garlic.

NUTRITIONAL INFORMATION

Calories 84	Sugars 1g
Protein 1g	Fat 8g
Carbohydrate 3g	Saturates 1g

 5 MINS   10 MINS

SERVES 4

I N G R E D I E N T S

4½ oz flat or open-cup mushrooms

½ cucumber

2 scallions

1 garlic clove

2 tbsp vegetable oil

¼ cup Chinese rice noodles

¾ tsp salt

1 tbsp soy sauce

1 Wash the mushrooms and pat dry on paper towels. Slice thinly. Do not remove the peel because this adds flavor.

2 Halve the cucumber lengthways. Scoop out the seeds, using a teaspoon, and slice the cucumber thinly.

3 Chop the scallions finely and cut the garlic clove into thin strips.

4 Heat the vegetable oil in a large saucepan or wok.

5 Add the scallions and garlic to the pan or wok and stir-fry for 30 seconds. Add the mushrooms and stir-fry for 2–3 minutes.

6 Stir in 2½ cups water. Break the noodles into short lengths and add to the soup. Bring to a boil, stirring occasionally.

7 Add the cucumber slices, salt, and soy sauce, and simmer for 2–3 minutes.

8 Serve the mushroom noodle soup in warm bowls, distributing the noodles and vegetables evenly.

COOK'S TIP

Scooping the seeds out from the cucumber gives it a pretty effect when sliced, and also helps to reduce any bitterness, but leave them in if you prefer.

Wonton Soup

The recipe for the wonton skins makes 24, but the soup requires only half that quantity. The other half can be frozen ready for another time.

NUTRITIONAL INFORMATION

Calories 278   Sugars 2g
Protein ....10g   Fat 5g
Carbohydrate ...50g   Saturates 1g

45 MINS   5 MINS

SERVES 4

I N G R E D I E N T S

WONTON SKINS

1 egg

6 tbsp water

2 cups all-purpose flour, plus extra for dusting

FILLING

½ cup frozen chopped spinach, defrosted

1 tbsp pine nuts, toasted and chopped

¼ cup ground quorn (TVP)

salt

SOUP

2½ cups vegetable stock

1 tbsp dry sherry

1 tbsp light soy sauce

2 scallions, chopped

1 To make the wonton skins, beat the egg lightly in a bowl and mix with the water. Stir in the flour to form a stiff dough. Knead lightly, then cover with a damp cloth, and leave to rest for 30 minutes.

2 Roll the dough out into a large sheet about ¼ inch thick. Cut out 3-inch squares. Dust each one lightly with flour. Only 12 squares are required for the soup so freeze the remainder to use on another occasion as needed.

3 To make the filling, squeeze out the excess water from the spinach. Mix the spinach with the pine nuts and quorn (TVP) until thoroughly combined. Season with salt.

4 Divide the mixture into 12 equal portions. Using a teaspoon, place one portion in the center of each square. Seal the wontons by bringing the opposite corners of each square together and squeezing well.

5 To make the soup, bring the vegetable stock, sherry, and soy sauce to the boil, add the wontons and boil rapidly for 2–3 minutes. Add the scallions and serve in warm bowls immediately.

Chicken Wonton Soup

This Chinese-style soup is delicious as a first course to an oriental meal or as a light meal in itself.

NUTRITIONAL INFORMATION

Calories 101	Sugars 0.3g	
Protein 14g	Fat 4g	
Carbohydrate 3g	Saturates 1g	

15 MINS

10 MINS

SERVES 4–6

I N G R E D I E N T S

FILLING

12 oz ground chicken

1 tbsp soy sauce

1 tsp grated, fresh gingerroot

1 garlic clove, crushed

2 tsp sherry

2 scallions, chopped

1 tsp sesame oil

1 egg white

½ tsp cornstarch

½ tsp sugar

about 35 wonton skins

SOUP

6 cups chicken stock

1 tbsp light soy sauce

1 scallion, shredded

1 small carrot, cut into very thin slices

1 Place all the ingredients for the filling in a large bowl and mix until thoroughly combined.

2 Place a small spoonful of the filling in the center of each wonton wrapper.

3 Dampen the edges and gather up the wonton wrapper to form a small pouch enclosing the filling.

4 Cook the filled wontons in boiling water for 1 minute or until they float to the top. Remove with a perforated spoon and set aside.

5 Bring the chicken stock to a boil. Add the soy sauce, scallion, and carrot.

6 Add the wontons to the soup and simmer gently for 2 minutes. Serve.

COOK'S TIP

Make double quantities of wonton skins and freeze the remainder. Place small squares of baking parchment between each skin, then place in a freezer bag and freeze. Defrost thoroughly before using.

Clear Chicken & Egg Soup

This tasty chicken soup has the addition of poached eggs, making it both delicious and filling. Use fresh, homemade stock for a better flavor.

NUTRITIONAL INFORMATION

Calories 138   Sugars 1g
Protein ....16g   Fat 7g
Carbohydrate ....1g   Saturates 2g

5 MINS   35 MINS

SERVES 4

INGREDIENTS

1 tsp salt

1 tbsp rice wine vinegar

4 eggs

3¾ cups chicken stock

1 leek, sliced

4½ oz broccoli flowerets

1 cup shredded cooked chicken

2 open-cap mushrooms, sliced

1 tbsp dry sherry

dash of chili sauce

chili powder, to garnish

VARIATION

Use 4 dried Chinese mushrooms, rehydrated according to the package directions, instead of the open-cap mushrooms, if you prefer.

1 Bring a large saucepan of water to a boil and add the salt and rice wine vinegar.

2 Reduce the heat so it is just simmering, and carefully break the eggs into the water, one at a time. Poach the eggs for 1 minute.

3 Remove the poached eggs with a perforated spoon and set aside.

4 Bring the chicken stock to a boil in a separate pan and add the leek, broccoli, chicken, mushrooms, and sherry and season with chili sauce to taste. Cook for 10–15 minutes.

5 Add the poached eggs to the soup and cook for 2 minutes. Carefully transfer the soup and poached eggs to 4 soup bowls. Dust with a little chili powder and serve immediately.

Chicken Soup with Almonds

This soup can also be made using pheasant breasts. For a really gamey flavor, make game stock from the carcass, and use in the soup.

NUTRITIONAL INFORMATION

Calories 219   Sugars 2g
Protein ....18g   Fat 15g
Carbohydrate ....2g   Saturates 2g

10 MINS   20 MINS

SERVES 4

I N G R E D I E N T S

1 large or 2 small boneless skinned
  chicken breast halves

1 tbsp sunflower oil

4 scallions, thinly sliced diagonally

1 carrot, cut into julienne strips

3 cups chicken stock

finely grated peel of ½ lemon

⅓ cup ground almonds

1 tbsp light soy sauce

1 tbsp lemon juice

¼ cup slivered almonds, toasted

salt and pepper

1 Cut each chicken breast into 4 strips lengthways, then slice very thinly across the grain to make shreds of chicken.

2 Heat the oil in a heated wok, swirling it around until really hot.

3 Add the scallions and cook for 2 minutes. Add the chicken and toss it for 3-4 minutes until sealed and almost cooked through, stirring all the time. Add the carrot strips and stir.

4 Add the stock to the wok and bring to a boil. Add the lemon peel, ground almonds, soy sauce, lemon juice, and plenty of seasoning. Bring back to a boil and simmer, uncovered, for 5 minutes, stirring from time to time.

5 Adjust the seasoning, add most of the toasted slivered almonds and continue to cook for a further 1-2 minutes.

6 Serve the soup very hot, in individual bowls, sprinkled with the remaining slivered almonds.

COOK'S TIP

To make game stock, break up a pheasant carcass and place in a pan with 2 quarts of water. Bring to a boil slowly, skimming off any scum. Add 1 bouquet garni, 1 peeled onion, and seasoning. Cover and simmer gently for 1½ hours. Strain and skim any surface fat.

Chicken & Corn Soup

A hint of chili and sherry flavor this soup while red bell pepper and tomato add color.

NUTRITIONAL INFORMATION

Calories ....199 Sugars 8g
Protein ....12g Fat 8g
Carbohydrate ...19g Saturates 1g

 5 MINS   20 MINS

SERVES 4

I N G R E D I E N T S

1 skinless, boneless chicken breast halves, about 6 oz

2 tbsp sunflower oil

2–3 scallions, thinly sliced diagonally

1 small or ½ large red bell pepper, thinly sliced

1 garlic clove, crushed

4½ oz baby corn-on-the-cob, thinly sliced

1 quart chicken stock

7 oz can of corn niblets, well drained

2 tbsp sherry

2–3 tsp bottled sweet chili sauce

2–3 tsp cornstarch

2 tomatoes, quartered, seeded, and sliced

salt and pepper

chopped fresh cilantro or parsley, to garnish

1 Cut the chicken breast halves into 4 strips lengthways, then cut each strip into narrow slices across the grain.

2 Heat the oil in a heated wok or skillet, swirling it around until it is really hot.

3 Add the chicken and stir-fry for 3–4 minutes, moving it around the wok until it is well sealed all over and almost cooked through.

4 Add the scallions, bell pepper, and garlic and stir-fry for 2–3 minutes. Add the corn and stock and bring them to a boil.

5 Add the corn niblets, sherry, sweet chili sauce, and salt to taste and simmer for 5 minutes, stirring from time to time.

6 Blend the cornstarch with a little cold water. Add to the soup and bring to a boil, stirring until the sauce thickens. Add the tomato slices, season to taste, and simmer for 1–2 minutes.

7 Serve the chicken and corn soup hot, sprinkled with chopped cilantro or parsley.

Curried Chicken & Corn Soup

Tender cooked chicken strips and baby corn-on-the-cobs are the main ingredients in this delicious clear soup, with just a hint of ginger.

NUTRITIONAL INFORMATION

Calories	206	Sugars	........5g
Protein	........29g	Fat	..........5g
Carbohydrate	...13g	Saturates	.......1g

5 MINS   30 MINS

SERVES 4

INGREDIENTS

6 oz can corn kernels, drained

3¾ cups chicken stock

2½ cups cooked, lean chicken, cut into strips

16 baby corn cobs

1 tsp Chinese curry powder

½-inch piece fresh gingerroot, grated

3 tbsp light soy sauce

2 tbsp chopped chives

1 Place the canned corn in a food processor, together with ⅔ cup of the chicken stock and process until the mixture forms a smooth purée.

2 Pass the sweetcorn purée through a fine strainer, pressing with the back of a spoon to remove any husks.

3 Pour the remaining chicken stock into a large saucepan and add the strips of cooked chicken. Stir in the corn purée.

4 Add the baby corn cobs and bring the soup to a boil. Boil the soup for 10 minutes.

5 Add the Chinese curry powder, grated fresh gingerroot, and light soy sauce and stir well. Cook for a further 10–15 minutes.

6 Stir the chopped chives into the soup.

7 Transfer the curried chicken and corn soup to warm soup bowls and serve immediately.

COOK'S TIP

Prepare the soup up to 24 hours in advance without adding the chicken, cool, cover, and store in the refrigerator. Add the chicken and heat the soup through thoroughly before serving.

Chicken Noodle Soup

Quick to make, this hot-and-spicy soup is hearty and warming. If you like your food fiery, add a chopped dried or fresh chili with its seeds.

NUTRITIONAL INFORMATION

Calories	196	Sugars	.........4g
Protein	........16g	Fat	...........11g
Carbohydrate	....8g	Saturates	.......2g

 10 MINS 25 MINS

SERVES 4–6

I N G R E D I E N T S

1 sheet of dried egg noodles from a 9 oz pack

1 tbsp oil

4 skinless, boneless chicken thighs, diced

1 bunch scallions, sliced

2 garlic cloves, chopped

¾ inch piece fresh gingerroot, finely chopped

3¾ cups chicken stock

scant 1 cup coconut milk

3 tsp red curry paste

3 tbsp peanut butter

2 tbsp light soy sauce

1 small red bell pepper, chopped

½ cup frozen peas

salt and pepper

VARIATION

Green curry paste can be used instead of red curry paste for a less fiery flavor.

1 Put the noodles in a shallow dish and soak in boiling water as the package directions.

2 Heat the oil in a large heated saucepan or wok.

3 Add the diced chicken to the pan or wok and fry for 5 minutes, stirring until lightly browned.

4 Add the white part of the scallions, the garlic, and ginger and fry for 2 minutes, stirring.

5 Stir in the chicken stock, coconut milk, red curry paste, peanut butter, and soy sauce.

6 Season with salt and pepper to taste. Bring to a boil, stirring, then simmer for 8 minutes, stirring occasionally.

7 Add the red bell pepper, peas, and green scallion tops and cook for 2 minutes.

8 Add the drained noodles and heat through. Spoon the chicken noodle soup into warm bowls and serve with a spoon and fork.

Spicy Chicken Noodle Soup

This filling soup is filled with spicy flavors and bright colors for a really attractive and hearty dish.

NUTRITIONAL INFORMATION

Calories ....286 Sugars 21g
Protein ....22g Fat 6g
Carbohydrate ...37g Saturates 1g

15 MINS   20 MINS

SERVES 4

I N G R E D I E N T S

2 tbsp tamarind paste

4 red chilies, finely chopped

2 cloves garlic, crushed

1-inch piece Thai ginger, peeled and very finely chopped

4 tbsp fish sauce

2 tbsp palm sugar or ordinary white sugar

8 lime leaves, roughly torn

5 cups chicken stock

12 oz boneless chicken breast halves

¾ cup carrots, very thinly sliced

2½ cups sweet potato, diced

3½ oz baby corn-on-the-cobs, halved

3 tbsp fresh cilantro, roughly chopped

3½ oz cherry tomatoes, halved

5½ oz flat rice noodles

fresh cilantro, chopped,to garnish

1 Heat a large wok or skillet. Place the tamarind paste, chilies, garlic, ginger, fish sauce, sugar, lime leaves, and chicken stock in the wok and bring to a boil, stirring constantly. Reduce the heat and cook for about 5 minutes.

2 Using a sharp knife, thinly slice the chicken. Add the chicken to the wok and cook for a further 5 minutes, stirring the mixture well.

3 Reduce the heat and add the carrots, sweet potato, and baby corn cobs to the wok. Leave to simmer, uncovered, for 5 minutes, or until the vegetables are just tender and the chicken is completely cooked through.

4 Stir in the chopped fresh cilantro, cherry tomatoes, and flat rice noodles.

5 Leave the soup to simmer for about 5 minutes, or until the noodles are tender.

6 Garnish the spicy chicken noodle soup with chopped fresh cilantro and serve hot.

Spicy Shrimp Soup

Lime leaves are used as a flavoring in this soup to add tartness. Look for them in Oriental grocery stores.

NUTRITIONAL INFORMATION

Calories 217   Sugars 16g
Protein . . . . .16g   Fat 4g
Carbohydrate . . .31g   Saturates 1g

    10 MINS   20 MINS

SERVES 4

INGREDIENTS

2 tbsp tamarind paste

4 red chilies, very finely chopped

2 cloves garlic, crushed

1-inch piece Thai ginger, peeled and very finely chopped

4 tbsp fish sauce

2 tbsp palm sugar or ordinary white sugar

5 cups fish stock

8 lime leaves

¾ cup carrots, very thinly sliced

12 oz sweet potato, diced

1 cup baby corn-on-the-cobs, halved

3 tbsp fresh cilantro, roughly chopped

3½ oz cherry tomatoes, halved

8 oz fan-tail shrimp

1 Place the tamarind paste, red chilies, garlic, ginger, fish sauce, sugar, and fish stock in a heated wok or large, heavy skillet. Roughly tear the lime leaves and add to the wok. Bring to a boil, stirring constantly to blend the flavors.

2 Reduce the heat and add the carrot, sweet potato, and baby corn cobs to the mixture in the wok.

3 Leave the soup to simmer, uncovered, for about 10 minutes, or until the vegetables are just tender.

4 Stir the cilantro, cherry tomatoes, and shrimp into the soup and heat through for 5 minutes.

5 Transfer the soup to a warm soup tureen or individual serving bowls and serve hot.

COOK'S TIP

Thai ginger or galangal is a member of the ginger family, but it is yellow in color with pink sprouts. The flavor is aromatic and less pungent than that of ginger.

Crab & Corn Soup

Crab and corn are classic ingredients in Chinese cooking. Here egg noodles are added for a filling dish.

NUTRITIONAL INFORMATION

Calories . . . . . . .324 Sugars 6g
Protein . . . . .27g Fat 8g
Carbohydrate . . .39g Saturates 2g

 5 MINS   20 MINS

SERVES 4

I N G R E D I E N T S

1 tbsp sunflower oil

1 tsp Chinese five-spice powder

1½ cups carrots, cut into sticks

½ cup canned or frozen corn kernels

¼ cup peas

6 scallions, trimmed and sliced

1 red chili, seeded and very thinly sliced

7 oz can white crab meat

6 oz egg noodles

7½ cups fish stock

3 tbsp soy sauce

1 Heat the sunflower oil in a large heated wok or heavy-based skillet.

2 Add the Chinese five-spice powder, carrots, corn, peas, scallions, and red chili to the wok and cook for about 5 minutes, stirring constantly.

3 Add the crabmeat to the wok and stir-fry the mixture for 1 minute, distributing the crabmeat evenly.

4 Roughly break up the egg noodles and add to the wok.

5 Pour the fish stock and soy sauce into the mixture in the wok and bring them to a boil.

6 Cover the wok or skillet and leave the soup to simmer for 5 minutes.

7 Stir once more, then transfer the soup to a warm soup tureen or individual serving bowls and serve at once.

COOK'S TIP

Chinese five-spice powder is a mixture of star anise, fennel, cloves, cinnamon, and Szechuan pepper. It has an unmistakeable flavor. Use it sparingly, as it is very pungent.

Peking Duck Soup

This is a hearty and robustly flavored soup, containing pieces of duck and vegetables cooked in a rich stock.

NUTRITIONAL INFORMATION

Calories	92	Sugars	....3g
Protein	....8g	Fat	....5g
Carbohydrate	....3g	Saturates	....1g

5 MINS   35 MINS

SERVES 4

INGREDIENTS

4½ oz lean duck breast meat

8 oz Chinese leaves cabbage

3¾ cups chicken or duck stock

1 tbsp dry sherry or rice wine

1 tbsp light soy sauce

2 garlic cloves, crushed

pinch of ground star anise

1 tbsp sesame seeds

1 tsp sesame oil

1 tbsp chopped fresh parsley

1 Remove the skin from the duck breast and finely dice the flesh.

2 Using a sharp knife, shred the Chinese cabbage.

3 Put the stock in a large saucepan and bring to a boil. Add the sherry or rice wine, soy sauce, diced duck meat, and shredded Chinese cabbage and stir to mix thoroughly. Reduce the heat and leave to simmer gently for 15 minutes.

4 Stir in the garlic and star anise and cook over a low heat for a further 10–15 minutes, until the duck is tender.

5 Meanwhile, dry-fry the sesame seeds in a heated, heavy-based skillet or wok, stirring constantly.

6 Remove the sesame seeds from the pan and stir them into the soup, together with the sesame oil and chopped fresh parsley.

7 Spoon the soup into warm bowls and serve immediately.

VARIATION

If Chinese cabbage is unavailable, use leafy green cabbage instead. You can to adjust the quantity to taste, as Western cabbage has a stronger flavor and aroma than Chinese cabbage.

Beef & Vegetable Noodle Soup

Thin strips of beef are marinated in soy sauce and garlic to form the basis of this delicious soup. Served with noodles, it is both filling and delicious.

NUTRITIONAL INFORMATION

Calories 186	Sugars 1g	
Protein 17g	Fat 5g	
Carbohydrate ...20g	Saturates 1g	

35 MINS   20 MINS

SERVES 4

INGREDIENTS

8 oz lean beef

1 garlic clove, crushed

2 scallions, chopped

3 tbsp soy sauce

1 tsp sesame oil

8 oz egg noodles

3¾ cups beef stock

3 baby corn-on-the-cobs, sliced

½ leek, shredded

1 cup broccoli, cut into flowerets

pinch of chili powder

1 Using a sharp knife, cut the beef into thin strips and place in a bowl with the garlic, scallions, soy sauce, and sesame oil.

2 Mix together the ingredients in the bowl, turning the beef to coat. Cover and leave to marinate in the refrigerator for 30 minutes.

3 Cook the noodles in a saucepan of boiling water for 3–4 minutes. Drain the noodles thoroughly and set aside.

4 Put the beef stock in a large saucepan and bring to a boil. Add the beef, together with the marinade, the baby corn, leek, and broccoli. Cover and leave to simmer over low heat for 7–10 minutes, or until the beef and vegetables are tender and cooked through.

5 Stir in the noodles and chili powder and cook for 2–3 minutes longer.

6 Transfer the soup to bowls and serve immediately.

VARIATION

Vary the vegetables used, or use those to hand. If preferred, use a few drops of chili sauce instead of chili powder, but remember it is very hot!

Lamb & Rice Soup

This is a very filling soup, because it contains rice and tender pieces of lamb. Serve before a light main course.

NUTRITIONAL INFORMATION

Calories	116	Sugars	.......0.2g
Protein	.........9g	Fat	..........4g
Carbohydrate	...12g	Saturates	.......2g

5 MINS   35 MINS

SERVES 4

I N G R E D I E N T S

5½ oz lean boneless lamb

¼ cup long-grain rice

3¾ cups lamb stock

1 leek, sliced

1 garlic clove, thinly sliced

2 tsp light soy sauce

1 tsp rice wine vinegar

1 medium open-cap mushroom, thinly
   sliced

salt

1 Using a sharp knife, trim any fat from the lamb and cut the meat into thin strips; set aside until required.

2 Bring a large pan of lightly salted water to a boil and add the rice. Bring back to a boil, stir once, reduce the heat, and cook for 10–15 minutes, until tender.

3 Drain the rice, rinse under cold running water, drain again, and set aside until required.

4 Meanwhile, put the lamb stock in a large saucepan and bring to a boil.

5 Add the lamb strips, leek, garlic, soy sauce, and rice wine vinegar to the stock in the pan. Reduce the heat, cover, and leave to simmer for 10 minutes, or until the lamb is tender and cooked through.

6 Add the mushroom slices and the rice to the pan and cook for 2–3 minutes longer, or until the mushroom is completely cooked through.

7 Ladle the soup into 4 individual warm soup bowls and serve immediately.

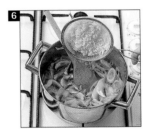

VARIATION

Use a few dried Chinese mushrooms, rehydrated according to the packet instructions and chopped, as an alternative to the open-cap mushroom. Add the Chinese mushrooms with the lamb in step 4.

Chinese Potato & Pork Broth

In this recipe the pork is seasoned with traditional Chinese flavorings – soy sauce, rice wine vinegar, and a dash of sesame oil.

NUTRITIONAL INFORMATION

Calories	166	Sugars	.........2g
Protein	........10g	Fat	...........5g
Carbohydrate	...26g	Saturates	.......1g

5 MINS   20 MINS

SERVES 4

I N G R E D I E N T S

4½ cups chicken stock

2 large potatoes, diced

2 tbsp rice wine vinegar

2 tbsp cornstarch

4 tbsp water

4½ oz pork tenderloin, sliced

1 tbsp light soy sauce

1 tsp sesame oil

1 carrot, cut into very thin strips

1 tsp gingerroot, chopped

3 scallions, sliced thinly

1 red bell pepper, sliced

8 oz can bamboo shoots, drained

VARIATION

For extra heat, add 1 chopped red chili or 1 tsp of chili powder to the soup in step 5.

1 Add the chicken stock, diced potatoes and 1 tbsp of the rice wine vinegar to a saucepan and bring to a boil. Reduce the heat until the stock is just simmering.

2 Mix the cornstarch with the water, then stir into the hot stock.

3 Bring the stock back to a boil, stirring until thickened, then reduce the heat until it is just simmering again.

4 Place the pork slices in a dish and season with the remaining rice wine vinegar, the soy sauce, and sesame oil.

5 Add the pork slices, carrot strips, and ginger to the stock and cook for 10 minutes. Stir in the scallions, red bell pepper, and bamboo shoots. Cook for 5 minutes longer. Pour the soup into warm bowls and serve immediately.

Pork & Szechuan Vegetable

Sold in cans, Szechuan preserved vegetable is pickled mustard root that is hot and salty, so rinse them in water before use.

NUTRITIONAL INFORMATION

Calories 135	Sugars 1g
Protein 14g	Fat 7g
Carbohydrate 3g	Saturates 2g

 5 MINS   5 MINS

SERVES 4

INGREDIENTS

9 oz pork tenderloin

2 tsp cornstarch paste (see page 15)

4½ oz Szechuan preserved vegetable

3 cups Chinese stock (see page 14) or water

salt and pepper

a few drops sesame oil (optional)

2-3 chives, sliced, to garnish

1 Heat a wok or large, heavy-based skillet.

2 Using a sharp knife, cut the pork across the grain into thin shreds.

3 Mix the pork with the cornstarch paste until the pork is completely coated in the mixture.

4 Thoroughly wash and rinse the Szechuan preserved vegetable, then pat dry on absorbent paper towels. Cut the Szechuan preserved vegetable into thin shreds the same size as the pork.

5 Pour either the Chinese stock or water into the wok or skillet and bring to a rolling boil. Add the pork to the wok and stir to separate the shreds. Return to a boil.

6 Add the shredded Szechuan preserved vegetable and bring back to a boil once more.

7 Adjust the seasoning to taste and sprinkle with sesame oil. Serve hot, garnished with chives.

COOK'S TIP

Szechuan preserved vegetable is mustard green root, pickled in salt and chilies. Available in cans from Chinese supermarkets, it gives a crunchy, spicy taste to dishes. Rinse in cold water before use and store in the refrigerator.

Chili Fish Soup

Chinese mushrooms add an intense flavor to this soup which is unique.
If they are unavailable, use sliced open-cap mushrooms.

NUTRITIONAL INFORMATION

Calories 166	Sugars 1g
Protein 23g	Fat 7g
Carbohydrate 4g	Saturates 1g

15 MINS   15 MINS

SERVES 4

INGREDIENTS

½ oz Chinese dried mushrooms

2 tbsp sunflower oil

1 onion, sliced

1½ cups snow peas

1½ cups bamboo shoots

3 tbsp sweet chili sauce

5 cups fish or vegetable stock

3 tbsp light soy sauce

2 tbsp fresh cilantro, plus extra to garnish

1 lb cod fillet, skinned and cubed

COOK'S TIP

Cod is used in this recipe as it is a meaty white fish. For real luxury, use monkfish tail instead. There are many different varieties of dried mushrooms, but shiitake are best. They are not cheap, but a small amount will go a long way.

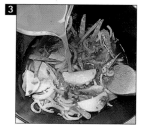

1 Place the mushrooms in a large bowl. Pour over enough boiling water to cover and leave to stand for 5 minutes. Drain the mushrooms thoroughly in a colander. Using a sharp knife, roughly chop the mushrooms.

2 Heat the sunflower oil in a heated wok or large skillet. Add the sliced onion to the wok and stir-fry for 5 minutes, or until softened.

3 Add the snow peas, bamboo shoots, chili sauce, stock, and soy sauce to the wok and bring to a boil.

4 Add the cilantro and cod and leave to simmer for 5 minutes or until the fish is cooked through.

5 Transfer the soup to warm bowls, garnish with extra cilantro, if wished, and serve hot.

Shrimp Dumpling Soup

These small dumplings filled with shrimp and pork can be made slightly larger and served as dim sum, if you prefer.

NUTRITIONAL INFORMATION

Calories	311	Sugars	.........2g
Protein	........18g	Fat	...........8g
Carbohydrate	...41g	Saturates	.......2g

20 MINS   10 MINS

SERVES 4

INGREDIENTS

DUMPLINGS

1⅝ cups all-purpose flour

¼ cup boiling water

⅛ cup cold water

1½ tsp vegetable oil

FILLING

4½ oz ground pork

4½ oz cooked peeled shrimp, chopped

⅓ cup canned water chestnuts, drained, rinsed and chopped

1 celery stick, chopped

1 tsp cornstarch

1 tbsp sesame oil

1 tbsp light soy sauce

SOUP

3¾ cups fish stock

1¾ oz cellophane noodles

1 tbsp dry sherry

chopped chives, to garnish

1 To make the dumplings, mix together the flour, boiling water, cold water, and oil in a bowl until a pliable dough is formed.

2 Knead the dough on a lightly floured surface for 5 minutes. Cut the dough into 16 equal size pieces.

3 Roll the dough pieces into circles about 3 inches in diameter.

4 Mix the filling ingredients together in a large bowl.

5 Spoon a little of the filling mixture into the center of each circle. Bring the edges of the dough together, scrunching them up to form a "moneybag" shape. Twist the gathered edges to seal.

6 Pour the fish stock into a large saucepan and bring to a boil.

7 Add the cellophane noodles, dumplings, and dry sherry to the pan and cook for 4–5 minutes until the noodles and dumplings are tender. Garnish with chopped chives and serve immediately.

Shrimp Soup

This soup is an interesting mix of colors and textures. The egg can be made into a flat omelet and added as thin strips, if preferred.

NUTRITIONAL INFORMATION

Calories 123	Sugars 0.2g	
Protein 13g	Fat 8g	
Carbohydrate 1g	Saturates 1g	

 5 MINS   20 MINS

SERVES 4

I N G R E D I E N T S

2 tbsp sunflower oil

2 scallions, thinly sliced diagonally

1 carrot, coarsely grated

4½ oz large closed cup mushrooms, thinly sliced

4 cups fish or vegetable stock

½ tsp Chinese five-spice powder

1 tbsp light soy sauce

4½ oz large or jumbo peeled shrimp or peeled tiger shrimp, defrosted if frozen

½ bunch watercress, trimmed and roughly chopped

1 egg, well beaten

salt and pepper

4 large shrimp in shells, to garnish (optional)

1 Heat the oil in a wok, swirling it around until really hot. Add the scallions and stir-fry for a minute, then add the carrots and mushrooms and continue to cook for about 2 minutes.

2 Add the stock and bring to a boil, then season to taste with salt and pepper, five-spice powder, and soy sauce and simmer for 5 minutes.

3 If the shrimp are really large, cut them in half before adding to the wok. Simmer for 3-4 minutes.

4 Add the watercress to the wok and mix well, then slowly pour in the beaten egg in a circular movement so it cooks in threads in the soup. Adjust the seasoning and serve each portion topped with a whole shrimp.

COOK'S TIP

The large open mushrooms with black gills give the best flavor but they tend to spoil the color of the soup, making it very dark. Oyster mushrooms can also be used.

Fish & Vegetable Soup

A chunky fish soup with strips of vegetables, all flavored with ginger and lemon, makes a meal in itself.

NUTRITIONAL INFORMATION

Calories 88   Sugars 1g
Protein . . . . .12g   Fat 3g
Carbohydrate . . . .3g   Saturates 0.5g

40 MINS   20 MINS

SERVES 4

INGREDIENTS

9 oz white fish fillets (cod, halibut, haddock, sole, and so on)

½ tsp ground ginger

½ tsp salt

1 small leek, trimmed

2-4 crab sticks, defrosted if frozen (optional)

1 tbsp sunflower oil

1 large carrot, cut into julienne strips

8 canned water chestnuts, thinly sliced

5 cups fish or vegetable stock

1 tbsp lemon juice

1 tbsp light soy sauce

1 large zucchini, cut into julienne strips

black pepper

1 Remove any skin from the fish and cut into 1-inch cubes. Combine the ground ginger and salt and use to rub into the pieces of fish. Leave to marinate for at least 30 minutes.

2 Meanwhile, divide the green and white parts of the leek. Cut each part into 1 inch pieces and then into julienne strips down the length of each piece, keeping the two parts separate. Slice the crabsticks into ½-inch pieces.

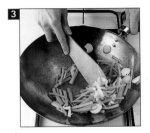

3 Heat the oil in the wok, swirling it around so it is really hot. Add the white part of the leek and stir-fry for a couple of minutes, then add the carrots and water chestnuts and continue to cook for 1-2 minutes, stirring thoroughly.

4 Add the stock and bring to a boil. Add the lemon juice and soy sauce and simmer for 2 minutes.

5 Add the fish and continue to cook for about 5 minutes until the fish begins to break up a little, then add the green part of the leek and the zucchini and simmer for about 1 minute. Add the sliced crabsticks, if using, and season to taste with black pepper. Simmer for a minute or so longer and serve very hot.

COOK'S TIP

To skin fish, place the fillet skin-side down and insert a sharp, flexible knife at one end between the flesh and the skin. Hold the skin at the end, keep the blade flat against the skin, slice the flesh using a sawing motion.

Oriental Fish Soup

This is a deliciously different fish soup that is cooked quickly and easily in a microwave.

NUTRITIONAL INFORMATION

Calories 105
Sugars 1g
Protein 13g
Fat 5g
Carbohydrate 1g
Saturates 1g

 20 MINS   10 MINS

SERVES 4

INGREDIENTS

1 egg

1 tsp sesame seeds, toasted

1 celery stick, chopped

1 carrot, cut into julienne strips

4 scallions, sliced on the diagonal

1 tbsp oil

1½ cups fresh spinach

3½ cups hot vegetable stock

4 tsp light soy sauce

9 oz haddock, skinned and cut into small chunks

salt and pepper

VARIATION

Instead of topping the soup with omelet shreds, pour the beaten egg, without the sesame seeds, into the hot stock at the end of the cooking time. The egg will set in pretty strands to give a flowery look.

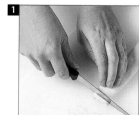

1 Beat the egg with the sesame seeds and seasoning. Lightly oil a plate and pour on the egg mixture. Cook on HIGH power for 1½ minutes until just setting in the center. Leave to stand for a few minutes then remove from the plate. Roll up the egg and shred thinly.

2 Mix together the celery, carrot, scallions, and oil. Cover and cook on HIGH power for 3 minutes.

3 Wash the spinach thoroughly under cold, running water. Cut off and discard any long stems and drain well. Shred the spinach finely.

4 Add the hot stock, soy sauce, haddock, and spinach to the vegetable mixture. Cover and cook on HIGH power for 5 minutes. Stir the soup and season to taste. Serve in warm bowls with the shredded egg scattered over.

Fish Soup with Wontons

This soup is topped with small wontons filled with shrimp, making it both very tasty and satisfying.

NUTRITIONAL INFORMATION

Calories	115	Sugars	.........0g
Protein	........16g	Fat	...........5g
Carbohydrate	....1g	Saturates	.......1g

10 MINS   15 MINS

SERVES 4

INGREDIENTS

4½ oz large, cooked, peeled shrimp

1 tsp chopped chives

1 small garlic clove, finely chopped

1 tbsp vegetable oil

12 wonton skins

1 small egg, beaten

3¾ cups fish stock

6 oz white fish fillet, diced

dash of chili sauce

sliced fresh red chili and chives, to garnish

1 Roughly chop a quarter of the shrimp and mix together with the chopped chives and garlic.

2 Heat the oil in a heated wok or large skillet until it is really hot.

3 Stir-fry the shrimp mixture for 1–2 minutes. Remove from the heat and set aside to cool completely.

4 Spread out the wonton skins on a work counter. Spoon a little of the shrimp filling into the center of each skin. Brush the edges of the skins with beaten egg and press the edges together, scrunching them to form a "moneybag" shape. Set aside while you are preparing the soup.

5 Pour the fish stock into a large saucepan and bring to a boil. Add the diced white fish and the remaining shrimp and cook for 5 minutes.

6 Season to taste with the chili sauce. Add the wontons and cook for a further 5 minutes.

7 Spoon into warm serving bowls, garnish with sliced red chili and chives, and serve immediately.

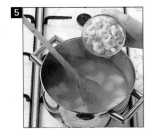

VARIATION

Replace the shrimp with cooked crabmeat for an alternative flavor.

Three-Flavor Soup

Ideally, use raw shrimp in this soup. If that is not possible, add cooked ones at the very last stage.

NUTRITIONAL INFORMATION

Calories 117	Sugars 0g
Protein 20g	Fat 3g
Carbohydrate 2g	Saturates 1g

3½ HOURS   10 MINS

SERVES 4

I N G R E D I E N T S

4½ oz skinned, boned chicken breast

4½ oz raw peeled shrimp

salt

½ egg white, lightly beaten

2 tsp cornstarch paste (see page 15)

4½ oz honey-roast ham

3 cups Chinese Stock (see page 14) or water

finely chopped scallions, to garnish

1 Using a sharp knife or meat cleaver, thinly slice the chicken into shreds. If the shrimp are large, cut each in half lengthways, otherwise leave them whole.

2 Place the chicken and shrimps in a bowl and mix with a pinch of salt, the egg white, and cornstarch paste until well coated. Set aside until required.

3 Cut the honey-roast ham into small thin slices roughly the same size as the chicken pieces.

4 In a heated wok or large, heavy skillet, bring the Chinese stock or water to a rolling boil and add the chicken, the raw shrimp, and the ham.

5 Bring the soup back to a boil, and simmer for 1 minute.

6 Adjust the seasoning to taste, then pour the soup into 4 warm individual serving bowls, garnish with the scallions, and serve immediately.

COOK'S TIP

Soups such as this are improved enormously in flavor if you use a well-flavored stock. Either use a bouillon cube, or find time to make Chinese stock. Better still, make double quantities and freeze some for future use.

Crab & Ginger Soup

Two classic ingredients in Chinese cooking are blended together in this recipe for a special soup.

NUTRITIONAL INFORMATION

Calories	32	Sugars	.........1g
Protein	.........6g	Fat	..........0.4g
Carbohydrate	....1g	Saturates	.......0g

🍲 10 MINS   🕐 25 MINS

SERVES 4

I N G R E D I E N T S

1 carrot

1 leek

1 bay leaf

3¾ cups fish stock

2 medium-sized cooked crabs

1-inch piece fresh gingerroot, grated

1 tsp light soy sauce

½ tsp ground star anise

salt and pepper

1 Using a sharp knife, chop the carrot and leek into small pieces and place in a large saucepan with the bay leaf and fish stock.

2 Bring the mixture in the saucepan to a boil.

3 Reduce the heat, cover, and leave to simmer for about 10 minutes, or until the vegetables are nearly tender.

4 Remove all of the meat from the cooked crabs. Break off and reserve the claws, break the joints, and remove the meat, using a fork or skewer.

5 Add the crabmeat to the pan of fish stock, together with the ginger, soy sauce, and star anise and bring to a boil. Leave to simmer for about 10 minutes, or until the vegetables are tender and the crab is heated through.

6 Season the soup then ladle into a warm soup tureen or individual serving bowls and garnish with crab claws. Serve immediately.

VARIATION

If fresh crabmeat is unavailable, use drained canned crabmeat or thawed frozen crabmeat instead.

Appetizers

This chapter contains a range of old favorites and traditional Chinese dishes, and there is sure to be something to suit every occasion. One of the advantages of these dishes is that they can be prepared well in advance. The Chinese usually serve a selection of appetizers together as an assorted hors d'oeuvres.

Remember not to have more than one type of the same food. The ingredients should be chosen for their harmony and balance in color, aroma, texture, and flavor. A suitable selection might contain Crispy Seaweed, Sesame Shrimp Toasts, Spareribs, and Egg Rolls. Many of these dishes also make an attractive addition to a buffet.

Egg Rolls

This classic dim sum dish is adaptable to almost any filling of your choice. Here the traditional mixture of pork and pak choi is used.

NUTRITIONAL INFORMATION

Calories	488	Sugars	........19g
Protein	........16g	Fat	.........24g
Carbohydrate	...55g	Saturates	.......4g

20 MINS   20 MINS

SERVES 4

INGREDIENTS

4 tsp vegetable oil

1-2 garlic cloves, crushed

8 oz ground pork

8 oz pak choi, shredded

4½ tsp light soy sauce

½ tsp sesame oil

8 egg roll wrappers, 10 inches square, thawed if frozen

oil, for deep-frying

CHILI SAUCE

¼ cup superfine sugar

¼ cup rice vinegar

2 tbsp water

2 red chilies, finely chopped

1 Heat the oil in a preheated wok. Add the garlic and stir-fry for 30 seconds. Add the pork and stir-fry for 2–3 minutes, until lightly colored.

2 Add the pak choi, soy sauce, and sesame oil to the wok and stir-fry for 2–3 minutes. Remove from the heat and set aside to cool.

3 Spread out the egg roll skins on a work counter and spoon 2 tablespoons of the pork mixture along one edge of each. Roll the skin over once and fold in the sides. Roll up completely to make a link-sausage shape, brushing the edges with a little water to seal. Set the rolls aside for 10 minutes to seal firmly.

4 To make the chili sauce, heat the sugar, vinegar, and water in a small saucepan, stirring until the sugar dissolves. Bring the mixture to a boil and boil rapidly until a light syrup forms. Remove from the heat and stir in the chopped red chilies; leave the sauce to cool before serving.

5 Heat the oil for deep-frying in a wok until almost smoking. Reduce the heat slightly and fry the egg rolls, in batches if necessary, for 3–4 minutes, until golden brown. Remove from the oil with a draining spoon and drain on absorbent paper towels. Serve with the chili sauce.

Filled Cucumber Cups

These attractive little cups would make an impressive appetizer at a dinner party.

NUTRITIONAL INFORMATION

Calories 256	Sugars 7g	
Protein 10g	Fat 21g	
Carbohydrate 8g	Saturates 4g	

10 MINS   0 MINS

SERVES 4

INGREDIENTS

1 cucumber

4 scallions, chopped finely

4 tbsp lime juice

2 small red chilies, seeded and chopped finely

3 tsp sugar

1¼ cups ground roasted peanuts

¼ tsp salt

3 shallots, sliced finely and deep-fried, to garnish

1 Wash the cucumber thoroughly and pat dry with absorbent paper towels.

2 To make the cucumber cups, cut the ends off the cucumber, and cut it into 3 equal pieces. Mark a line around the center of each one as a guide.

3 Make a zigzag cut all the way around the center of each section, always pointing the knife towards the center of the cucumber.

4 Pull apart the two halves. Scoop out the center of each cup with a melon baller or teaspoon, leaving a base on the bottom of each cup.

5 Put the scallions, lime juice, red chilies, sugar, ground roasted peanuts, and salt in a bowl and mix well to combine.

6 Divide the filling evenly between the 6 cucumber cups and arrange on a serving plate.

7 Garnish the cucumber cups with the deep-fried shallots and serve.

COOK'S TIP

Cherry tomatoes can also be hollowed out very simply with a melon baller and filled with this mixture. The two look very pretty arranged together on a serving dish.

Little Golden Bundles

These little bundles will draw admiring gasps from your guests, but they are simple to prepare.

NUTRITIONAL INFORMATION

Calories 320	Sugars 1g	
Protein 6g	Fat 21g	
Carbohydrate ...28g	Saturates 5g	

 35 MINS   🕐 35 MINS

SERVES 4

INGREDIENTS

1 garlic clove, crushed

1 tsp chopped cilantro root

1 tsp pepper

1 cup boiled mashed potato

1 cup water chestnuts, chopped finely

1 tsp grated gingerroot

2 tbsp ground roasted peanuts

2 tsp light soy sauce

½ tsp salt

½ tsp sugar

30 wonton skins, defrosted

1 tsp cornstarch, made into a paste with a little water

vegetable oil, for deep-frying

fresh chives, to garnish

sweet chili sauce, to serve

1 Mix together all the ingredients except the wonton sheets, cornstarch, and oil.

2 Keeping the remainder of the wonton skins covered with a damp cloth, lay 4 skins out on a work counter. Put a teaspoon of the mixture on each. Make a line of the cornstarch paste around each sheet, about ½ inch from the edge.

3 Bring all four corners to the center and press together to form little bags. Repeat with all the wonton skins.

4 Heat 2 inches of the oil in a pan until a light haze appears on top and fry the bundles, in batches of 3, until golden brown. Remove and drain on paper towels. Tie a chive around the neck of each bag to garnish, and serve with a sweet chili sauce for dipping.

VARIATION

If wonton skins are not available, use egg roll skins or phyllo pastry dough, and cut large squares to about 4 inches square.

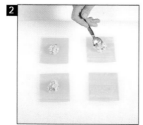

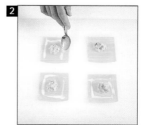

Stuffed Zucchini

Hollow out eight zucchini, fill them with a spicy beef mixture, and bake them for a delicious side dish.

NUTRITIONAL INFORMATION

Calories	208	Sugars	.........3g
Protein	........12g	Fat	..........9g
Carbohydrate	...20g	Saturates	.......4g

45 MINS   35 MINS

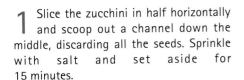

SERVES 4

I N G R E D I E N T S

8 medium zucchini

1 tbsp sesame or vegetable oil

1 garlic clove, crushed

2 shallots, chopped finely

1 small red chili, seeded and chopped finely

1 cup lean ground beef

1 tbsp fish sauce or mushroom catsup

1 tbsp chopped fresh cilantro or basil

2 tsp cornstarch, blended with a little cold water

½ cup cooked long-grain rice

salt and pepper

T O   G A R N I S H

sprigs of fresh cilantro or basil

carrot slices

1 Slice the zucchini in half horizontally and scoop out a channel down the middle, discarding all the seeds. Sprinkle with salt and set aside for 15 minutes.

2 Heat the oil in a wok or skillet and add the garlic, shallots, and chili. Stir-fry for 2 minutes, until golden. Add the ground beef and stir-fry briskly for about 5 minutes. Stir in the fish sauce or mushroom catsup, the chopped cilantro or basil, and the blended cornstarch, and cook for 2 minutes, stirring until thickened. Season with salt and pepper, then remove from the heat.

3 Rinse the zucchini in cold water and arrange them in a greased shallow baking dish, cut side uppermost. Mix the cooked rice into the ground beef, then use this mixture to stuff the zucchini.

4 Cover with foil and bake in a preheated oven at 375°F for 20–25 minutes, removing the foil for the last 5 minutes of cooking time.

5 Serve at once, garnished with sprigs of fresh cilantro or basil, and carrot slices.

Aubergine Dipping Platter

Dipping platters are a very sociable dish, bringing together all the diners at the table.

NUTRITIONAL INFORMATION

Calories 81   Sugars 4g
Protein . . . . .4g   Fat 5g
Carbohydrate . . . .5g   Saturates 1g

15 MINS   10 MINS

SERVES 4

I N G R E D I E N T S

1 eggplant, peeled and cut into 1-inch cubes

3 tbsp sesame seeds, roasted in a dry pan over a low heat

1 tsp sesame oil

grated rind and juice of ½ lime

1 small shallot, diced

1 tsp sugar

1 red chili, seeded and sliced

1¼ cups broccoli flowerets

2 carrots, cut into matchsticks

8 baby corn-on-the-cobs, cut in half lengthways

2 celery stalks, cut into matchsticks

1 baby red cabbage, cut into 8 wedges, the leaves of each wedge held together by the core

salt and pepper

1 Cook the diced eggplant in a saucpan of boiling water for 7–8 minutes.

2 Meanwhile, grind the sesame seeds with the oil in a food processor or mortar and pestle.

3 Add the eggplant, lime rind, and juice, shallot, ½ tsp salt, pepper, sugar, and chili in that order to the sesame seeds.

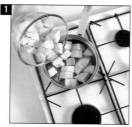 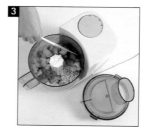 

Process, or chop and mash by hand, until smooth.

4 Adjust the seasoning to taste then spoon the dip into a bowl.

5 Serve the eggplant dipping platter surrounded by the broccoli, carrots, baby corn, celery, and red cabbage.

VARIATION

You can vary the selection of vegetables depending on your preference or whatever you have at hand. Other vegetables you could use are cauliflower flowerets and cucumber sticks.

Eggplant Satay

Eggplants and mushrooms are broiled on skewers and served with a satay sauce.

NUTRITIONAL INFORMATION

Calories 155	Sugars 2g	
Protein 4g	Fat 14g	
Carbohydrate 3g	Saturates 3g	

 2¼ HOURS 25 MINS

SERVES 4

I N G R E D I E N T S

2 eggplants, cut into 1 inch pieces

1½ cups small crimini mushrooms

M A R I N A D E

1 tsp cumin seeds

1 tsp coriander seeds

1 inch piece gingerroot, grated

2 garlic cloves, crushed lightly

½ stalk lemongrass, chopped roughly

4 tbsp light soy sauce

8 tbsp sunflower oil

2 tbsp lemon juice

P E A N U T   S A U C E

½ tsp cumin seeds

½ tsp coriander seeds

3 garlic cloves

1 small onion, puréed in a food processor or chopped very finely by hand

1 tbsp lemon juice

1 tsp salt

½ red chili, seeded and sliced

½ cup coconut milk

1 cup crunchy peanut butter

1 cup water

1 Thread the vegetables onto eight metal or soaked wooden skewers.

2 For the marinade, grind the cumin and coriander seeds, ginger, garlic, and lemongrass. Stir-fry over a high heat until fragrant. Remove from the heat and add the remaining marinade ingredients. Place the skewers in a dish and spoon the marinade over. Leave to marinate for at least 2 hours and up to 8 hours.

3 To make the sauce, grind the cumin and coriander seeds with the garlic. Add all the ingredients, except the water. Transfer to a pan and stir in the water. Bring to a boil and cook until thick.

4 Cook the skewers under a heated very hot broiler for 15–20 minutes. Brush with the marinade frequently and turn once. Serve with the peanut sauce.

Spinach Meatballs

Balls of pork mixture are coated in spinach and steamed before being served with a sesame and soy sauce dip.

NUTRITIONAL INFORMATION

Calories 137   Sugars 2g
Protein ....13g   Fat 7g
Carbohydrate ....6g   Saturates 2g

 20 MINS   25 MINS

SERVES 4

INGREDIENTS

4½ oz lean boneless pork

1 small egg

½-inch piece fresh gingerroot, chopped

1 small onion, finely chopped

1 tbsp boiling water

2 tbsp canned bamboo shoots, drained, rinsed and chopped

2 slices smoked ham, chopped

2 tsp cornstarch

1 lb fresh spinach

2 tsp sesame seeds

SAUCE

⅔ cup vegetable stock

½ tsp cornstarch

1 tsp cold water

1 tsp light soy sauce

½ tsp sesame oil

1 tbsp chopped chives

1 Grind the pork very finely in a food processor. Lightly beat the egg in a bowl and stir into the pork.

2 Put the ginger and onion in a separate bowl, add a boiling water and let stand for 5 minutes. Drain and add to the pork mixture with the bamboo shoots, ham, and cornstarch. Mix thoroughly and roll into 12 balls.

3 Wash the spinach and remove the stems. Blanch in boiling water for 10 seconds, drain well then slice into very thin strips and mix with the sesame seeds. Roll the meatballs in the mixture to coat.

4 Place the meatballs on a heatproof plate in the base of a steamer. Cover and steam for 8–10 minutes until cooked through and tender.

5 Meanwhile, make the sauce. Put the stock in a saucepan and bring to a boil. Mix together the cornstarch and water to a smooth paste and stir it into the stock. Stir in the soy sauce, sesame oil, and chives. Transfer the cooked meatballs to a warm plate and serve with the sauce.

Crispy Wontons

Mushroom-filled crispy wontons are served on skewers with a dipping sauce flavored with chilies.

  45 MINS   20 MINS

SERVES 4

INGREDIENTS

8 wooden skewers, soaked in cold water
for 30 minutes

1 tbsp vegetable oil

1 tbsp chopped onion

1 small garlic clove, chopped

½ tsp chopped gingerroot

½ cup flat mushrooms, chopped

16 wonton skins

vegetable oil for deep-frying

salt

SAUCE

2 tbsp vegetable oil

2 scallions, shredded thinly

1 red and 1 green chili, seeded and
shredded finely

3 tbsp light soy sauce

1 tbsp vinegar

1 tbsp dry sherry

pinch of sugar

1 Heat the vegetable oil in a preheated wok or skillet.

2 Add the onion, garlic, and gingerroot to the wok or pan and stir-fry for 2 minutes. Stir in the mushrooms and fry for 2 minutes longer. Season well with salt and leave to cool.

3 Place 1 teaspoon of the cooled mushroom filling in the center of each wonton skin.

4 Bring two opposite corners of each wonton skin together to cover the mixture and pinch together to seal. Repeat with the remaining corners.

5 Thread 2 wontons onto each skewer. Heat enough oil in a large saucepan to deep-fry the wontons in batches until golden and crisp. Do not overheat the oil or the wontons will brown on the outside before they are properly cooked inside. Remove the wontons with a perforated spoon and drain on paper towels.

6 To make the sauce, heat the vegetable oil in a small saucepan until quite hot or until a small cube of bread dropped in the oil browns in a few seconds. Put the scallions and chilies in a bowl and pour the hot oil slowly ontop. Mix in the remaining ingredients.

7 Transfer the crispy wontons to a serving dish and serve with the dipping sauce.

Bean Curd Tempura

Crispy coated vegetables and bean curd accompanied by a sweet, spicy dip give a real taste of the Orient in this Japanese-style dish.

NUTRITIONAL INFORMATION

Calories 582	Sugars 10g	
Protein 16g	Fat 27g	
Carbohydrate . . .65g	Saturates 4g	

15 MINS   20 MINS

SERVES 4

INGREDIENTS

4½ oz baby zucchini

4½ oz baby carrots

4½ oz baby corn-on-the-cobs

4½ oz baby leeks

2 baby eggplants

8 oz bean curd

vegetable oil, for deep-frying

julienne strips of carrot, gingerroot, and
  baby leek to garnish

noodles, to serve

BATTER

2 egg yolks

1¼ cups water

2 cups all-purpose flour

DIPPING SAUCE

5 tbsp mirin or dry sherry

5 tbsp Japanese soy sauce

2 tsp honey

1 garlic clove, crushed

1 tsp grated gingerroot

1 Slice the zucchini and carrots in half lengthways. Trim the corn. Trim the leeks at both ends. Quarter the eggplants. Cut the bean curd into 1-inch cubes.

2 To make the batter, mix the egg yolks with the water. Sift in 1½ cups of the flour and beat with a balloon whisk to form a thick batter. Don't worry if there are any lumps. Heat the oil for deep-frying to 350°F or until a cube of bread browns in 30 seconds.

3 Place the remaining flour on a large plate and toss the vegetables and bean curd until lightly coated.

4 Dip the bean curd in the batter and deep-fry for 2–3 minutes, until lightly golden. Drain on paper towels and keep warm.

5 Dip the vegetables in the batter and deep-fry, a few at a time, for 3–4 minutes, until golden. Drain and place on a warmed serving plate.

6 To make the dipping sauce, mix all the ingredients together. Serve with the vegetables and bean curd, accompanied with noodles and garnished with julienne strips of vegetables.

Son-in-Law Eggs

This recipe is supposedly so called because it is an easy dish for a son-in-law to cook to impress his new mother-in-law!

NUTRITIONAL INFORMATION

Calories 229	Sugars 8g	
Protein 9g	Fat 18g	
Carbohydrate 8g	Saturates 3g	

15 MINS   15 MINS

SERVES 4

I N G R E D I E N T S

6 eggs, hard-cooked and shelled

4 tbsp sunflower oil

1 onion, sliced thinly

2 fresh red chilies, sliced

2 tbsp sugar

1 tbsp water

2 tsp tamarind pulp

1 tbsp liquid seasoning

rice, to serve

1 Prick the hard-cooked eggs 2 or 3 times with a toothpick.

2 Heat the sunflower oil in a wok and fry the eggs until crispy and golden. Drain on paper towels.

3 Halve the eggs lengthways and put on a serving dish.

4 Reserve 1 tablespoon of the oil, pour off the rest, then heat the tablespoonful in the wok. Cook the onion and chilies over a high heat until golden and slightly crisp. Drain the mixture on paper towels.

5 Heat the sugar, water, tamarind pulp, and liquid seasoning in the wok and simmer for 5 minutes until thickened.

6 Pour the sauce over the eggs and spoon over the onion and chilies. Serve immediately with rice.

COOK'S TIP

Tamarind pulp is sold in oriental grocery stores, and is very sour. If it is not available, use twice the amount of lemon juice in its place.

Vegetable Egg rolls

There are many different versions of egg rolls throughout the Far East, a vegetable filling being the classic.

NUTRITIONAL INFORMATION

Calories 189   Sugars 4g
Protein . . . . .2g   Fat 16g
Carbohydrate . . . .11g   Saturates 5g

10 MINS   15 MINS

SERVES 4

I N G R E D I E N T S

8 oz carrots

1 red bell pepper

1 tbsp sunflower oil, plus extra for frying

¾ cup bean sprouts

finely grated peel and juice of 1 lime

1 red chili, seeded and very finely chopped

1 tbsp soy sauce

½ tsp arrowroot

2 tbsp chopped fresh cilantro

8 sheets phyllo pastry

1 oz butter

2 tsp sesame oil

TO SERVE

chili sauce

scallion tassels

1 Using a sharp knife, cut the carrots into thin sticks. Seed the bell pepper and cut into thin slices.

2 Heat the sunflower oil in a large preheated wok.

3 Add the carrot, red bell pepper, and bean sprouts and cook, stirring, for 2 minutes, or until softened. Remove the wok from the heat and toss in the lime peel and juice, and the red chili.

4 Mix the soy sauce with the arrowroot. Stir the mixture into the wok, return to the heat, and cook for 2 minutes or until the juices thicken.

5 Add the chopped fresh cilantro to the wok and mix well.

6 Lay the sheets of phyllo pastry dough out. Melt the butter and sesame oil and brush each sheet with the mixture.

7 Spoon a little of the vegetable filling at the top of each sheet, fold over each long side, and roll up.

8 Add a little oil to the wok and cook the egg rolls in batches, for 2–3 minutes, or until crisp and golden.

9 Transfer the egg rolls to a serving dish, garnish and serve hot with chili dipping sauce.

Crispy Seaweed

This tasty appetizer is not all that it seems – the seaweed is, in fact, pak choi which is fried, salted, and tossed with pine kernels.

NUTRITIONAL INFORMATION

Calories . . . . .214 Sugars 14g
Protein . . . . .6g Fat 15g
Carbohydrate . . .15g Saturates 2g

 10 MINS   5 MINS

SERVES 4

INGREDIENTS

2 lb 4 oz pak choi

peanut oil, for deep-frying (about 3¾ cups)

1 tsp salt

1 tbsp superfine sugar

2½ tbsp toasted pine nuts

1 Rinse the pak choi leaves under cold running water and then pat dry thoroughly with paper towels.

2 Discarding any tough outer leaves, roll each pak choi leaf up, then slice through thinly so that the leaves are finely

shredded. Alternatively, use a food processor to shred the pak choi.

3 Heat the peanut oil in a large wok or heavy-based skillet.

4 Carefully add the shredded pak choi leaves to the wok or skillet and fry for about 30 seconds or until they shrivel and become crispy: you may need to do this in batches, depending on the size of the wok.

5 Remove the crispy seaweed from the wok with a draining spoon and drain on absorbent paper towels.

6 Transfer the crispy seaweed to a large bowl and toss with the salt, sugar, and pine nuts. Serve immediately.

COOK'S TIP

The tough, outer leaves of pak choi are discarded because these will spoil the overall taste and texture of the dish. Use savoy cabbage instead of the pak choi if it is unavailable, drying the leaves thoroughly before frying.

Moneybags

These traditional steamed dumplings can be eaten on their own or dipped in a mixture of soy sauce, sherry, and slivers of gingerroot.

NUTRITIONAL INFORMATION

Calories 315   Sugars 3g
Protein . . . . .8g   Fat 8g
Carbohydrate . . .56g   Saturates 1g

45 MINS   20 MINS

SERVES 4

INGREDIENTS

3 Chinese dried mushrooms
(if unavailable, use thinly sliced
open-cap mushrooms)

2 cups all-purpose flour

1 egg, beaten

⅓ cup water

1 tsp baking powder

¾ tsp salt

2 tbsp vegetable oil

2 scallions, chopped

½ cup sweetcorn kernels

½ red chili, seeded and chopped

1 tbsp black bean sauce

1 Place the dried mushrooms in a small bowl, cover with warm water, and leave to soak for 20–25 minutes.

2 To make the skins, sift the all-purpose flour into a bowl. Add the beaten egg and mix in lightly. Stir in the water, baking powder, and salt. Mix to make a soft dough.

3 Knead the dough lightly on a floured board. Cover with a damp dish cloth and set aside for 5–6 minutes. This allows the baking powder time to activate, so the dumplings swell when steaming.

4 Drain the mushrooms, squeezing them dry. Remove the tough centers and chop the mushrooms.

5 Heat the vegetable oil in a wok or large skillet and stir-fry the mushrooms, scallions, sweetcorn, and chili for 2 minutes.

6 Stir in the black bean sauce and remove from the heat.

7 Roll the dough into a large rope and cut into 24 even-sized pieces. Roll each piece out into a thin circle and place a teaspoonful of the filling in the center. Gather up the edges to a point, pinch together and twist to seal.

8 Stand the dumplings in an oiled steaming basket. Place over a saucepan of simmering water, cover, and steam for 12–14 minutes before serving.

Vegetable Dim Sum

Dim sum are small Chinese bundles which are filled with a variety of ingredients, steamed or fried, and served with a dipping sauce.

NUTRITIONAL INFORMATION

Calories 295	Sugars 1g	
Protein 5g	Fat 22g	
Carbohydrate ...20g	Saturates 6g	

15 MINS   15 MINS

SERVES 4

INGREDIENTS

2 scallions, chopped

1 oz green beans, chopped

½ small carrot, finely chopped

1 red chili, chopped

⅓ cup bean sprouts, chopped

⅓ cup button mushrooms, chopped

¼ cup unsalted cashew
nuts, chopped

1 small egg, beaten

2 tbsp cornstarch

1 tsp light soy sauce

1 tsp hoisin sauce

1 tsp sesame oil

32 wonton skins

oil, for deep-frying

1 tbsp sesame seeds

1 Mix all of the vegetables together in a bowl. Add the nuts, egg, cornstarch, soy sauce, hoisin sauce, and sesame oil to the bowl.

2 Lay the wonton skins out on a chopping board and spoon small quantities of the mixture into the center of each. Gather the skins around the filling at the top, to make little bundles, leaving the top open.

3 Heat the oil for deep-frying in a wok to 350°F, or until a cube of bread browns in 30 seconds. Fry the wontons, in batches, for 1–2 minutes or until golden brown. Drain on paper towels and keep warm whilst frying the remaining wontons.

4 Sprinkle the sesame seeds over the wontons. Serve the vegetable dim sum with a soy or plum dipping sauce.

COOK'S TIP

If preferred, arrange the wontons on a heatproof plate and then steam in a steamer for 5-7 minutes for a healthier cooking method.

Spicy Corn Fritters

Cornmeal can be found in all supermarkets and health food stores. Yellow in color, it acts as a binding agent in this recipe.

NUTRITIONAL INFORMATION

Calories 213   Sugars 6g
Protein . . . . .5g   Fat 8g
Carbohydrate . . .30g   Saturates 1g

5 MINS   15 MINS

SERVES 4

I N G R E D I E N T S

¾ cup canned or frozen corn kernels

2 red chilies, seeded and very finely chopped

2 cloves garlic, crushed

10 lime leaves, very finely chopped

2 tbsp fresh cilantro, chopped

1 large egg

½ cup cornmeal

¾ cup fine green beans, very finely sliced

peanut oil, for frying

1 Place the corn, chilies, garlic, lime leaves, cilantro, egg, and cornmeal in a large mixing bowl, and stir to combine.

2 Add the green beans to the ingredients in the bowl and mix well, using a wooden spoon.

3 Divide the mixture into small, evenly sized balls. Flatten the balls of mixture between the palms of your hands to form patties.

4 Heat a little peanut oil in a preheated wok or large skillet until really hot. Cook the fritters, in batches, until brown and crispy on the outside, turning occasionally.

5 Leave the fritters to drain on paper towels while frying the remaining fritters.

6 Transfer the fritters to warm serving plates and serve immediately.

COOK'S TIP

Kaffir lime leaves are dark green, glossy leaves that have a lemony-lime flavor. They can be bought from Asian food stores either fresh or dried. Fresh leaves impart the most delicious flavor.

Deep-Fried Chili Corn Balls

These small corn balls have a wonderful hot-and-sweet flavor, offset by the pungent cilantro.

NUTRITIONAL INFORMATION

Calories	248	Sugars	.........6g
Protein	.........6g	Fat	12
Carbohydrate	...30g	Saturates	.......5g

15 MINS   30 MINS

SERVES 4

I N G R E D I E N T S

6 scallions, sliced

3 tbsp fresh cilantro, chopped

8 oz canned corn kernels

1 tsp mild chili powder

1 tbsp sweet chili sauce

¼ cup shredded coconut

1 egg

⅓ cup cornmeal

oil, for deep-frying

extra sweet chili sauce, to serve

1 In a large bowl, mix together the scallions, cilantro, corn, chili powder, chili sauce, coconut, egg, and cornmeal until well blended.

2 Cover the bowl with plastic wrap and leave to stand for 10 minutes.

3 Heat the oil for deep-frying in a large preheated wok or skillet to 350°F, or until a cube of bread browns in 30 seconds.

4 Carefully drop spoonfuls of the chili and cornmeal mixture into the hot oil. Deep-fry the chili corn balls, in batches, for 4–5 minutes or until crispy and a deep golden brown color.

5 Remove the chili corn balls with a draining spoon, transfer to paper towels and leave to drain thoroughly.

6 Transfer the chili corn balls to serving plates and serve with an extra sweet chili sauce for dipping.

COOK'S TIP

For safe deep-frying in a round-bottomed wok, place it on a wok rack so that it rests securely. Only half-fill the wok with oil. Never leave the wok unattended over a high heat.

Aspagarus Rolls

These small rolls are ideal as part of a main meal and irresistible as a quick snack with extra plum sauce for dipping.

NUTRITIONAL INFORMATION

Calories	194	Sugars	.........2g
Protein	.........3g	Fat	..........16g
Carbohydrate	....11g	Saturates	.......4g

 5 MINS   25 MINS

SERVES 4

I N G R E D I E N T S

3½ oz fine tip asparagus

1 red bell pepper, seeded and thinly sliced

½ cup bean sprouts

2 tbsp plum sauce

1 egg yolk

8 sheets phyllo pastry dough

oil, for deep-frying

1 Place the asparagus, bell pepper, and beansprouts in a large mixing bowl.

2 Add the plum sauce to the vegetables and mix until well-combined.

3 Beat the egg yolk and set aside until required.

4 Lay the sheets of phyllo pastry out onto a clean work counter.

5 Place a little of the asparagus and red bell pepper filling at the top end of each phyllo pastry sheet. Brush the edges of the phyllo pastry dough with a little of the beaten egg yolk.

6 Roll up the phyllo dough, tucking in the ends and enclosing the filling like an egg roll. Repeat with the remaining phyllo sheets.

7 Heat the oil for deep-frying in a large heated wok. Carefully cook the rolls, 2 at a time, in the hot oil for 4–5 minutes, or until crispy.

8 Remove the rolls with a draining spoon and leave to drain on paper towels.

9 Transfer the rolls to warm serving plates and serve immediately.

COOK'S TIP

Be sure to use fine-tipped asparagus as it is more tender than the larger stems.

Chicken Egg rolls

A cucumber dipping sauce tastes perfect with these delicious egg rolls, filled with chicken and fresh, crunchy vegetables.

NUTRITIONAL INFORMATION

Calories	367	Sugars	........18g
Protein	........13g	Fat	..........21g
Carbohydrate	...32g	Saturates	.......3g

🥗 10 MINS   🕐 25 MINS

SERVES 4

I N G R E D I E N T S

2 tbsp vegetable oil

4 scallions, trimmed and sliced very finely

1 carrot, cut into matchstick pieces

1 small green or red bell pepper, cored, seeded, and sliced finely

⅔ cup button mushrooms, sliced

1 cup beansprouts

1 cup cooked chicken, shredded

1 tbsp light soy sauce

1 tsp sugar

2 tsp cornstarch, blended in 2 tbsp cold water

12 × 8 inch egg roll skins

oil for deep-frying

salt and pepper

scallion brushes to garnish

S A U C E

¼ cup light malt vinegar

¼ cup light muscovado sugar

½ tsp salt

2 inch piece of cucumber, peeled and chopped finely

4 scallions, trimmed and sliced finely

1 small red or green chili, seeded and chopped very finely

1 Stir-fry the scallions, carrot, and bell pepper for 2–3 minutes. Add the mushrooms, beansprouts, and chicken and cook for 2 minutes. Season. Mix the soy sauce, sugar and blended cornstarch. Add to the wok and stir-fry for 1 minute. Leave to cool slightly. Spoon the chicken and vegetable mixture onto the egg roll skins. Dampen the edges and roll them up to enclose the filling completely.

2 To make the sauce, heat the vinegar, water, sugar, and salt in a pan. Boil for 1 minute. Combine the cucumber, scallions, and chili and pour over the vinegar mixture. Leave to cool.

3 Heat the oil and fry the rolls until crisp and golden brown. Drain on paper towels, garnish with scallion brushes, and serve with the cucumber dipping sauce.

Pot Stickers

These dumplings obtain their name from the fact that they will stick to the pot when steamed if they are not fried crisply enough initially.

NUTRITIONAL INFORMATION

Calories 345	Sugar 3g	
Protein 13g	Fat 17g	
Carbohydrate ...36g	Saturates 2g	

50 MINS   25 MINS

SERVES 4

INGREDIENTS

DUMPLINGS

1½ cups all-purpose flour

pinch of salt

3 tbsp vegetable oil

6–8 tbsp boiling water

oil, for deep-frying

½ cup water, for steaming

sliced scallions and chives, to garnish

soy sauce or hoisin sauce, to serve

FILLING

1 cup lean chicken, very finely chopped

1 tbsp canned bamboo shoots, drained and chopped

2 scallions, finely chopped

½ small red bell pepper, seeded and finely chopped

½ tsp Chinese curry powder

1 tbsp light soy sauce

1 tsp superfine sugar

1 tsp sesame oil

1 To make the dumplings, mix together the flour and salt in a bowl. Make a well in the center, add the oil and water, and mix well to form a soft dough. Knead the dough on a lightly floured surface, wrap in plastic wrap and let stand for 30 minutes. Meanwhile, mix all of the filling ingredients together in a large bowl.

2 Divide the dough into 12 equal-sized pieces and roll each piece into a 5-inch circle. Spoon a portion of the filling onto one half of each round. Fold the dough over the filling to form a pasty, pressing the edges together to seal.

3 Pour a little oil into a skillet and cook the dumplings, in batches, until browned and slightly crisp.

4 Return all of the dumplings to the pan and add about ½ cup water. Cover and steam for 5 minutes, or until the dumplings are cooked through. Remove with a draining spoon and garnish with scallions and chives. Serve with soy sauce or hoisin sauce.

Chinese Omelet

This is a filling omelet, as it contains chicken and shrimp. It is cooked as a whole omelet and then sliced for serving.

NUTRITIONAL INFORMATION

Calories	309	Sugars 0g
Protein	........34g	Fat 19g
Carbohydrate	...0.2g	Saturates 5g

🥚 5 MINS   🕐 5 MINS

SERVES 4

I N G R E D I E N T S

8 eggs

2 cups cooked chicken, shredded

12 jumbo shrimp, peeled and deveined

2 tbsp chopped chives

2 tsp light soy sauce

dash of chili sauce

2 tbsp vegetable oil

1 Lightly beat the eggs in a large mixing bowl.

2 Add the shredded chicken and jumbo shrimp to the eggs, mixing well.

3 Stir in the chopped chives, light soy sauce, and chili sauce, mixing well to combine all the ingredients.

4 Heat the vegetable oil in a large heated skillet over a medium heat.

5 Add the egg mixture to the skillet, tilting the pan to coat the base completely.

6 Cook over a medium heat, gently stirring the omelet with a fork until the surface is just set and the underside is a golden brown color.

7 When the omelette is set, slide it out of the pan, with the aid of a spatula.

8 Cut the Chinese omelet into squares or slices and serve immediately. Alternatively, serve the omelet as a main course for two people.

VARIATION

You could add extra flavor to the omelette by stirring in 3 tablespoons of finely chopped fresh cilantro or 1 teaspoon of sesame seeds with the chives in step 3.

Honeyed Chicken Wings

Chicken wings are ideal for a first course because they are small and perfect for eating with the fingers.

NUTRITIONAL INFORMATION

Calories 131   Sugars 4g
Protein . . . . .10g   Fat 8g
Carbohydrate . . . .4g   Saturates 2g

5 MINS   40 MINS

SERVES 4

INGREDIENTS

1 lb chicken wings

2 tbsp peanut oil

2 tbsp light soy sauce

2 tbsp hoisin sauce

2 tbsp honey

2 garlic cloves, crushed

1 tsp sesame seeds

MARINADE

1 dried red chili

½–1 tsp chili powder

½–1 tsp ground ginger

finely grated peel of 1 lime

1 To make the marinade, crush the dried chili in a mortar and pestle. Mix together the crushed dried chili, chili powder, ground ginger, and lime peel in a small mixing bowl.

2 Thoroughly rub the spice mixture into the chicken wings with your fingertips. Set aside for at least 2 hours to allow the flavors to penetrate the chicken wings.

3 Heat the peanut oil in a large wok or skillet.

4 Add the chicken wings and fry, turning frequently, for about 10–12 minutes until golden and crisp. Drain off any excess oil.

5 Add the soy sauce, hoisin sauce, honey, garlic, and sesame seeds to the wok, turning the chicken wings to coat.

6 Reduce the heat and cook for 20–25 minutes, turning the chicken wings frequently, until completely cooked through. Serve hot.

COOK'S TIP

Make the dish in advance and freeze the chicken wings. Defrost thoroughly, cover with foil, and heat right through in a moderate oven.

Bang-Bang Chicken

The cooked chicken meat is tenderized by being beaten with a rolling pin, hence the name for this very popular Szechuan dish.

NUTRITIONAL INFORMATION

Calories	82	Sugars	.........1g
Protein	........13g	Fat	...........3g
Carbohydrate	....2g	Saturates	.......1g

  1¼ HOURS 40 MINS

SERVES 4

I N G R E D I E N T S

4 cups water

2 chicken quarters (breast half and leg)

1 cucumber, cut into matchstick shreds

S A U C E

2 tbsp light soy sauce

1 tsp sugar

1 tbsp finely chopped scallion, plus extra to garnish

1 tsp red chili oil

¼ tsp pepper

1 tsp white sesame seeds

2 tbsp peanut butter, creamed with a little sesame oil, plus extra to garnish

1 Bring the water to a rolling boil in a wok or a large saucepan. Add the chicken pieces, reduce the heat, cover, and cook for 30-35 minutes.

2 Remove the chicken from the wok or pan and immerse in a bowl of cold water for at least 1 hour to cool it, ready for shredding.

3 Remove the chicken pieces, drain, and dry on paper towels. Take the meat off the bone.

4 On a flat surface, pound the chicken with a rolling pin, then tear the meat

into shreds with 2 forks. Mix the chicken with the shredded cucumber and arrange in a serving dish.

5 To serve, mix together all the sauce ingredients until thoroughly combined and pour over the chicken and cucumber in the serving dish. Sprinkle some sesame seeds and chopped scallions over the sauce and serve.

COOK'S TIP

Take the time to tear the chicken meat into similar-sized shreds, to make an elegant-looking dish. You can do this quite efficiently with 2 forks, although Chinese cooks do it with their fingers.

Sesame Ginger Chicken

Chunks of chicken breast are marinated in a mixture of lime juice, garlic, sesame oil, and fresh gingerroot to give them a great flavor.

NUTRITIONAL INFORMATION

Calories	204	Sugars	.........0g
Protein	........28g	Fat	..........10g
Carbohydrate	....1g	Saturates	.......2g

  2¼ HOURS   10 MINS

SERVES 4

I N G R E D I E N T S

4 wooden satay sticks, soaked in
    warm water

1 lb 2 oz boneless chicken breasts

sprigs of fresh mint, to garnish

M A R I N A D E

1 garlic clove, crushed

1 shallot, chopped very finely

2 tbsp sesame oil

1 tbsp fish sauce or light soy sauce

finely grated peel of 1 lime or
    ½ lemon

2 tbsp lime juice or lemon juice

1 tsp sesame seeds

2 tsp finely grated fresh gingerroot

2 tsp chopped fresh mint

salt and pepper

1 To make the marinade, put the crushed garlic, chopped shallot, sesame oil, fish sauce or soy sauce, lime or lemon peel, and juice, sesame seeds, grated gingerroot and chopped mint into a large nonmetallic bowl. Season with a little salt and pepper and mix together until all the ingredients are thoroughly combined.

2 Remove the skin from the chicken breasts and cut the flesh into chunks.

3 Add the chicken to the marinade, stirring to coat the chicken completely in the mixture. Cover with plastic wrap and chill in the refrigerator for at least 2 hours so that the flavors are absorbed.

4 Thread the chicken onto wooden satay sticks. Place them on the rack of a broiler pan and baste with the marinade.

5 Place the kabobs under a preheated broiler for about 8–10 minutes. Turn them frequently, basting them with the remaining marinade.

6 Serve the chicken skewers at once, garnished with sprigs of fresh mint.

COOK'S TIP

The kabobs taste delicious if dipped into an accompanying bowl of hot chili sauce.

Steamed Duck Buns

The dough used in this recipe can also be wrapped around chicken, pork or shrimp, or sweet fillings as an alternative.

NUTRITIONAL INFORMATION

Calories	...307	Sugars	...11g
Protein	...17g	Fat	...6g
Carbohydrate	...50g	Saturates	...1g

1½ HOURS   1 HOUR

SERVES 4

INGREDIENTS

DUMPLING DOUGH

2⅔ cups plain all-purpose flour

½ oz active-dried yeast

1 tsp superfine sugar

2 tbsp warm water

¾ cup warm milk

FILLING

10½ oz duck breast

1 tbsp light brown sugar

1 tbsp light soy sauce

2 tbsp clear honey

1 tbsp hoisin sauce

1 tbsp vegetable oil

1 leek, finely chopped

1 garlic clove, crushed

½-inch piece fresh gingerroot, grated

1 Place the duck breast in a large bowl. Mix together the light brown sugar, soy sauce, honey, and hoisin sauce. Pour the mixture over the duck and marinate for 20 minutes.

2 Remove the duck from the marinade and cook on a rack set over a roasting pan in a preheated oven 400°F for 35–40 minutes, or until cooked through. Leave to

cool, remove the meat from the bones, and cut the meat into small cubes.

3 Heat the vegetable oil in a heated wok or skillet until really hot.

4 Add the leek, garlic, and ginger to the wok and fry for 3 minutes. Mix with the duck meat.

5 Sift the all-purpose flour into a large bowl. Mix the yeast, superfine sugar, and warm water in a separate bowl and leave in a warm place for 15 minutes.

6 Pour the yeast mixture into the flour, together with the warm milk, mixing to form a firm dough. Knead the dough on a floured surface for 5 minutes. Roll into a long rope shape, 1 inch in diameter. Cut into 16 pieces, cover, and let stand for 20–25 minutes.

7 Flatten the dough pieces into 4-inch circles. Place a spoonful of filling in the center of each, draw up the sides to form a moneybag shape, and twist to seal.

8 Place the dumplings on a clean, damp dish cloth in the base of a steamer, cover, and steam for 20 minutes. Serve immediately.

Beef Satay

In this dish, strips of beef are threaded onto skewers, broiled, and served with a spicy peanut sauce.

NUTRITIONAL INFORMATION

Calories	.314	Sugars	.8g
Protein	.32g	Fat	.16g
Carbohydrate	.10g	Saturates	.4g

2¼ HOURS   15 MINS

SERVES 6

INGREDIENTS

4 boneless, skinned chicken breast halves or 1 lb 10 oz sirloin steak, trimmed

MARINADE

1 small onion, finely chopped

1 garlic clove, crushed

1-inch piece gingerroot, peeled and grated

2 tbsp dark soy sauce

2 tsp chili powder

1 tsp ground coriander

2 tsp dark brown sugar

1 tbsp lemon or lime juice

1 tbsp vegetable oil

SAUCE

1¼ cups coconut milk

⅓ cup crunchy peanut butter

1 tbsp fish sauce

1 tsp lemon or lime juice

salt and pepper

1 Using a sharp knife, trim any fat from the chicken or beef then cut into thin strips, about 3 inches long.

2 To make the marinade, place all the ingredients in a shallow dish and mix well. Add the chicken or beef strips and stir in the marinade until well coated.

Cover with plastic wrap and leave to marinate for 2 hours or overnight in the refrigerator.

3 Remove the meat from the marinade and thread the pieces, concertina style, on soaked bamboo or thin wooden skewers.

4 Broil the chicken and beef satays for 8-10 minutes, turning and brushing occasionally with the marinade, until cooked through.

5 Meanwhile, to make the sauce, mix the coconut milk with the peanut butter, fish sauce, and lemon or lime juice in a saucepan. Bring to a boil and cook for 3 minutes. Season to taste.

6 Transfer the sauce to a serving bowl and serve with the cooked satays.

Pork with Chili & Garlic

Any leftovers from this dish can be used for a number of other dishes, such as stir-fries.

NUTRITIONAL INFORMATION

Calories ....137 Sugars 0.1g
Protein ....16g Fat 8g
Carbohydrate ....1g Saturates 2g

5 HOURS   35 MINS

SERVES 4

INGREDIENTS

1 lb 2 oz leg of pork, boned but not skinned

SAUCE

1 tsp finely chopped garlic

1 tsp finely chopped scallion

2 tbsp light soy sauce

1 tsp red chili oil

½ tsp sesame oil

sprig of fresh cilantro, to garnish (optional)

1 Place the pork, tied together in one piece, in a large saucepan, add enough cold water to cover, and bring to a rolling boil over a medium heat.

2 Using a draining spoon, skim off the scum that rises to the surface, cover the pan with a lid, and simmer gently for 25-30 minutes.

3 Leave the meat in the liquid to cool, under cover, for at least 1-2 hours.

4 Lift out the meat with 2 draining spoons and leave to cool completely, skin-side up, for 2-3 hours.

5 To serve, cut off the skin, leaving a very thin layer of fat ontop like a ham joint. Cut the meat in small thin slices across the grain, and arrange on a plate in an overlapping pattern.

6 In a small bowl, mix together the sauce ingredients, and pour the sauce evenly over the pork.

7 Garnish the pork with a sprig of fresh cilantro, if wished, and serve at once.

COOK'S TIP

This is a very simple dish, but beautifully presented. Make sure you slice the meat as thinly and evenly as possible to make an elegantly arranged dish.

Pork Dim Sum

These small steamed bundles are traditionally served as an appetizer and are very adaptable to your favorite fillings.

NUTRITIONAL INFORMATION

Calories 478	Sugars 3g	
Protein 33g	Fat 29g	
Carbohydrate ...21g	Saturates 9g	

 10 MINS   15 MINS

SERVES 4

I N G R E D I E N T S

14 oz ground pork

2 scallions, chopped

1¾ oz canned bamboo shoots, drained, rinsed, and chopped

1 tbsp light soy sauce

1 tbsp dry sherry

2 tsp sesame oil

2 tsp superfine sugar

1 egg white, lightly beaten

4½ tsp cornstarch

24 wonton skins

1 Place the ground pork, scallions, bamboo shoots, soy sauce, dry sherry, sesame oil, superfine sugar, and beaten egg white in a large mixing bowl and mix until all the ingredients are thoroughly combined.

2 Stir in the cornstarch, mixing until thoroughly incorporated with the other ingredients.

3 Spread out the wonton skins on a work counter. Place a spoonful of the pork and vegetable mixture in the center of each wonton wrapper and lightly brush the edges of the skins with water.

4 Bring the sides of the skins together in the center of the filling, pinching firmly together.

5 Line a steamer with a clean, damp dish cloth and arrange the wontons inside.

6 Cover and steam for 5–7 minutes, until the dim sum are cooked through. Serve immediately.

COOK'S TIP

Bamboo steamers are designed to rest on the sloping sides of a wok above the water. They are available in a range of sizes.

Pork Sesame Toasts

This classic Chinese appetizer is also a great nibble for serving at parties – but be sure to make plenty!

NUTRITIONAL INFORMATION

Calories 674	Sugars 2g	
Protein 33g	Fat 46g	
Carbohydrate . . .33g	Saturates 7g	

5 MINS   35 MINS

SERVES 4

I N G R E D I E N T S

9 oz lean pork

⅔ cup uncooked peeled shrimp, deveined

4 scallions, trimmed

1 garlic clove, crushed

1 tbsp chopped fresh cilantro leaves and stems

1 tbsp fish sauce

1 egg

8-10 slices of thick-cut white bread

3 tbsp sesame seeds

⅔ cup vegetable oil

salt and pepper

TO GARNISH

sprigs of fresh cilantro

red bell pepper, sliced finely

1 Put the pork, shrimp, scallions, garlic, cilantro, fish sauce, egg, and seasoning into a food processor or blender. Process for a few seconds until the ingredients are finely chopped. Transfer the mixture to a bowl. Alternatively, chop the pork, shrimp, and scallions very finely, and mix with the garlic, cilantro, fish sauce, beaten egg, and seasoning until all the ingredients are well combined.

2 Spread the pork and shrimp mixture thickly over the bread so that it reaches right up to the edges. Cut off the crusts and slice each piece of bread into 4 squares or triangles.

3 Sprinkle the topping liberally with sesame seeds.

4 Heat the oil in a wok or skillet. Fry a few pieces of the bread, topping side down first so that it sets the egg, for about 2 minutes or until golden brown. Turn the pieces over to cook on the other side, about 1 minute.

5 Drain the pork and shrimp toasts and place them on paper towels. Fry the remaining pieces. Serve garnished with sprigs of fresh cilantro and strips of red bell pepper.

Barbecue Spareribs

This is a simplified version of the half saddle of pork ribs seen hanging in the windows of Cantonese restaurants.

NUTRITIONAL INFORMATION

Calories	271	Sugars	4g
Protein	13g	Fat	22g
Carbohydrate	5g	Saturates	8g

6½ HOURS   50 MINS

SERVES 4

INGREDIENTS

1 lb 2 oz pork finger spareribs

1 tbsp sugar

1 tbsp light soy sauce

1 tbsp dark soy sauce

3 tbsp hoisin sauce

1 tbsp rice wine or dry sherry

4-5 tbsp water or Chinese Stock (see page 14)

mild chili sauce, to dip

cilantro leaves, to garnish

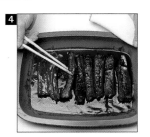

1 Using a sharp knife, trim off any excess fat from the spare ribs and cut into pieces. Place the ribs in a baking dish.

2 Mix together the sugar, light and dark soy sauces, hoisin sauce, and wine. Pour over the ribs in the baking dish. Turn to coat the ribs thoroughly in the mixture and leave to marinate for about 2-3 hours.

3 Add the water or Chinese stock to the ribs and spread them out in the dish. Roast in a preheated hot oven for 15 minutes.

4 Turn the ribs over, lower the oven temperature, and cook for 30-35 minutes longer.

5 To serve, chop each rib into 3-4 small, bite-sized pieces with a large knife or Chinese cleaver, and arrange neatly on a serving dish.

6 Pour the sauce from the baking dish over the spareribs and garnish with a few cilantro leaves. Place some mild chili sauce into a small dish and serve with the ribs as a dip. Serve immediately.

COOK'S TIP

Finger ribs are especially small, thin ribs. Ask your local butcher to cut some if you can't find the right size in the supermarket. Don't throw away any trimmings from the ribs – they can be used for soup or stock.

Spicy Salt & Pepper Shrimp

For best results, use raw tiger shrimp in their shells. You can buy them with or without their heads attached, as you prefer.

NUTRITIONAL INFORMATION

Calories	160	Sugars	.......0.2g
Protein	........17g	Fat	..........10g
Carbohydrate	...0.5g	Saturates	.......1g

  35 MINS   20 MINS

SERVES 4

INGREDIENTS

9-10½ oz raw shrimp in their shells, defrosted if frozen

1 tbsp light soy sauce

1 tsp Chinese rice wine or dry sherry

2 tsp cornstarch

vegetable oil, for deep-frying

2-3 scallions, to garnish

SPICY SALT AND PEPPER

1 tbsp salt

1 tsp ground Szechuan peppercorns

1 tsp five-spice powder

1 Pull the soft legs off the shrimp, but keep the body shells on. Dry well on paper towels.

2 Place the shrimp in a bowl with the soy sauce, rice wine or sherry and cornstarch. Turn the shrimp to coat thoroughly in the mixture and leave to marinate for about 25-30 minutes.

3 To make the Spicy Salt and Pepper, mix the salt, ground Szechuan peppercorns, and five-spice powder together. Place in a dry skillet and stir-fry for about 3-4 minutes over a low heat, stirring constantly to prevent the spices burning on the bottom of the pan. Remove from the heat and allow to cool.

4 Heat the vegetable oil in a preheated wok or large skillet until smoking, then deep-fry the shrimp in batches until golden brown. Remove the shrimp from the wok with a draining spoon and drain on paper towels.

5 Place the scallions in a bowl, pour on 1 tablespoon of the hot oil, and leave for 30 seconds. Serve the shrimp garnished with the scallions, and with the Spicy Salt and Pepper as a dip.

COOK'S TIP

The roasted spice mixture made with Szechuan peppercorns is used throughout China as a dip for deep-fried food. The peppercorns are sometimes roasted first and then ground. Dry-frying is a way of releasing the flavors of the spices.

Shrimp Rolls

These small shrimp bites are packed with the flavor of lime and cilantro for a quick and tasty appetizer.

NUTRITIONAL INFORMATION

Calories	305	Sugars	.........2g
Protein	........15g	Fat	..........21g
Carbohydrate	...14g	Saturates	.......8g

 15 MINS   20 MINS

SERVES 4

INGREDIENTS

1 tbsp sunflower oil

1 red bell pepper, seeded and very thinly sliced

¾ cup beansprouts

finely grated peel and juice of 1 lime

1 red chili, seeded and very finely chopped

½ inch piece of gingerroot, peeled and grated

8 oz peeled shrimp

1 tbsp fish sauce

½ tsp arrowroot

2 tbsp chopped fresh cilantro

8 sheets phyllo pastry dough

2 tbsp butter

2 tsp sesame oil

oil, for frying

scallion tassels, to garnish

chili sauce, to serve

COOK'S TIP

If using cooked shrimp, cook for 1 minute only otherwise they will toughen.

1 Heat the sunflower oil in a large preheated wok. Add the red bell pepper and beansprouts and stir-fry for 2 minutes, or until the vegetables have softened.

2 Remove the wok from the heat and toss in the lime peel and juice, red chili, ginger, and shrimp, stirring well.

3 Mix the fish sauce with the arrowroot and stir the mixture into the wok juices. Return the wok to the heat and cook, stirring, for 2 minutes, or until the juices thicken. Toss in the cilantro and mix well.

4 Lay the sheets of phyllo pastry dough out on a board. Melt the butter and sesame oil and brush each dough sheet with the mixture.

5 Spoon a little of the shrimp filling onto the top of each sheet, fold over each end, and roll up to enclose the filling.

6 Heat the oil in a large wok. Cook the rolls, in batches, for 2–3 minutes, or until crisp and golden. Garnish with scallion tassels and serve hot with a chili dipping sauce.

Fat Horses

A mixture of meats is flavored with coconut milk, fish sauce, and cilantro in this curious-sounding dish.

NUTRITIONAL INFORMATION

Calories 195	Sugars 1g
Protein 23g	Fat 11g
Carbohydrate 1g	Saturates 6g

🍲 🍲 🍲

🥘 10 MINS   🕐 30 MINS

SERVES 4

INGREDIENTS

2 tbsp creamed coconut

4½ oz boneless lean pork

4½ oz chicken breast, skin removed

½ cup canned crabmeat, drained

2 eggs

2 garlic cloves, crushed

4 scallions, trimmed and chopped

1 tbsp fish sauce

1 tbsp chopped fresh cilantro leaves and stems

1 tbsp dark muscovado sugar

salt and pepper

TO GARNISH

finely sliced daikon or turnip

chives

red chili

sprigs of fresh cilantro

3 Add the coconut mixture to the food processor or blender with the eggs, garlic, scallions, fish sauce, cilantro, and sugar. Seasonto taste and process for a few more seconds. Alternatively, mix these ingredients into the chopped pork, chicken, and crabmeat.

4 Grease 6 ramekins with a little butter. Spoon in the ground mixture, leveling the surface. Place them in a steamer, then set the steamer over a pan of gently boiling water. Cook until set, which will take about 30 minutes.

5 Lift out the dishes and leave to cool for a few minutes. Run a knife around the edge of each dish, then invert onto warmed plates. Serve garnished with finely sliced daikon or turnip, chives, red chili, and sprigs of fresh cilantro.

1 Mix the coconut with 3 tbsp of hot water. Stir to dissolve the coconut.

2 Put the pork, chicken and crabmeat into a food processor or blender and process for 10–15 seconds until ground, or chop them finely by hand and put in a mixing bowl.

Chili Fish Cakes

These small fish cakes are quick to make and are delicious served with a chili dip.

NUTRITIONAL INFORMATION

Calories 164   Sugars 1g
Protein . . . . .23g   Fat 6g
Carbohydrate . . . .6g   Saturates 1g

 5 MINS   40 MINS

SERVES 4

INGREDIENTS

1 lb cod fillets, skinned

2 tbsp fish sauce

2 red chilies, seeded and very finely chopped

2 cloves garlic, crushed

10 lime leaves, very finely chopped

2 tbsp fresh cilantro, chopped

1 large egg

¼ cup all-purpose flour

¾ cup fine green beans, very finely sliced

peanut oil, for frying

chili dip, to serve

VARIATION

Almost any kind of fish fillets and seafood can used in this recipe, try haddock, crabmeat or lobster.

1 Using a sharp knife, roughly cut the cod fillets into bite-sized pieces.

2 Place the cod in a food processor together with the fish sauce, chilies, garlic, lime leaves, cilantro, egg, and flour. Process until finely chopped and turn out into a large mixing bowl.

3 Add the green beans to the cod mixture and combine.

4 Divide the mixture into small balls. Flatten the balls between the palms of your hands to form patties.

5 Heat a little oil in a preheated wok or large skillet. Fry the fish cakes on both sides until brown and crispy on the outside.

6 Transfer the fish cakes to serving plates and serve hot with a chili dip.

Sweet & Sour Shrimp

Shrimp are marinated in a soy sauce mixture, coated in a light batter, fried, and served with a delicious sweet-and-sour dip.

NUTRITIONAL INFORMATION

Calories 294	Sugars 11g	
Protein 14g	Fat 12g	
Carbohydrate . . .34g	Saturates 2g	

40 MINS   20 MINS

SERVES 4

I N G R E D I E N T S

16 large raw shrimp, peeled

1 tsp grated fresh root ginger

1 garlic clove, crushed

2 scallions, sliced

2 tbsp dry sherry

2 tsp sesame oil

1 tbsp light soy sauce

vegetable oil, for deep-frying

shredded scallions, to garnish

B A T T E R

4 egg whites

4 tbsp cornstarch

2 tbsp all-purpose flour

S A U C E

2 tbsp tomato paste

3 tbsp white wine vinegar

4 tsp light soy sauce

2 tbsp lemon juice

3 tbsp light brown sugar

1 green bell pepper, seeded and cut into thin matchsticks

½ tsp chili sauce

1¼ cups vegetable stock

2 tsp cornstarch

1 Using tweezers, devein the shrimp, then flatten them with a large knife.

2 Place the shrimp in a dish and add the ginger, garlic, scallions, dry sherry, sesame oil, and soy sauce. Cover with plastic wrap and leave to marinate for 30 minutes.

3 Make the batter by beating the egg whites until thick. Fold in the cornstarch and all-purpose flour to form a light batter.

4 Place all of the sauce ingredients in a saucepan and bring to a boil. Reduce the heat and leave to simmer for 10 minutes.

5 Remove the shrimp from the marinade and dip them into the batter to coat.

6 Heat the vegetable oil in a preheated wok or large skillet until almost smoking. Reduce the heat and fry the shrimp for 3–4 minutes, until crisp and golden brown.

7 Garnish the shrimp with shredded scallion and serve with the sauce.

Poultry

Second to pork, poultry is one of the most popular foods throughout China. It also plays an important symbolic role in Chinese cooking. The cockerel symbolizes the male, positiveness, and aggression, while the duck represents happiness and fidelity. Being uniformly tender, poultry is ideal for Chinese cooking methods that rely on the rapid

cooking of small, even-sized pieces of meat. Poultry can be cut into wafer-thin slices, thin matchstick strips, or cubes, and can be quickly cooked without any loss of moisture or tenderness. This chapter contains dishes which are stir-fried, braised, steamed, and roasted, and old favorites as well as more unusual dishes.

Chicken Chop Suey

Chop suey is a well-known and popular dish containing beansprouts and soy sauce with a meat or vegetables.

NUTRITIONAL INFORMATION

Calories	337	Sugars	.........7g
Protein	........32g	Fat	..........18g
Carbohydrate	...14g	Saturates	.......3g

25 MINS   15 MINS

SERVES 4

I N G R E D I E N T S

4 tbsp light soy sauce

2 tsp light brown sugar

1 lb 2 oz skinless, boneless chicken breast halves

3 tbsp vegetable oil

2 onions, quartered

2 garlic cloves, crushed

3 cups beansprouts

1 tbsp sesame oil

1 tbsp cornstarch

3 tbsp water

2 cups chicken stock

shredded leek, to garnish

VARIATION

This recipe may be made with strips of lean steak, pork, or with mixed vegetables. Change the type of stock accordingly.

1 Mix the soy sauce and sugar together, stirring until the sugar has dissolved.

2 Trim any fat from the chicken and cut into thin strips. Place the meat in a shallow dish and spoon the soy mixture over them, turning to coat. Marinate in the refrigerator for 20 minutes.

3 Heat the oil in a wok and stir-fry the chicken for 2–3 minutes until golden brown. Add the onions and garlic and cook for a further 2 minutes. Add the beansprouts, cook for 4–5 minutes, then add the sesame oil.

4 Mix the cornstarch and water to form a smooth paste. Pour the stock into the wok, add the cornstarch paste and bring to a boil, stirring until the sauce is thickened and clear. Serve, garnished with shredded leek.

Cashew Chicken

Yellow bean sauce is available from supermarkets and Chinese food stores. Buy a chunky sauce, rather than a smooth one, for texture.

NUTRITIONAL INFORMATION

Calories	398	Sugars	.........2g
Protein	........31g	Fat	..........27g
Carbohydrate	....8g	Saturates	.......4g

10 MINS   15 MINS

SERVES 4

I N G R E D I E N T S

1 lb boneless chicken breast halves

2 tbsp vegetable oil

1 red onion, sliced

1½ cups flat mushrooms, sliced

⅓ cup cashew nuts

¼ cup yellow bean sauce

fresh cilantro, to garnish

egg fried rice or plain boiled rice, to serve

1 Using a sharp knife, remove the excess skin from the chicken breasts, if desired. Cut the chicken into small, bite-sized chunks.

2 Heat the vegetable oil in a preheated wok or skillet.

3 Add the chicken to the wok and stir-fry for 5 minutes.

4 Add the red onion and mushrooms to the wok and continue to stir-fry for a further 5 minutes.

5 Place the cashew nuts on a cookie sheet and toast under a heated medium broiler until just browning – toasting nuts brings out their flavour.

6 Toss the toasted cashew nuts into the wok together with the yellow bean sauce and heat through.

7 Allow the sauce to bubble for 2–3 minutes.

8 Transfer the chop suey to warm serving bowls and garnish with fresh cilantro. Serve hot with egg fried rice or plain boiled rice.

VARIATION

Chicken thighs could be used instead of the chicken breast halves for a more economical dish.

Lemon Chicken

This is on everyone's list of favorite Chinese dishes, and it is so simple to make. Serve with stir-fried vegetables for a truly delicious meal.

NUTRITIONAL INFORMATION

Calories	272	Sugars	.........1g
Protein	........36g	Fat	...........11g
Carbohydrate	....5g	Saturates	.......2g

  5 MINS   15 MINS

SERVES 4

INGREDIENTS

vegetable oil, for deep-frying

1 lb 7 oz skinless, boneless chicken, cut into strips

lemon slices and shredded scallion, to garnish

SAUCE

1 tbsp cornstarch

6 tbsp cold water

3 tbsp fresh lemon juice

2 tbsp sweet sherry

½ tsp superfine sugar

1 Heat the oil for deep-frying in a preheated wok or skillet to 350°F or until a cube of bread browns in 30 seconds.

2 Reduce the heat and stir-fry the chicken strips for 3–4 minutes, until cooked through.

3 Remove the chicken with a slotted spoon, set aside and keep warm. Drain the oil from the wok.

4 To make the sauce, mix the cornstarch with 2 tablespoons of the water to form a paste.

5 Pour the lemon juice and remaining water into the mixture in the wok.

6 Add the sweet sherry and superfine sugar and bring to a boil, stirring until the sugar has completely dissolved.

7 Stir in the cornstarch mixture and return to a boil. Reduce the heat and simmer, stirring constantly, for 2–3 minutes, until the sauce is thickened and clear.

8 Transfer the chicken to a warm serving plate and pour the sauce over the top.

9 Garnish the chicken with the lemon slices and shredded scallion and serve immediately.

COOK'S TIP

If you would prefer to use chicken portions rather than strips, cook them in the oil, covered, over a low heat for about 30 minutes, or until cooked through.

Stir-Fried Ginger Chicken

The oranges add color and piquancy to this refreshing dish, which complements the chicken well.

NUTRITIONAL INFORMATION

Calories 289	Sugars 15g
Protein 20g	Fat 9g
Carbohydrate ...17g	Saturates 2g

 5 MINS   20 MINS

SERVES 4

I N G R E D I E N T S

2 tbsp sunflower oil

1 onion, sliced

1½ cups carrots, cut into thin sticks

1 clove garlic, crushed

12 oz boneless skinless chicken breasts

2 tbsp fresh gingerroot, peeled and grated

1 tsp ground ginger

4 tbsp sweet sherry

1 tbsp tomato paste

1 tbsp demerara sugar

⅓ cup orange juice

1 tsp cornstarch

1 orange, peeled and segmented

fresh snipped chives, to garnish

1 Heat the oil in a large preheated wok. Add the onion, carrots, and garlic and stir-fry over a high heat for 3 minutes or until the vegetables begin to soften.

2 Slice the chicken into thin strips. Add to the wok with the fresh and ground ginger. Stir-fry for a further 10 minutes, or until the chicken is well cooked through and golden in color.

3 Mix together the sherry, tomato paste, sugar, orange juice, and cornstarch in a bowl. Stir the mixture into the wok and heat through until the mixture bubbles and the juices start to thicken.

4 Add the orange segments and carefully toss to mix.

5 Transfer the stir-fried chicken to warm serving bowls and garnish with freshly snipped chives. Serve immediately.

COOK'S TIP

Make sure that you do not continue cooking the dish once the orange segments have been added in step 4, otherwise they will break up.

Kung Po Chicken

In this recipe, cashew nuts are used, but peanuts, walnuts, or almonds can be substituted, if preferred.

NUTRITIONAL INFORMATION

Calories 294	Sugars 3g	
Protein 21g	Fat 18g	
Carbohydrate ...10g	Saturates 4g	

 10 MINS   5 MINS

SERVES 4

INGREDIENTS

9-10½ oz chicken meat, boned and skinned

¼ tsp salt

⅓ egg white

1 tsp cornstarch paste (see page 15)

1 medium green bell pepper, cored and seeded

4 tbsp vegetable oil

1 scallion, cut into short sections

a few small slices of gingerroot

4-5 small dried red chilies, soaked, seeded, and shredded

2 tbsp crushed yellow bean sauce

1 tsp rice wine or dry sherry

1 cup roasted cashew nuts

a few drops of sesame oil

boiled rice, to serve

1 Cut the chicken into small cubes about the size of sugar lumps. Place the chicken in a small bowl and mix with a pinch of salt, the egg white, and the cornstarch paste, in that order.

2 Cut the green bell pepper into cubes or triangles about the same size as the chicken pieces.

3 Heat the oil in a wok, add the chicken and stir-fry for 1 minute. Remove with a draining spoon and keep warm.

4 Add the scallion, ginger, chilies, and green bell pepper. Stir-fry for 1 minute, then add the chicken with the yellow bean sauce and wine. Blend well and stir-fry for another minute. Finally stir in the cashew nuts and sesame oil. Serve hot with boiled rice.

VARIATION

Any nuts can be used in place of the cashew nuts, if preferred. The important point is the crunchy texture, which is very much a feature of Szechuan cooking.

Green Chicken Stir-Fry

Tender chicken is mixed with a selection of spring greens and flavored with yellow bean sauce in this crunchy stir-fry.

NUTRITIONAL INFORMATION

Calories	297	Sugars	.........5g
Protein	........30g	Fat	..........16g
Carbohydrate	....8g	Saturates	.......3g

5 MINS   15 MINS

SERVES 4

INGREDIENTS

2 tbsp sunflower oil

1 lb skinless, boneless chicken breast

2 cloves garlic, crushed

1 green bell pepper

1½ cups snow peas

6 scallions, sliced, plus extra to garnish

3 cups spring greens or cabbage, shredded

¾ cup yellow bean sauce

3 tbsp roasted cashew nuts

1 Heat the sunflower oil in a large preheated wok.

2 Slice the chicken into thin strips and add to the wok together with the garlic. Stir-fry for about 5 minutes, or until the chicken is sealed on all sides and beginning to turn golden.

3 Using a sharp knife, seed the green bell pepper and cut into thin strips.

4 Add the snow peas, scallions, green bell pepper strips, and spring greens or cabbage to the wok. Stir-fry for a further 5 minutes, or until the vegetables are just tender.

5 Stir in the yellow bean sauce and heat through for about 2 minutes, or until the mixture starts to bubble.

6 Scatter the roasted cashew nuts into the wok.

7 Transfer the stir-fry to warm serving plates and garnish with extra scallions, if desired. Serve the stir-fry immediately.

COOK'S TIP

Do not add salted cashew nuts to this dish because this will make the dish too salty.

Orange Chicken Stir-Fry

Chicken thighs are inexpensive, meaty portions that are readily available. Although not as tender as breast, they are perfect for stir-frying.

NUTRITIONAL INFORMATION

Calories 267   Sugars 11g
Protein . . . . .23g   Fat 11g
Carbohydrate . . .15g   Saturates 2g

10 MINS   15 MINS

SERVES 4

INGREDIENTS

3 tbsp sunflower oil

12 oz boneless chicken thighs, skinned and cut into thin strips

1 onion, sliced

1 clove garlic, crushed

1 red bell pepper, seeded, and sliced

1¼ cups snow peas

4 tbsp light soy sauce

4 tbsp sherry

1 tbsp tomato paste

finely grated peel and juice of 1 orange

1 tsp cornstarch

2 oranges

1 cup beansprouts

cooked rice or noodles, to serve

1 Heat the oil in a large preheated wok. Add the chicken and stir-fry for 2–3 minutes, or until sealed on all sides.

2 Add the onion, garlic, bell pepper, and snow peas to the wok. Stir-fry for a further 5 minutes, or until the vegetables are just tender and the chicken is completely cooked through.

3 Mix together the soy sauce, sherry, tomato paste, orange peel and juice, and the cornstarch. Add to the wok and cook, stirring, until the juices start to thicken.

4 Using a sharp knife, peel and segment the oranges. Add the segments to the mixture in the wok with the beansprouts and heat through for a further 2 minutes.

5 Transfer the stir-fry to serving plates and serve at once with cooked rice or noodles.

COOK'S TIP

beansprouts are sprouting mung beans and are a regular ingredient in Chinese cooking. They require very little cooking and may even be eaten raw, if wished.

Chili Coconut Chicken

This tasty dish combines the flavors of lime, peanut, coconut, and chili. You'll find coconut cream in Oriental grocery stores.

NUTRITIONAL INFORMATION

Calories	348	Sugars	........2g
Protein	........36g	Fat	..........21g
Carbohydrate	....3g	Saturates	.......8g

4 MINS   15 MINS

SERVES 4

INGREDIENTS

⅔ cup hot chicken stock

⅓ cup creamed coconut

1 tbsp sunflower oil

8 skinless, boneless chicken thighs, cut into long, thin strips

1 small red chili, sliced thinly

4 scallions, sliced thinly

4 tbsp smooth or crunchy peanut butter

finely grated peel and juice of 1 lime

1 fresh red chili and scallion tassel, to garnish

boiled rice, to serve

1 Pour the chicken stock into a measuring jug or small bowl. Crumble the creamed coconut into the chicken stock and stir the mixture until the creamed coconut dissolves.

2 Heat the oil in a heated wok or large heavy pan.

3 Add the chicken strips and cook, stirring, until the chicken turns a golden color.

4 Stir in the chopped red chili and scallions and cook gently for a few minutes.

5 Add the peanut butter, dissolved creamed coconut, and chicken stock mixture, lime peel and juice, and simmer, uncovered, for about 5 minutes, stirring frequently to prevent the mixture sticking.

6 Transfer the chili coconut chicken to a warm serving dish, garnish with the red chili and scallion tassel and serve with boiled rice.

COOK'S TIP

Serve jasmine rice with this spicy dish. It has a fragrant aroma that is well-suited to the flavors in this dish.

Chicken with Black Bean Sauce

This tasty chicken stir-fry is quick and easy to make, and is full of fresh flavors and crunchy vegetables.

NUTRITIONAL INFORMATION

Calories 205	Sugars 4g
Protein 25g	Fat 9g
Carbohydrate 6g	Saturates 2g

  40 MINS   10 MINS

SERVES 4

INGREDIENTS

3 cups chicken breasts, sliced thinly

pinch of salt

pinch of cornstarch

2 tbsp oil

1 garlic clove, crushed

1 tbsp black bean sauce

1 each small red and green bell pepper, cut into strips

1 red chili, chopped finely

1 cup mushrooms, sliced

1 onion, chopped

6 scallions, chopped

salt and pepper

SEASONING

½ tsp salt

½ tsp sugar

3 tbsp chicken stock

1 tbsp dark soy sauce

2 tbsp beef stock

2 tbsp rice wine

1 tsp cornstarch, blended with a little rice wine

1 Put the chicken strips in a bowl. Add a pinch of salt and a pinch of cornstarch and cover with water. Leave to stand for 30 minutes.

2 Heat 1 tablespoon of the oil in a wok or deep-sided skillet and stir-fry the chicken for 4 minutes.

3 Remove the chicken to a warm serving dish and clean the wok.

4 Add the remaining oil to the wok and add the garlic, black bean sauce, green and red bell peppers, chili, mushrooms, onion, and scallions. Stir-fry for 2 minutes then return the chicken to the wok.

5 Add the seasoning ingredients, fry for 3 minutes, and thicken with a little of the cornstarch blend. Serve with fresh noodles.

Szechuan Chili Chicken

In China, the chicken pieces are chopped through the bone for this dish, but if you do not possess a cleaver, use boned chicken meat.

NUTRITIONAL INFORMATION

Calories 218   Sugars 4g
Protein . . . . .23g   Fat 9g
Carbohydrate . . . .8g   Saturates 2g

45 MINS   15 MINS

SERVES 4

INGREDIENTS

1 lb 2 oz chicken thighs

¼ tsp pepper

1 tbsp sugar

2 tsp light soy sauce

1 tsp dark soy sauce

1 tbsp rice wine or dry sherry

2 tsp cornstarch

2-3 tbsp vegetable oil

1-2 garlic cloves, crushed

2 scallions, cut into short sections, with the green and white parts separated

4-6 small dried red chilies, soaked and seeded

2 tbsp crushed yellow bean sauce

⅔ cup Chinese stock (see page 14) or water

1 Cut or chop the chicken thighs into bite-sized pieces and marinate with the pepper, sugar, soy sauce, wine, and cornstarch for 25-30 minutes.

2 Heat the oil in a heated wok and stir-fry the chicken for about 1–2 minutes until lightly brown. Remove with a draining spoon, transfer to a warm dish and reserve. Add the garlic, the white parts of the scallions, the chilies, and yellow bean sauce to the wok and stir-fry for about 30 seconds.

3 Return the chicken to the wok, stirring constantly for about 1–2 minutes, then add the stock or water, bring to a boil, and cover. Braise over a medium heat for 5-6 minutes, stirring once or twice. Garnish with the green parts of the scallions and serve immediately.

COOK'S TIP

One of the striking features of Szechuan cooking is the quantity of chilies used. Food generally in this region is much hotter than elsewhere in China – people tend to keep a string of dry chilies hanging from the eaves of their houses.

Cumin-Spiced Chicken

Cumin seeds are more frequently associated with Indian cooking, but they are used in this Chinese recipe for their earthy flavor.

NUTRITIONAL INFORMATION

Calories ....245 Sugars 9g
Protein ....28g Fat 10g
Carbohydrate ....11g Saturates 2g

 5 MINS   15 MINS

SERVES 4

INGREDIENTS

1 lb boneless, skinless chicken breast halves

2 tbsp sunflower oil

1 clove garlic, crushed

1 tbsp cumin seeds

1 tbsp grated fresh gingerroot

1 red chili, seeded and sliced

1 red bell pepper, seeded and sliced

1 green bell pepper, seeded and sliced

1 yellow bell pepper, seeded and sliced

1 cup beansprouts

12 oz pak choi or other green leaves

2 tbsp sweet chili sauce

3 tbsp light soy sauce

deep-fried crispy gingerroot, to garnish (see Cook's Tip)

COOK'S TIP

To make the deep-fried ginger garnish, peel and thinly slice a large piece of gingerroot. Carefully lower the slices of gingerroot into a wok or small pan of hot oil and cook for about 30 seconds. Transfer to paper towels and leave to drain thoroughly.

1 Using a sharp knife, slice the chicken breasts into thin strips.

2 Heat the oil in a large preheated wok.

3 Add the chicken to the wok and stir-fry for 5 minutes.

4 Add the garlic, cumin seeds, ginger and chili to the wok, stirring to mix.

5 Add all the bell peppers to the wok and stir-fry for a further 5 minutes.

6 Toss in the beansprouts and pak choi together with the sweet chili sauce and soy sauce and continue to cook until the pak choi leaves start to wilt.

7 Transfer to warm serving bowls and garnish with deep-fried gingerroot (see Cook's Tip).

Spicy Peanut Chicken

This quick dish has many variations, but this version includes the classic combination of peanuts, chicken, and chilies.

NUTRITIONAL INFORMATION

Calories	342	Sugars	........3g
Protein	........25g	Fat	..........24g
Carbohydrate	....6g	Saturates	.......5g

5 MINS   10 MINS

SERVES 4

INGREDIENTS

10½ oz skinless, boneless chicken breast halves

2 tbsp peanut oil

1 cup shelled peanuts

1 fresh red chili, sliced

1 green bell pepper, seeded and cut into strips

fried rice, to serve

SAUCE

⅔ cup chicken stock

1 tbsp Chinese rice wine or dry sherry

1 tbsp light soy sauce

1½ tsp light brown sugar

2 garlic cloves, crushed

1 tsp grated fresh gingerroot

1 tsp rice wine vinegar

1 tsp sesame oil

1 Trim any fat from the chicken and cut the meat into 1-inch cubes. Set aside until required.

2 Heat the peanut oil in a heated wok or skillet.

3 Add the peanuts to the wok and stir-fry for 1 minute. Remove the peanuts with a draining spoon and set aside.

4 Add the chicken to the wok and cook for 1–2 minutes.

5 Stir in the chili and green bell pepper and cook for 1 minute. Remove from the wok with a draining spoon and set aside.

6 Put half of the peanuts in a food processor and process until almost smooth. If necessary, add a little stock to form a softer paste. Alternatively, place them in a plastic bag and crush them with a rolling pin.

7 To make the sauce, add the chicken stock, Chinese rice wine or dry sherry, light soy sauce, light brown sugar, crushed garlic cloves, grated fresh gingerroot and rice wine vinegar to the wok.

8 Heat the sauce without boiling and stir in the peanut paste, remaining peanuts, chicken, sliced red chili, and green bell pepper strips. Mix well until all the ingredients are thoroughly combined.

9 Sprinkle the sesame oil into the wok, stir, and cook for 1 minute. Transfer the spicy peanut chicken to a warm serving dish and serve hot with fried rice.

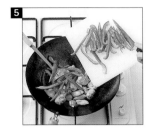

Yellow Bean Chicken

Yellow bean sauce is available from supermarkets and Chinese food stores. It is made from yellow soy beans and is quite salty.

NUTRITIONAL INFORMATION

Calories	234	Sugars 1g
Protein	........26g	Fat 12g
Carbohydrate	....6g	Saturates 2g

25 MINS   10 MINS

SERVES 4

INGREDIENTS

1 lb skinless, boneless chicken breast halves

1 egg white, beaten

1 tbsp cornstarch

1 tbsp rice wine vinegar

1 tbsp light soy sauce

1 tsp superfine sugar

3 tbsp vegetable oil

1 garlic clove, crushed

½-inch piece fresh root gingerroot, grated

1 green bell pepper, seeded and diced

2 large mushrooms, sliced

3 tbsp yellow bean sauce

yellow or green bell pepper strips, to garnish

1 Trim any fat from the chicken and cut the meat into 1-inch cubes.

2 Mix the egg white and cornstarch in a shallow bowl. Add the chicken and turn in the mixture to coat. Set aside for 20 minutes.

3 Mix the rice wine vinegar, soy sauce, and superfine sugar in a bowl.

4 Remove the chicken from the egg-white mixture.

5 Heat the oil in a preheated wok, add the chicken and stir-fry for 3–4 minutes, until golden brown. Remove the chicken from the wok with a draining spoon, set aside, and keep warm.

6 Add the garlic, ginger, bell pepper, and mushrooms to the wok and stir-fry for 1–2 minutes.

7 Add the yellow bean sauce and cook for 1 minute. Stir in the vinegar mixture and return the chicken to the wok. Cook for 1–2 minutes and serve hot, garnished with bell pepper strips.

VARIATION

Black bean sauce will work equally well with this recipe. Although this would affect the appearance of the dish, as the sauce is much darker in color, the flavors would be compatible.

Peppered Chicken

Crushed mixed peppercorns coat tender, thin strips of chicken that are cooked with green and red bell peppers to make a really colorful dish.

NUTRITIONAL INFORMATION

Calories 219	Sugars 6g
Protein 22g	Fat 10g
Carbohydrate 11g	Saturates 2g

 5 MINS   15 MINS

SERVES 4

INGREDIENTS

2 tbsp tomato catsup

2 tbsp soy sauce

1 lb boneless, skinless chicken breast halves

2 tbsp crushed mixed peppercorns

2 tbsp sunflower oil

1 red bell pepper

1 green bell pepper

2½ cups sugar snap peas

2 tbsp oyster sauce

1 Mix the tomato catsup with the soy sauce in a bowl.

2 Using a sharp knife, slice the chicken into thin strips.

3 Toss the chicken in the tomato catsup and soy sauce mixture until the chicken is well coated.

4 Sprinkle the crushed peppercorns on to a plate. Dip the coated chicken in the peppercorns until evenly coated.

5 Heat the sunflower oil in a preheated wok or large skillet, until the oil is smoking.

6 Add the chicken to the wok and stir-fry for 5 minutes.

7 Using a sharp knife, seed and slice the bell peppers.

8 Add the bell peppers to the wok together with the sugar snap peas and stir-fry for a further 5 minutes.

9 Add the oyster sauce and allow to bubble for 2 minutes. Transfer the peppered chicken to serving bowls and serve immediately.

VARIATION

Use snow peas instead of the sugar snap peas, if you prefer.

Chicken & Corn Stir-Fry

This quick and healthy dish is stir-fried, which means you use only the minimum of fat.

NUTRITIONAL INFORMATION

Calories 280	Sugars 7g
Protein 31g	Fat 11g
Carbohydrate 9g	Saturates 2g

5 MINS   10 MINS

SERVES 4

INGREDIENTS

4 skinless, boneless chicken breast halves

1⅓ cups baby corn-on-the-cob

9 oz snow peas

2 tbsp sunflower oil

1 tbsp sherry vinegar

1 tbsp honey

1 tbsp light soy sauce

1 tbsp sunflower seeds

pepper

rice or Chinese egg noodles, to serve

1 Using a sharp knife, slice the chicken breasts into long, thin strips.

2 Cut the baby corn in half lengthways and top and tail the snow peas.

3 Heat the sunflower oil in a preheated wok or a wide skillet.

4 Add the chicken and fry over a fairly high heat, stirring, for 1 minute.

5 Add the baby corn and snow peas and stir-fry over a medium heat for 5–8 minutes, until evenly cooked. The vegetables should still be slightly crunchy.

6 Mix together the sherry vinegar, honey and soy sauce in a small bowl.

7 Stir the vinegar mixture into the pan with the sunflower seeds.

8 Season well with pepper. Cook, stirring, for 1 minute.

9 Serve the chicken and corn stir-fry hot with rice or Chinese egg noodles.

VARIATION

Rice vinegar or balsamic vinegar makes a good substitute for the sherry vinegar.

Chicken with bell Peppers

Red bell pepper or celery can also be used in this recipe, as can lean turkey meat.

NUTRITIONAL INFORMATION

Calories	113	Sugars	.........1g
Protein	.........17g	Fat	..........3g
Carbohydrate	....4g	Saturates	.......1g

5 MINS   5 MINS

SERVES 4

INGREDIENTS

10½ oz boned, skinned chicken breast

1 tsp salt

½ egg white

2 tsp cornstarch paste (see page 15)

1 medium green bell pepper, cored and seeded

1¼ cups vegetable oil

1 scallion, finely shredded

a few strips of gingerroot, thinly shredded

1-2 red chilies, seeded and thinly shredded

½ tsp sugar

1 tbsp rice wine or dry sherry

a few drops of sesame oil

1 Cut the chicken breast into strips. Mix the chicken with a pinch of the salt, the egg white, and cornstarch.

2 Cut the green bell pepper into fairly thin shreds.

3 Heat the oil in a preheated wok, and deep-fry the chicken strips in batches for about 1 minute, or until the chicken changes color. Remove the chicken strips with a draining spoon, pat dry on paper towels, and keep warm.

4 Pour off the excess oil from the wok, leaving about 1 tablespoon. Add the scallion, ginger, chilies, and green bell pepper and stir-fry for 1 minute.

5 Return the chicken to the wok with the remaining salt, the sugar and wine or sherry. Stir-fry for another minute, sprinkle with sesame oil, and serve immediately.

COOK'S TIP

Rice wine is used everywhere in China for both cooking and drinking. Made from glutinous rice, it is known as yellow wine because of its rich amber color. Sherry is the best substitute as a cooking ingredient.

Braised Chicken

This is a delicious way to cook a whole chicken. It has a wonderful glaze, which is served as a sauce.

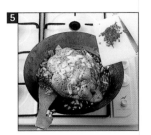

NUTRITIONAL INFORMATION

Calories 294	Sugars 9g	
Protein 31g	Fat 15g	
Carbohydrate ...10g	Saturates 3g	

 5 MINS   1¼ HOURS

SERVES 4

I N G R E D I E N T S

3 lb 5 oz chicken

3 tbsp vegetable oil

1 tbsp peanut oil

2 tbsp dark brown sugar

5 tbsp dark soy sauce

⅔ cup water

2 cloves garlic, crushed

1 small onion, chopped

1 fresh red chili, chopped

celery leaves and chives,
   to garnish

1 Preheat a large wok or large skillet on a high heat.

2 Clean the chicken inside and out with damp paper towels.

3 Put the vegetable oil and peanut oil in the wok, add the dark brown sugar, and heat gently until the sugar caramelizes.

4 Stir the soy sauce into the wok. Add the chicken and turn it in the mixture to coat thoroughly on all sides.

5 Add the water, garlic, onion, and chili. Cover and simmer, turning the chicken occasionally, for about 1 hour, or until cooked through. Test by piercing a thigh with the point of a knife or a skewer – the juices will run clear when the chicken is cooked.

6 Remove the chicken from the wok and set aside. Increase the heat and reduce the sauce in the wok until thickened. Transfer the chicken to a serving plate, garnish with celery leaves and chives, and serve with the sauce.

COOK'S TIP

For a spicier sauce, add 1 tbsp finely chopped fresh gingerroot and 1 tbsp ground Szechuan peppercorns with the chili in step 5.

Honey & Soy Chicken

Honey is often added to Chinese recipes for sweetness, and it combines well with the saltiness of the soy sauce.

NUTRITIONAL INFORMATION

Calories	279	Sugars	........10g
Protein	........38g	Fat	...........8g
Carbohydrate	...12g	Saturates	.......2g

35 MINS   25 MINS

SERVES 4

INGREDIENTS

2 tbsp honey

3 tbsp light soy sauce

1 tsp Chinese five-spice powder

1 tbsp sweet sherry

1 clove garlic, crushed

8 chicken thighs

1 tbsp sunflower oil

1 red chili

1¼ cups baby corn-on-the-cobs, halved

8 scallions, sliced

1½ cups beansprouts

1 Mix together the honey, soy sauce, Chinese five-spice powder, sherry, and garlic in a large bowl.

2 Using a sharp knife, make 3 slashes in the skin of each chicken thigh. Brush the honey and soy marinade over the chicken thighs, cover, and leave to stand for at least 30 minutes.

3 Heat the oil in a large heated wok. Add the chicken and cook over a fairly high heat for 12–15 minutes, or until the chicken browns and the skin begins to crispen. Remove the chicken with a draining spoon and keep warm until required.

4 Using a sharp knife, seed and very finely chop the chili.

5 Add the chili, corn cobs, scallions, and beansprouts to the wok and stir-fry for 5 minutes.

6 Return the chicken to the wok and mix all of the ingredients together until completely heated through. Transfer to serving plates and serve immediately.

COOK'S TIP

Chinese five-spice powder is found in most large supermarkets and is a blend of star anise, fennel seeds, cloves, cinnamon bark, and Szechuan pepper.

Peanut Sesame Chicken

Sesame seeds and peanuts give extra crunch and flavor to this stir-fry, and the fruit juice glaze gives a shiny coating to the sauce.

NUTRITIONAL INFORMATION

Calories ....435 Sugars 10g
Protein ....38g Fat 26g
Carbohydrate ...14g Saturates 4g

10 MINS   15 MINS

SERVES 4

I N G R E D I E N T S

2 tbsp vegetable oil

2 tbsp sesame oil

1 lb 2 oz boneless, skinned chicken breast halves, sliced into strips

1½ cups broccoli, divided into small flowerets

9 oz baby corn-on-the-cobs, halved if large

1 small red bell pepper, cored, seeded, and sliced

2 tbsp soy sauce

1 cup orange juice

2 tsp cornstarch

2 tbsp toasted sesame seeds

⅓ cup roasted, shelled, unsalted peanuts

rice or noodles, to serve

1 Heat the vegetable oil and sesame oil in a large, heavy-based skillet or wok until smoking. Add the chicken strips and stir-fry until browned, about 4-5 minutes.

2 Add the broccoli, corn, and red bell pepper and stir-fry for a further 1-2 minutes.

3 Meanwhile, mix the soy sauce with the orange juice, and cornstarch. Stir into the chicken and vegetable mixture, stirring constantly until the sauce has slightly thickened and a glaze develops.

4 Stir in the sesame seeds and peanuts, mixing well. Heat the stir-fry for a further 3-4 minutes.

5 Transfer the stir-fry to a warm serving dish and serve with rice or noodles.

COOK'S TIP

Make sure you use the unsalted peanuts or the dish will be too salty, because the soy sauce adds saltiness.

Chicken Fu-Yung

Although commonly described as an omelet, a fu-yung (white lotus petals) should be made with egg whites only to create a delicate texture.

NUTRITIONAL INFORMATION

Calories 220	Sugars 1g	
Protein 16g	Fat 14g	
Carbohydrate 7g	Saturates 3g	

  5 MINS   5 MINS

SERVES 4

INGREDIENTS

6 oz chicken breast fillet, skinned

½ tsp salt

pepper

1 tsp rice wine or dry sherry

1 tbsp cornstarch

3 eggs

½ tsp finely chopped scallions

3 tbsp vegetable oil

1 cup green peas

1 tsp light soy sauce

salt

few drops of sesame oil

1 Cut the chicken across the grain into very small, paper-thin slices, using a cleaver. Place the chicken slices in a shallow dish.

2 In a small bowl, mix together ½ teaspoon salt, pepper, rice wine or dry sherry, and cornstarch.

3 Pour the mixture over the chicken slices in the dish, turning the chicken until well coated.

4 Beat the eggs in a small bowl with a pinch of salt and the scallions.

5 Heat the vegetable oil in a preheated wok, add the chicken slices, and stir-fry for about 1 minute, making sure that the slices are kept separated.

6 Pour the beaten eggs over the chicken, and lightly scramble until set. Do not stir too vigorously, or the mixture will break up in the oil. Stir the oil from the bottom of the wok so that the foo-yung rises to the surface.

7 Add the peas, light soy sauce, and salt to taste and blend well. Transfer to warm serving dishes, sprinkle with sesame oil, and serve.

COOK'S TIP

If available, chicken strips can be used for this dish.

Crispy Chicken

In this recipe, the chicken is brushed with a syrup and deep-fried until golden. The dish is a little time consuming, but well worth the effort.

NUTRITIONAL INFORMATION

Calories 283	Sugars 8g
Protein 29g	Fat 15g
Carbohydrate 8g	Saturates 3g

15 HOURS   35 MINS

SERVES 4

INGREDIENTS

3 lb 5 oz oven-ready chicken

2 tbsp honey

2 tsp Chinese five-spice powder

2 tbsp rice wine vinegar

3 ¾ cups vegetable oil, for deep-frying

chili sauce, to serve

1 Rinse the chicken inside and out under cold running water and pat dry with paper towels.

2 Bring a large saucepan of water to a boil and remove from the heat. Place the chicken in the water, cover, and set aside for 20 minutes.

3 Remove the chicken from the water and pat dry with absorbent paper towels. Cool and leave to chill in the refrigerator overnight.

4 To make the glaze, mix the honey, Chinese five-spice powder, and rice wine vinegar together.

5 Brush some of the glaze all over the chicken and return to the refrigerator for 20 minutes.

6 Repeat this process of glazing and refrigerating the chicken until all of the glaze has been used. Return the chicken to the refrigerator for at least 2 hours after the final coating.

7 Using a cleaver or heavy kitchen knife, open the chicken out by splitting it through the center through the breast and then cut each half into 4 pieces.

8 Heat the oil for deep-frying in a wok until almost smoking. Reduce the heat and fry each piece of chicken for 5–7 minutes until golden and cooked through. Remove from the oil with a draining spoon and drain on paper towels.

9 Transfer to a serving dish and serve hot with a little chili sauce.

COOK'S TIP

If it is easier, use chicken portions instead of a whole chicken. You could also use chicken legs for this recipe, if you prefer.

Lemon & Sesame Chicken

Sesame seeds have a strong flavor and also add nuttiness to recipes.
They are perfect for coating these thin chicken strips.

NUTRITIONAL INFORMATION

Calories	273	Sugars	.........5g
Protein	........29g	Fat	..........13g
Carbohydrate	....11g	Saturates	.......3g

10 MINS   10 MINS

SERVES 4

I N G R E D I E N T S

4 boneless, skinless chicken breast halves

1 egg white

2 tbsp sesame seeds

2 tbsp vegetable oil

1 onion, sliced

1 tbsp brown crystal sugar

finely grated peel and juice of 1 lemon

3 tbsp lemon curd

7 oz canned water chestnuts, drained

lemon peel, to garnish

COOK'S TIP

Water chestnuts are commonly added to Chinese recipes for their crunchy texture because they do not have a great deal of flavor.

1 Place the chicken pieces between 2 sheets of plastic wrap and pound with a rolling pin to flatten. Slice the chicken into thin strips.

2 Whisk the egg white until light and foamy. Dip the chicken strips into the egg white, then coat in the sesame seeds.

3 Heat the oil in a wok and stir-fry the onion for 2 minutes until softened.

4 Add the chicken to the wok and stir-fry for 5 minutes, or until the chicken turns golden.

5 Mix the sugar, lemon peel, lemon juice, and lemon curd and add to the wok.; allow it to bubble slightly.

6 Slice the water chestnuts thinly, add to the wok, and cook for 2 minutes. Garnish with lemon peel and serve hot.

Chicken with Chili & Basil

Chicken drumsticks are cooked in a delicious sauce and served with deep-fried basil for color and flavor.

NUTRITIONAL INFORMATION

Calories 196	Sugars 2g
Protein 23g	Fat 10g
Carbohydrate 3g	Saturates 2g

5 MINS   30 MINS

SERVES 4

I N G R E D I E N T S

8 chicken drumsticks

2 tbsp soy sauce

1 tbsp sunflower oil

1 red chili

¾ cup carrots, cut into thin sticks

6 celery stalks, cut into sticks

3 tbsp sweet chili sauce

vegetable oil, for frying

about 50 fresh basil leaves

1 Remove the skin from the chicken drumsticks, if desired. Make 3 slashes in each drumstick. Brush the drumsticks with the soy sauce.

2 Heat the sunflower oil in a preheated wok and fry the drumsticks for 20 minutes, turning frequently, until they are cooked through.

3 Seed and finely chop the chili. Add the chili, carrots, and celery to the wok and cook for a further 5 minutes. Stir in the chili sauce, cover, and allow to bubble gently whilst preparing the basil leaves.

4 Heat a little oil in a heavy-based pan. Carefully add the basil leaves – stand well away from the pan and protect

your hand with a dish cloth as they will spit. Cook the basil leaves for about 30 seconds, or until they begin to curl up but not brown. Leave the leaves to drain on paper towels.

5 Arrange the cooked chicken, vegetables, and pan juices on to a warm serving plate, garnish with the deep-fried crispy basil leaves, and serve immediately.

COOK'S TIP

Basil has a very strong flavor that is perfect with chicken and Chinese flavorings. You could use baby spinach instead of the basil, if you prefer.

Aromatic & Crispy Duck

As it is very time-consuming to make the pancakes, buy prepared ones from Oriental food stores, or use crisp lettuce leaves as the wrapper.

NUTRITIONAL INFORMATION

Calories	169	Sugars	.........1g
Protein	.........7g	Fat	...........11g
Carbohydrate	....7g	Saturates	.......3g

7 HOURS   5 HOURS

SERVES 4

INGREDIENTS

2 large duckling quarters

1 tsp salt

3-4 pieces star anise

1 tsp Szechuan red peppercorns

1 tsp cloves

2 cinnamon sticks, broken into pieces

2-3 scallions, cut into short sections

4-5 small slices gingerroot

3-4 tbsp rice wine or dry sherry

vegetable oil, for deep-frying

TO SERVE

12 pancakes or 12 crisp lettuce leaves

hoisin or plum sauce

¼ cucumber, finley shredded

3-4 scallions, finely shredded

1 Rub the duck with the salt and arrange the star anise, peppercorns, cloves, and cinnamon on top. Sprinkle with the scallions, ginger, and wine and marinate for at least 3-4 hours.

2 Arrange the duck pieces on a plate that will fit inside a bamboo steamer. Pour some hot water into a wok, and place the bamboo steamer on top, sitting on a trivet. Add the duck and cover with the bamboo lid. Steam the duck over a high heat for 2-3 hours, until tender and cooked through. Top up the hot water from time to time as required. Remove the duck and leave to cool for at least 4-5 hours so the skin becomes crispy.

3 Pour off the water and wipe the wok dry. Pour in the oil and heat until smoking. Deep-fry the duck pieces, skin-side down, for 4-5 minutes, or until crisp and brown; remove and drain.

4 To serve, scrape the meat off the bone, place about 1 teaspoon of hoisin or plum sauce on the center of a pancake (or lettuce leaf), and add a few pieces of cucumber and scallion with a portion of the duck meat. Wrap up to form a small roll and eat with your fingers.

Fruity Duck Stir-Fry

The pineapple and plum sauce add a sweetness and fruity flavor to this colorful recipe that blends well with the duck.

NUTRITIONAL INFORMATION

Calories 241	Sugars 7g
Protein 26g	Fat 8g
Carbohydrate . . .16g	Saturates 2g

 5 MINS   25 MINS

SERVES 4

INGREDIENTS

4 duck breast halves

1 tsp Chinese five-spice powder

1 tbsp cornstarch

1 tbsp chili oil

1½ cups baby onions, peeled

2 cloves garlic, crushed

1 cup baby corn-on-the-cobs

1¼ cups canned pineapple chunks

6 scallions, sliced

1 cup beansprouts

2 tbsp plum sauce

1 Remove any skin from the duck breasts. Cut the duck into thin slices.

2 Mix the five-spice powder and the cornstarch together. Toss the duck in the mixture until well coated.

3 Heat the oil in a preheated wok. Stir-fry the duck for 10 minutes, or until just begining to crispen around the edges. Remove from the wok and set aside.

4 Add the onions and garlic to the wok and stir-fry for 5 minutes, or until softened. Add the baby corn-on-the-cobs and stir-fry for a further 5 minutes. Add the pineapple, scallions, and beansprouts and stir-fry for 3–4 minutes. Stir in the plum sauce.

5 Return the cooked duck to the wok and toss until well mixed. Transfer to warm serving dishes and serve hot.

COOK'S TIP

Buy pineapple chunks in natural juice rather than syrup for a fresher flavor. If you can only find pineapple in syrup, rinse it in cold water and drain thoroughly before using.

Duck with Ginger & Lime

Just the thing for a lazy summer day – roasted duck sliced and served with a dressing made of ginger, lime juice, sesame oil, and fish sauce.

NUTRITIONAL INFORMATION

Calories	529	Sugars	.........3g
Protein	........38g	Fat	..........41g
Carbohydrate	....3g	Saturates	.......6g

20 MINS   25 MINS

SERVES 4

INGREDIENTS

3 boneless Barbary duck breast halves, about 9 oz each

salt

DRESSING

½ cup olive oil

2 tsp sesame oil

2 tbsp lime juice

grated peel and juice of 1 orange

2 tsp fish sauce

1 tbsp grated gingerroot

1 garlic clove, crushed

2 tsp light soy sauce

3 scallions, finely chopped

1 tsp sugar

about 9 oz assorted salad leaves

orange slices, to garnish (optional)

1 Wash the duck pieces, dry on paper towels, and then cut in half. Prick the skin all over with a fork and season well with salt. Place the duck pieces, skin-side down, on a wire rack or trivet over a roasting pan.

2 Cook the duck in a preheated oven for 10 minutes, then turn over and cook for a further 12-15 minutes, or until the duck is cooked, but still pink in the center, and the skin is crisp.

3 To make the dressing, beat the olive oil and sesame oil with the lime juice, orange peel and juice, fish sauce, grated gingerroot, garlic, light soy sauce, scallions, and sugar until well blended.

4 Remove the duck from the oven, and allow to cool. Using a sharp knife, cut the duck into thick slices.

5 Add a little of the dressing to moisten and coat the duck.

6 To serve, arrange assorted salad leaves on a serving dish. Top with the sliced duck breasts and drizzle with the remaining salad dressing.

7 Garnish with orange slices, if using, then serve at once.

Barbecued Duck Breasts

The sweet, spicy marinade used in this recipe gives the duck a subtle flavor of the Orient.

NUTRITIONAL INFORMATION

Calories 249   Sugars 20g
Protein . . . . .27g   Fat 6g
Carbohydrate . . .23g   Saturates 2g

6¼ HOURS   30 MINS

SERVES 4

INGREDIENTS

3 cloves garlic, crushed

⅔ cup light soy sauce

5 tbsp light muscovado sugar

1-inch piece gingerroot, grated

1 tbsp chopped, fresh cilantro

1 tsp five-spice powder

4 duck breast halves

sprig of fresh cilantro, to garnish (optional)

1 To make the marinade, mix together the garlic, soy sauce, sugar, grated ginger, chopped cilantro, and five-spice powder in a small bowl until well combined.

2 Place the duck pieces in a shallow, nonmetallic dish and pour over the marinade. Carefully turn over the duck so it is coated with the marinade on both sides.

3 Cover the bowl with plastic wrap and leave to marinate for 1–6 hours, turning the duck once or twice so that the marinade is fully absorbed.

4 Remove the duck from the marinade, reserving the marinade for basting.

5 Barbecue the duckling breast halves over hot coals for about 20–30 minutes, turning and basting frequently with the reserved marinade, using a pastry brush.

6 Cut the duckling into slices and transfer to warm serving plates. Serve the barbecued duck garnished with a sprig of fresh cilantro, if using.

COOK'S TIP

Duck is quite a fatty meat so there is no need to add oil to the marinade. However, you must remember to oil the barbecue rack to prevent the duck from sticking. Oil the barbecue rack standing well away from the barbecue to avoid any danger of a flare-up.

Sweet Mango Chicken

The sweet, scented flavor of mango gives this dish its characteristic sweetness.

NUTRITIONAL INFORMATION

Calories 244   Sugars 18g
Protein . . . . .27g   Fat 7g
Carbohydrate . . .2.1g   Saturates 2g

🍲 10 MINS   🕐 15 MINS

SERVES 4

I N G R E D I E N T S

1 tbsp sunflower oil

6 skinless, boneless chicken thighs

1 ripe mango

2 cloves garlic, crushed

2 cups leeks, shredded

1 cup beansprouts

⅔ cup mango juice

1 tbsp white wine vinegar

2 tbsp honey

2 tbsp tomato catsup

1 tsp cornstarch

1 Heat the sunflower oil in a large preheated wok.

2 Cut the chicken into bite-sized cubes, add to the wok, and stir-fry over a high heat for 10 minutes, tossing frequently until the chicken is cooked through and golden in color.

3 Peel and slice the mango and add to the wok with the garlic, leeks, and beansprouts. Stir-fry for a further 2–3 minutes, or until softened.

4 Mix together the mango juice, white wine vinegar, honey, tomato catsup, and cornstarch. Pour into the wok and stir-fry for a further 2 minutes, or until the juices start to thicken.

5 Transfer to a warmed serving dish and serve immediately.

COOK'S TIP

Mango juice is available in jars from most supermarkets and is thick and sweet. If it is unavailable, paste and strain a ripe mango and add a little water to make up the required quantity.

Duck in Spicy Sauce

Chinese five-spice powder adds an authentic flavor to this sliced duck, and the chili adds a little subtle heat.

NUTRITIONAL INFORMATION

Calories	162	Sugars	........2g
Protein	........20g	Fat	..........7g
Carbohydrate	....3g	Saturates	.......2g

5 MINS   25 MINS

SERVES 4

INGREDIENTS

1 tbsp vegetable oil

1 tsp grated fresh root ginger

1 clove garlic , crushed

1 fresh red chili, chopped

2 oz skinless, boneless duck meat, cut into strips

1 cup cauliflower, cut into flowerets

2 oz snow peas

2 oz baby corn-on-the-cobs, halved lengthways

1¼ cups chicken stock

1 tsp Chinese five-spice powder

2 tsp Chinese rice wine or dry sherry

1 tsp cornstarch

2 tsp water

1 tsp sesame oil

1 Heat the oil in a wok. Lower the heat slightly, add the ginger, garlic, chili, and duck and stir-fry for 2-3 minutes. Remove from the wok and set aside.

2 Add the vegetables to the wok and stir-fry for 2-3 minutes. Pour off any excess oil from the wok and push the vegetables to one side.

3 Return the duck to the wok and pour in the stock. Sprinkle the Chinese five-spice powder over the top, stir in the wine or sherry and cook over a low heat for 15 minutes, or until the duck is tender.

4 Blend the cornstarch with the water to form a paste and stir into the wok with the sesame oil. Bring to a boil, stirring until the sauce has thickened and cleared. Transfer the duck and spicy sauce to a warm serving dish and serve immediately.

COOK'S TIP

Omit the chili for a milder dish, or seed the chili before adding it to remove some of the heat.

Duck with Leek & Cabbage

Duck is a strongly-flavored meat that benefits from the added citrus peel to counteract this rich taste.

NUTRITIONAL INFORMATION

Calories 192	Sugars 5g
Protein 26g	Fat 7g
Carbohydrate 6g	Saturates 2g

10 MINS   40 MINS

SERVES 4

INGREDIENTS

4 duck breasts

5 cups green cabbage, thinly shredded

1½ cups leeks, sliced

finely grated peel of 1 orange

6 tbsp oyster sauce

1 tsp toasted sesame seeds,
   to serve

1 Heat a large wok and dry-fry the duck breasts, with the skin on, for about 5 minutes on each side; you may need to do this in 2 batches.

2 Remove the duck breast halves from the wok and transfer to a clean board.

3 Using a sharp knife, cut the duck breast halves into thin slices.

4 Remove all but 1 tablespoon of the fat from the duck left in the wok; discard the rest.

5 Using a sharp knife, thinly shred the green cabbage.

6 Add the leeks, green cabbage, and orange peel to the wok and stir-fry for about 5 minutes, or until the vegetables have softened.

7 Return the duck to the wok and heat through for 2–3 minutes.

8 Drizzle the oyster sauce over the mixture in the wok, toss well until all the ingredients are combined, and then heat through.

9 Scatter with toasted sesame seeds, transfer to a warm serving dish, and serve hot.

VARIATION

Use Chinese leaves cabbage for a lighter, sweeter flavor instead of the green cabbage, if you prefer.

 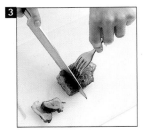 

Duck with Lime & Kiwi Fruit

Tender breast meat is served in thin slices, with a sweet but very tangy lime and wine sauce, full of pieces of kiwi fruit.

NUTRITIONAL INFORMATION

Calories 264   Sugars 20g
Protein . . . . .20g   Fat 10g
Carbohydrate . . .21g   Saturates 2g

1¼ HOURS   15 MINS

SERVES 4

I N G R E D I E N T S

4 boneless or part-boned duck breast halves

grated peel and juice of 2 large limes

2 tbsp sunflower oil

4 scallions, thinly sliced diagonally

1 cup carrots, cut into matchsticks

6 tbsp dry white wine

¼ cup sugar

2 kiwi fruit, peeled, halved, and sliced

salt and pepper

parsley sprigs and lime halves tied in knots (see Cook's Tip), to garnish

1 Trim any fat from the duck, then prick the skin all over with a fork, and lay in a shallow dish. Add half the grated lime and half the juice to the ducks, rubbing in thoroughly. Leave to stand in a cool place for at least 1 hour, turning the meat over at least once.

2 Drain the duck pieces, reserving the marinade. Heat 1 tablespoon of oil in a wok. Add the duck and fry quickly to seal all over, lower the heat, and continue to cook for about 5 minutes, turning several times until just cooked through and well browned all over. Remove and keep warm.

3 Wipe the wok and heat the remaining oil. Add the scallions and carrots and stir-fry for 1 minute, then add the remaining lime marinade, wine, and sugar. Bring to a boil and simmer for 2-3 minutes until syrupy.

4 Add the duck pieces to the sauce, season, and add the kiwi fruit. Stir-fry for a minute or until really hot and both the duck and kiwi fruit are well coated in the sauce.

5 Cut each duck breast into slices, leaving a hinge at one end. Open out into a fan shape and arrange on plates. Spoon the sauce over the duck, sprinkle with the remaining pieces of lime peel, garnish, and serve.

COOK'S TIP

To make the garnish, trim a piece off the base of each lime half so they stand upright. Pare off a thin strip of peel from the top of the lime halves, about ¼ inch thick, but do not detach it. Tie the strip into a knot with the end bending over the cut surface of the lime.

Duck with Broccoli & Peppers

This is a colorful dish using different colored bell peppers and broccoli to make it both tasty and appealing to the eye.

NUTRITIONAL INFORMATION

Calories 261	Sugars 3g
Protein 26g	Fat 13g
Carbohydrate 11g	Saturates 2g

🖐 🖐 🖐

🍲 35 MINS 🕐 15 MINS

SERVES 4

INGREDIENTS

1 egg white

2 tbsp cornstarch

1 lb skinless, boneless duck meat

vegetable oil, for deep-frying

1 red bell pepper, seeded and diced

1 yellow bell pepper, seeded and diced

4½ oz small broccoli flowerets

1 garlic clove, crushed

2 tbsp light soy sauce

2 tsp Chinese rice wine or dry sherry

1 tsp light brown sugar

½ cup chicken stock

2 tsp sesame seeds

1 In a mixing bowl, beat together the egg white and cornstarch.

2 Using a sharp knife, cut the duck into 1-inch cubes and stir into the egg white mixture. Leave to stand for 30 minutes.

3 Heat the oil for deep-frying in a preheated wok or heavy-based skillet until almost smoking.

4 Remove the duck from the egg white mixture, add to the wok, and fry in the oil for 4–5 minutes, until crisp.

Remove the duck from the oil with a draining spoon and drain on paper towels.

5 Add the bell peppers and broccoli to the wok and fry for 2–3 minutes. Remove with a draining spoon and drain on paper towels.

6 Pour all but 2 tablespoons of the oil from the wok and return to the heat. Add the garlic and stir-fry for 30 seconds.

Stir in the soy sauce, Chinese rice wine or sherry, sugar, and chicken stock and bring to a boil.

7 Stir in the duck and reserved vegetables and cook for 1–2 minutes.

8 Carefully spoon the duck and vegetables onto a warmed serving dish and sprinkle with the sesame seeds. Serve immediately.

Duck with Mangoes

Use fresh mangoes in this recipe for a terrific flavor and color. If they are unavailable, use canned mangoes and rinse them before using.

NUTRITIONAL INFORMATION

Calories	235	Sugars	.........6g
Protein	........23g	Fat	..........14g
Carbohydrate	....6g	Saturates	.......2g

5 MINS   35 MINS

SERVES 4

INGREDIENTS

2 medium-size ripe mangoes

1¼ cups chicken stock

2 garlic cloves, crushed

1 tsp grated gingerroot

3 tbsp vegetable oil

2 large skinless duck breast halves, about 8 oz each

1 tsp wine vinegar

1 tsp light soy sauce

1 leek, sliced

freshly chopped parsley, to garnish

1 Peel the mangoes and cut the flesh from each side of the pits. Cut the flesh into strips.

2 Put half of the mango pieces and the chicken stock in a food processor and process until smooth. Alternatively, press half of the mangoes through a fine strainer and mix with the stock.

3 Rub the garlic and ginger over the duck. Heat the vegetable oil in a preheated wok and cook the duck breasts, turning, until sealed. Reserve the oil in the wok and remove the duck.

4 Place the duck on a rack set over a roasting pan and cook in a preheated oven at 425°F for 20 minutes, until the duck is cooked through.

5 Meanwhile, place the mango and stock mixture in a saucepan and add the wine vinegar and light soy sauce.

6 Bring the mixture in the saucepan to a boil and cook over a high heat, stirring, until reduced by half.

7 Heat the oil reserved in the wok and stir-fry the sliced leek and remaining mango for 1 minute. Remove from the wok, transfer to a serving dish, and keep warm until required.

8 Slice the cooked duck breast halves and arrange the slices on top of the leek and mango mixture. Pour the sauce over the duck slices, garnish, and serve.

Duck with Pineapple

For best results, use cooked duck meat, widely available from Chinese restaurants and take-outs.

NUTRITIONAL INFORMATION

Calories ....187 Sugars 7g
Protein ....10g Fat 12g
Carbohydrate ....11g Saturates 2g

     25 MINS 🕐 10 MINS

SERVES 4

I N G R E D I E N T S

4½-6 oz cooked duck meat

3 tbsp vegetable oil

1 small onion, thinly shredded

2-3 slices gingerroot, thinly shredded

1 scallion, thinly shredded

1 small carrot, thinly shredded

1 cup canned pineapple, cut into small slices

½ tsp salt

1 tbsp red rice vinegar

2 tbsp syrup from the pineapple

1 tbsp cornstarch paste (see page 15)

black bean sauce, to serve (optional)

1 Using a sharp knife or metal cleaver, cut the cooked duck meat into thin even-sized strips, and set aside until required.

2 Heat the oil in a preheated wok or large heavy-based skillet.

3 Add the shredded onion and stir-fry until the shreds are opaque.

4 Add the slices of gingerroot, scallion shreds, and carrot shreds to the wok and stir-fry for about 1 minute.

5 Add the duck shreds and pineapple to the wok together with the salt, rice vinegar, and the pineapple syrup. Stir until the mixture is well blended.

6 Add the cornstarch paste and stir for 1-2 minutes until the sauce has thickened.

7 Transfer to a serving dish and serve with black bean sauce, if desired.

COOK'S TIP

Red rice vinegar is made from fermented rice. It has a distinctive dark color and depth of flavor. If unavailable, use red wine vinegar, which is similar in flavor.

Honey-Glazed Duck

The honey-and-soy glaze gives a wonderful sheen and flavor to the duck skin. Such a simple recipe, yet the result is unutterably delicious.

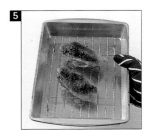

NUTRITIONAL INFORMATION

Calories	176	Sugars	....8g
Protein	....22g	Fat	....5g
Carbohydrate	...10g	Saturates	....1g

2¼ HOURS   30 MINS

SERVES 4

INGREDIENTS

1 tsp dark soy sauce

2 tbsp honey

1 tsp garlic vinegar

2 garlic cloves, crushed

1 tsp ground star anise

2 tsp cornstarch

2 tsp water

2 large boneless duck breast halves, about 8 oz each

celery leaves, cucumber wedges and snipped chives, to garnish

1 Mix together the soy sauce, honey, garlic vinegar, garlic, and star anise.

2 Blend the cornstarch with the water to form a smooth paste and stir it into the soy sauce mixture.

3 Place the duck breast halves in a shallow baking dish. Brush with the soy marinade, turning to coat them completely. Cover and leave to marinate in the refrigerator for at least 2 hours, or overnight if possible.

4 Remove the duck from the marinade and roast in a heated oven at 425°F for 20–25 minutes, basting frequently with the glaze.

5 Remove the duck from the oven and transfer to a heated broiler. Broil for about 3–4 minutes to caramelize the top.

6 Remove the duck from the broiler pan and cut into thin slices. Arrange the duck slices in a warm serving dish, garnish with celery leaves, cucumber wedges, and snipped chives and serve immediately.

COOK'S TIP

If the duck begins to burn slightly while it is cooking in the oven, cover with foil. Check that the duck breast halves are cooked through by inserting the point of a sharp knife into the thickest part of the flesh – the juices should run clear.

Turkey with Cranberry Glaze

Traditional Christmas ingredients are given a Chinese twist in this stir-fry that contains cranberries, ginger, chestnuts, and soy sauce!

NUTRITIONAL INFORMATION

Calories 167	Sugars 11g	
Protein 8g	Fat 7g	
Carbohydrate ...20g	Saturates 1g	

5 MINS   15 MINS

SERVES 4

I N G R E D I E N T S

1 turkey breast

2 tbsp sunflower oil

2 tbsp stem ginger

½ cup fresh or frozen cranberries

¼ cup canned chestnuts

4 tbsp cranberry sauce

3 tbsp light soy sauce

salt and pepper

1 Remove any skin from the turkey meat. Using a sharp knife, thinly slice the turkey breast.

2 Heat the sunflower oil in a large preheated wok or heavy-based skillet.

3 Add the turkey to the wok and stir-fry for 5 minutes, or until cooked through.

4 Using a sharp knife, finely chop the stem ginger.

5 Add the ginger and the cranberries to the wok or skillet and stir-fry for 2–3 minutes or until the cranberries have softened.

6 Add the chestnuts, cranberry sauce, and soy sauce. Season to taste with salt and pepper and allow to bubble for 2–3 minutes.

7 Transfer the turkey stir-fry to warm serving dishes and serve immediately.

COOK'S TIP

It is very important that the wok is very hot before you stir-fry. Test by by holding your hand flat about 3 inches above the base of the interior – you should be able to feel the heat radiating from it.

Meat

Pork is the most popular meat in China because it is tender and suitable for all Chinese cooking methods. Lamb is popular in northern China, where religious laws forbid the eating of pork. Beef, although it is used in some dishes, is less popular than pork. This is partly because of economic and religious reasons, but also because it is less versatile in

cooking. One of the favorite cooking methods in China is stir-frying because it is a simple and easy way of preparing meat, as well as being healthy and economical. Stir-frying gives a dry texture, whereas braising and steaming, which are other popular cooking methods, ensure a tender result. This is also true of double-cooking in which the meat is first tenderized by long, slow simmering in water, following by a quick crisping or stir-frying in a sauce.

Beef & Broccoli Stir-Fry

This is a great combination of ingredients in terms of color and flavor, and it is so simple to prepare.

NUTRITIONAL INFORMATION

Calories 232	Sugars 1g
Protein 12g	Fat 19g
Carbohydrate 4g	Saturates 6g

 4¼ HOURS   15 MINS

SERVES 4

I N G R E D I E N T S

8 oz lean steak, trimmed

2 garlic cloves, crushed

dash of chili oil

½-inch piece fresh gingerroot, grated

½ tsp Chinese five-spice powder

2 tbsp dark soy sauce

2 tbsp vegetable oil

1¼ cups broccoli flowerets

1 tbsp light soy sauce

⅔ cup beef stock

2 tsp cornstarch

4 tsp water

carrot strips, to garnish

1 Using a sharp knife, cut the steak into thin strips and place in a shallow glass dish.

2 Mix together the garlic, chili oil, grated ginger, Chinese five-spice powder, and dark soy sauce in a small bowl and pour over the beef, tossing to coat the strips evenly.

3 Cover the bowl and leave the meat to marinate in the refrigerator for several hours to allow the flavors to develop fully.

4 Heat 1 tablespoon of the vegetable oil in a preheated wok or large skillet. Add the broccoli and stir-fry over a medium heat for 4–5 minutes. Remove from the wok with a draining spoon and set aside until required.

5 Heat the remaining oil in the wok. Add the steak together with the marinade and stir-fry for 2-3 minutes until the steak is browned and sealed.

6 Return the broccoli to the wok and stir in the light soy sauce and stock.

7 Blend the cornstarch with the water to form a smooth paste and stir into the wok. Bring to a boil, stirring, until thickened and clear. Cook for 1 minute. Transfer the beef and broccoli stir-fry to a warm serving dish, arrange the carrot strips in a lattice on top, and serve immediately.

Beef with Bamboo Shoots

Tender beef, marinated in a soy and tomato sauce, is stir-fried with crisp bamboo shoots and snow peas in this simple recipe.

NUTRITIONAL INFORMATION

Calories 275	Sugars 3g
Protein 21g	Fat 19g
Carbohydrate 6g	Saturates 6g

 1¼ HOURS 10 MINS

SERVES 4

I N G R E D I E N T S

12 oz rump steak

3 tbsp dark soy sauce

1 tbsp tomato catsup

2 cloves garlic, crushed

1 tbsp fresh lemon juice

1 tsp ground coriander

2 tbsp vegetable oil

2¾ cups snow peas

7 oz can bamboo shoots

1 tsp sesame oil

COOK'S TIP

Leave the meat to marinate for at least 1 hour for the flavors to penetrate and increase the tenderness of the meat. If possible, leave for a little longer for a fuller flavor to develop.

1 Thinly slice the meat and place in a nonmetallic dish together with the dark soy sauce, tomato catsup, garlic, lemon juice, and ground coriander. Mix well so that all of the meat is coated in the marinade, cover, and leave for at least 1 hour.

2 Heat the vegetable oil in a preheated wok. Add the meat to the wok and stir-fry for 2–4 minutes (depending on how well cooked you like your meat) or until cooked through.

3 Add the snow peas and bamboo shoots to the mixture in the wok and stir-fry over a high heat, tossing frequently, for a further 5 minutes.

4 Drizzle with the sesame oil and toss well to combine. Transfer to serving dishes and serve hot.

Beef & Beans

The green of the beans complements the dark color of the beef, which is served in a rich sauce.

NUTRITIONAL INFORMATION

Calories 381	Sugars 3g
Protein 25g	Fat 27g
Carbohydrate ...10g	Saturates 8g

35 MINS   15 MINS

SERVES 4

I N G R E D I E N T S

1 lb sirloin steak, cut into 1-inch pieces

M A R I N A D E

2 tsp cornstarch

2 tbsp dark soy sauce

2 tsp peanut oil

S A U C E

2 tbsp vegetable oil

3 garlic cloves, crushed

1 small onion, cut into 8

1½ cups thin green beans, halved

¼ cup unsalted cashews

1 oz canned bamboo shoots, drained and rinsed

2 tsp dark soy sauce

2 tsp Chinese rice wine or dry sherry

½ cup beef stock

2 tsp cornstarch

4 tsp water

salt and pepper

1 To make the marinade, mix together the cornstarch, soy sauce, and peanut oil.

2 Place the steak in a shallow glass bowl. Pour the marinade over the steak, turn to coat thoroughly, cover and leave to marinate in the refrigerator for at least 30 minutes.

3 To make the sauce, heat the oil in a preheated wok. Add the garlic, onion, beans, cashews, and bamboo shoots and stir-fry for 2–3 minutes.

4 Remove the steak from the marinade, drain, add to the wok, and stir-fry for 3–4 minutes.

5 Mix the soy sauce, Chinese rice wine or sherry, and beef stock together. Blend the cornstarch with the water and add to the soy sauce mixture, mixing to combine.

6 Stir the mixture into the wok and bring the sauce to a boil, stirring until thickened and clear. Reduce the heat and leave to simmer for 2–3 minutes. Season to taste and serve immediately.

Spicy Beef

In this recipe, beef is marinated in a mixture of Chinese five-spice and chili marinade for a spicy flavor.

NUTRITIONAL INFORMATION

Calories	246	Sugars	.........2g
Protein	........21g	Fat	..........13g
Carbohydrate	...10g	Saturates	.......3g

1¼ HOURS   10 MINS

SERVES 4

INGREDIENTS

8 oz beef tenderloin

2 garlic cloves, crushed

1 tsp powdered star anise

1 tbsp dark soy sauce

scallion tassels, to garnish

SAUCE

2 tbsp vegetable oil

1 bunch scallions, halved lengthways

1 tbsp dark soy sauce

1 tbsp dry sherry

¼ tsp chili sauce

⅔ cup water

2 tsp cornstarch

4 tsp water

1 Cut the steak into thin strips and place in a shallow dish.

2 Mix together the garlic, star anise and dark soy sauce in a bowl.

3 Pour the sauce mixture over the steak strips, turning them to coat thoroughly. Cover and leave to marinate in the refrigerator for at least 1 hour.

4 To make the sauce, heat the oil in a preheated wok or large skillet. Reduce the heat and stir-fry the scallions for 1-2 minutes.

5 Remove the scallions from the wok with a draining spoon, drain on paper towels, and set aside until required.

6 Add the beef to the wok, together with the marinade, and stir-fry for 3-4 minutes. Return the scallions to the wok and add the soy sauce, sherry, chili sauce, and two-thirds of the water.

7 Blend the cornstarch with the remaining water and stir into the wok. Bring to a boil, stirring until the sauce thickens and clears.

8 Transfer to a warm serving dish, garnish and serve immediately.

Beef & Bok Choy

In this recipe, a colorful selection of vegetables is stir-fried with tender strips of steak.

NUTRITIONAL INFORMATION

Calories 369	Sugars 9g	
Protein 29g	Fat 23g	
Carbohydrate ...12g	Saturates 8g	

 15 MINS 5 MINS

SERVES 4

INGREDIENTS

1 large head of bok choy, about 9-9½ oz, torn into large pieces

2 tbsp vegetable oil

2 garlic cloves, crushed

1 lb 2 oz sirloin or tenderloin steak, cut into thin strips

5½ oz snow peas, trimmed

5½ oz baby or dwarf corn

6 scallions, chopped

2 red bell peppers, cored, seeded, and thinly sliced

2 tbsp oyster sauce

1 tbsp fish sauce

1 tbsp sugar

rice or noodles, to serve

1 Steam the bok choy over boiling water until just tender; keep warm.

2 Heat the oil in a large, heavy-based skillet or wok, add the garlic and steak strips, and stir-fry until just browned, about 1-2 minutes.

3 Add the snow peas, baby corn, scallions, red bell pepper, oyster sauce, fish sauce, and sugar to the pan, mixing well. Stir-fry for a further 2-3 minutes until the vegetables are just tender, but still crisp.

4 Arrange the bok choy leaves in the base of a heated serving dish and spoon the beef and vegetable mixture into the center.

5 Serve the stir-fry immediately, with rice or noodles.

COOK'S TIP

Bok choy is one of the most important ingredients in this dish. If unavailable, use Chinese cabbage, mustard leaves, or pak choy.

Beef & Black Bean Sauce

It is not necessary to use the expensive cuts of beef steak for this recipe: the meat will be tender because it is cut into thin slices and marinated.

NUTRITIONAL INFORMATION

Calories 392	Sugars 2g	
Protein 13g	Fat 36g	
Carbohydrate 3g	Saturates 7g	

3¼ HOURS   10 MINS

SERVES 4

I N G R E D I E N T S

9-10½ oz beef steak, such as sirloin

1 small onion

1 small green bell pepper, cored and seeded

1¼ cups vegetable oil

1 scallion, cut into short sections

a few small slices of gingerroot

1-2 small green or red chilies, seeded and sliced

2 tbsp crushed black bean sauce

M A R I N A D E

½ tsp bicarbonate of baking soda or baking powder

½ tsp sugar

1 tbsp light soy sauce

2 tsp rice wine or dry sherry

2 tsp cornstarch paste (see page 15)

2 tsp sesame oil

1 Using a sharp knife or meat cleaver, cut the beef into small, thin strips.

2 To make the marinade, mix together all the ingredients in a shallow dish. Add the beef strips, turn to coat, and leave to marinate for at least 2-3 hours.

3 Cut the onion and green bell pepper into small cubes.

4 Heat the vegetable oil in a heated wok or large skillet. Add the beef strips and stir-fry for about 1 minute or until the color changes. Remove the beef strips with a draining spoon and drain on paper towels. Keep warm and set aside until required.

5 Pour off the excess oil, leaving about 1 tablespoon in the wok. Add the scallion, ginger, chilies, onion, and green bell pepper and stir-fry for about 1 minute.

6 Add the black bean sauce and stir until smooth. Return the beef strips to the wok, blend well, and stir-fry for another minute. Transfer the stir-fry to a warm serving dish and serve hot.

Oyster Sauce Beef

Like Pork with Vegetables (see page 143), the vegetables used in this recipe can be varied as you wish.

NUTRITIONAL INFORMATION

Calories . . . . . . .462 Sugars 2g
Protein . . . . .16g Fat 42g
Carbohydrate . . . .4g Saturates 8g

4 HOURS   10 MINS

SERVES 4

INGREDIENTS

10½ oz beef steak

1 tsp sugar

1 tbsp light soy sauce

1 tsp rice wine or dry sherry

1 tsp cornstarch paste (see page 15)

½ small carrot

2 oz snow peas

2 oz canned bamboo shoots

2 oz canned straw mushrooms

about 1¼ cups vegetable oil

1 scallion, cut into short sections

2-3 small slices gingerroot

½ tsp salt

2 tbsp oyster sauce

2-3 tbsp Chinese stock (see page 14) or water

1 Cut the beef into small, thin slices. Place in a shallow dish with the sugar, soy sauce, wine, and cornstarch paste and leave to marinate for 25-30 minutes.

2 Slice the carrot, snow peas, bamboo shoots, and straw mushrooms into roughly the same size pieces as each other.

3 Heat the oil in a wok and add the beef slices. Stir-fry for 1 minute, then remove and keep warm.

4 Pour off the oil, leaving about 1 tablespoon in the wok. Add the sliced vegetables with the scallion and ginger and stir-fry for about 2 minutes. Add the salt, beef, and oyster sauce with stock or water. Blend well until heated through and serve.

VARIATION

You can use whatever vegetables are available for this dish, but it is important to get a good contrast of color – don't use all red or all green.

Peppered Beef Cashew

A simple but stunning dish of tender strips of beef mixed with crunchy cashew nuts, coated in a hot sauce. Serve with rice noodles.

NUTRITIONAL INFORMATION

Calories 403	Sugars 7g
Protein 26g	Fat 29g
Carbohydrate 11g	Saturates 9g

  10 MINS   10 MINS

SERVES 4

I N G R E D I E N T S

1 tbsp peanut or sunflower oil

1 tbsp sesame oil

1 onion, sliced

1 garlic clove, crushed

1 tbsp grated gingerroot

1 lb 2 oz tenderloin or sirloin steak, cut into thin strips

2 tsp palm sugar

2 tbsp light soy sauce

1 small yellow bell pepper, cored, seeded, and sliced

1 red bell pepper, cored, seeded, and sliced

4 scallions, chopped

2 celery sticks, chopped

4 large open-cap mushrooms, sliced

4 tbsp roasted cashew nuts

3 tbsp stock or white wine

1 Heat the oils in a large, heavy-based skillet or wok. Add the onion, garlic, and ginger and stir-fry for about 2 minutes until softened.

2 Add the steak strips and stir-fry for a further 2-3 minutes until the meat has browned.

3 Add the sugar and soy sauce, stirring to mix well.

4 Add the bell peppers, scallions, celery, mushrooms, and cashews, mixing well.

5 Add the stock or white wine and stir-fry for 2-3 minutes until the beef is cooked through and the vegetables are tender-crisp.

6 Serve the stir-fry immediately with rice noodles.

COOK'S TIP

Palm sugar is a thick brown sugar with a slightly caramel taste. It is sold in cakes, or in small containers. If not available, use dark brown or brown crystal sugar.

Red Spiced Beef

A spicy stir-fry flavored with paprika, chili, and tomato, with a crisp bite to it from the celery strips.

NUTRITIONAL INFORMATION

Calories	431	Sugars	.........0g
Protein	........32g	Fat	..........28g
Carbohydrate	...14g	Saturates	......10g

40 MINS   10 MINS

SERVES 4

INGREDIENTS

1 lb 6 oz sirloin steak

2 tbsp paprika

2-3 tsp mild chili powder

½ tsp salt

6 celery sticks

4 tomatoes, peeled, seeded, and sliced

6 tbsp stock or water

2 tbsp tomato paste

2 tbsp honey

3 tbsp wine vinegar

1 tbsp Worcestershire sauce

2 tbsp sunflower oil

4 scallions, thinly sliced diagonally

1-2 garlic cloves, crushed

Chinese noodles, to serve

celery leaves, to garnish (optional)

1 Using a sharp knife or meat cleaver, cut the steak across the grain into narrow strips ½ inch thick and place in a bowl.

2 Combine the paprika, chili powder and salt, add to the beef and mix thoroughly until the meat strips are evenly coated with the spices. Leave the beef to marinate in a cool place for at least 30 minutes.

3 Cut the celery into 2 inch lengths, then cut the lengths into strips about ¼ inch thick.

4 Combine the stock, tomato paste, honey, Worcestershire sauce, and wine vinegar, and set aside.

5 Heat the oil in the wok until really hot. Add the scallions, celery, and garlic and stir-fry for about 1 minute until the vegetables are beginning to soften, then add the steak strips. Stir-fry over a high heat for 3-4 minutes until the meat is well sealed.

6 Add the sauce to the wok and continue to stir-fry briskly until thoroughly coated and sizzling.

7 Serve with noodles and garnish with celery leaves, if liked.

Soy & Sesame Beef

Soy sauce and sesame seeds are classic ingredients in Chinese cooking.
Use a dark soy sauce for fuller flavor and richness.

NUTRITIONAL INFORMATION

Calories 324	Sugars 2g	
Protein 25g	Fat 22g	
Carbohydrate 3g	Saturates 6g	

 5 MINS   10 MINS

SERVES 4

INGREDIENTS

2 tbsp sesame seeds

1 lb beef tenderloin

2 tbsp vegetable oil

1 green bell pepper, seeded and thinly
   sliced

4 cloves garlic, crushed

2 tbsp dry sherry

4 tbsp soy sauce

6 scallions, sliced

noodles, to serve

1 Heat a large wok or heavy-based
skillet until it is very hot.

2 Add the sesame seeds to the wok or
skillet and dry fry, stirring, for 1–2
minutes or until they just begin to brown.
Remove the sesame seeds from the wok
and set aside until required.

3 Using a sharp knife or meat cleaver,
thinly slice the beef.

4 Heat the vegetable oil in the wok or
skillet. Add the beef and stir-fry for
2–3 minutes or until sealed on all sides.

5 Add the sliced bell pepper and
crushed garlic to the wok and
continue stir-frying for 2 minutes.

6 Add the dry sherry and soy sauce to
the wok together with the scallions.
Allow the mixture in the wok to bubble,
stirring occasionally, for about 1 minute,
but do not let the mixture burn.

7 Transfer the garlic beef stir-fry to
warm serving bowls and scatter with
the dry-fried sesame seeds. Serve hot with
boiled noodles.

COOK'S TIP

Spread the
sesame seeds out on a
cookie sheet and toast them under a
preheated broiler until browned
all over, if you prefer.

Beef with Green Peas

This recipe is the perfect example of quick stir-frying ingredients for a delicious, crisp, colorful dish.

NUTRITIONAL INFORMATION

Calories 325	Sugars 2g	
Protein 26g	Fat 22g	
Carbohydrate 8g	Saturates 7g	

5 MINS   10 MINS

SERVES 4

I N G R E D I E N T S

1 lb sirloin steak

2 tbsp sunflower oil

1 onion

2 cloves garlic

1 cup fresh or frozen peas

5 ¾ oz black bean sauce

2 ½ cups Chinese cabbage, shredded

1 Using a sharp knife, trim away any fat from the beef. Cut the beef into thin slices.

2 Heat the sunflower oil in a large preheated wok.

3 Add the beef to the wok and stir-fry for 2 minutes.

4 Using a sharp knife, peel and slice the onion and crush the garlic cloves in a mortar and pestle.

5 Add the onion, garlic, and peas to the wok and stir-fry for 5 minutes.

6 Add the black bean sauce and Chinese cabbage to the wok.

7 Heat the mixture in the wok for a further 2 minutes until the Chinese cabbage has wilted.

8 Transfer to warm serving bowls then serve immediately.

COOK'S TIP

Buy a chunky black bean sauce if you can for the best texture and flavor. Chinese cabbage is now widely available. They look like a pale, elongated head of lettuce with light green, tightly packed crinkly leaves.

Caramelized Beef

Palm sugar or brown crystal sugar is used in this recipe to give the beef a slightly caramelized flavor.

NUTRITIONAL INFORMATION

Calories	335	Sugars	.........8g
Protein	........23g	Fat	..........21g
Carbohydrate	...14g	Saturates	.......7g

 1¼ HOURS   10 MINS

SERVES 4

I N G R E D I E N T S

1 lb tenderloin beef

2 tbsp soy sauce

1 tsp chili oil

1 tbsp tamarind paste

2 tbsp palm sugar or brown crystal sugar

2 cloves garlic, crushed

2 tbsp sunflower oil

1½ cups pearl onions

2 tbsp chopped fresh cilantro, to garnish

1 Using a sharp knife or meat cleaver, thinly slice the beef.

2 Place the slices of beef in a large, shallow nonmetallic dish.

3 Mix together the soy sauce, chili oil, tamarind paste, palm or brown crystal sugar and garlic in a mixing bowl.

4 Spoon the sugar mixture over the beef. Toss well to coat the beef in the mixture, cover with plastic wrap and leave to marinate for at least 1 hour, the longer the better.

5 Heat the oil in a preheated wok or large skillet.

6 Peel the onions and cut them in half. Add the onion pieces to the wok and stir-fry for 2–3 minutes, or until just browning.

7 Add the beef and marinade juices to the wok and stir-fry over a high heat for about 5 minutes.

8 Scatter with chopped fresh cilantro and serve at once.

COOK'S TIP

Use the chili oil carefully as it is very hot and could easily spoil the dish if too much is added.

Crispy Shredded Beef

A very popular Szechuan dish served in most Chinese restaurants all over the world.

NUTRITIONAL INFORMATION

Calories . . . . .341 Sugars 17g
Protein . . . . .20g Fat 17g
Carbohydrate . . .29g Saturates 4g

 10 MINS   15 MINS

SERVES 4

INGREDIENTS

10½-12 oz beef steak, such as sirloin

2 eggs

¼ tsp salt

4-5 tbsp all-purpose flour

vegetable oil, for deep-frying

2 carrots, finely shredded

2 scallions, thinly shredded

1 garlic clove, finely chopped

2-3 small fresh green or red chilies, seeded and thinly shredded

4 tbsp sugar

3 tbsp rice vinegar

1 tbsp light soy sauce

2-3 tbsp Chinese stock (see page 14) or water

1 tsp cornstarch paste (see page 15)

1 Cut the steak across the grain into thin strips. Beat the eggs in a bowl with the salt and flour, adding a little water if necessary. Add the beef strips to the batter and mix well until coated.

2 Heat the oil in a preheated wok until smoking. Add the beef strips and deep-fry for 4-5 minutes, stirring to separate the shreds. Remove with a draining spoon and drain on paper towels.

3 Add the carrots to the wok and deep-fry for about 1-1½ minutes, then remove with a draining spoon and drain.

4 Pour off the excess oil. Add the scallions, garlic, chilies, and carrots and stir-fry for 1 minute.

5 Add the sugar, rice vinegar, light soy sauce, and Chinese stock or water to the wok, blend well and bring to a boil.

6 Stir in the cornstarch paste and simmer for a few minutes to thicken the sauce.

7 Return the beef to the wok and stir until the shreds of meat are well coated with the sauce. Serve hot.

Meatballs in Peanut Sauce

Choose very lean ground beef to make these meatballs – or better still, buy lean beef and grind it yourself.

NUTRITIONAL INFORMATION

Calories	553	Sugars	10g
Protein	32g	Fat	43g
Carbohydrate	21g	Saturates	12g

  5 MINS · 30 MINS

SERVES 4

INGREDIENTS

2 cups lean ground beef

2 tsp finely grated fresh gingerroot

1 small red chili, seeded and chopped finely

1 tbsp chopped fresh basil or cilantro

1 tbsp sesame oil

1 tbsp vegetable oil

salt and pepper

SAUCE

2 tbsp red curry paste

1¼ cups coconut milk

1 cup ground peanuts

1 tbsp fish sauce

TO GARNISH

chopped fresh basil

sprigs of fresh basil or cilantro

1 Put the beef, ginger, chili, and basil or cilantro into a food processor or blender. Add ¹/₂ teaspoon of salt and plenty of pepper. Process for about 10–15 seconds until finely chopped. Alternatively, chop the ingredients finely and mix together.

2 Form the beef mixture into about 12 balls. Heat the sesame oil and vegetable oil in a wok or skillet and fry the meatballs over a medium-high heat until well browned on all sides, about 10 minutes. Lift them out and drain on paper towels.

3 To make the sauce, stir-fry the red curry paste in the wok or skillet for 1 minute. Add the coconut milk, peanuts, and fish sauce. Heat, stirring, until just simmering.

4 Return the meatballs to the wok or skillet and cook gently in the sauce for 10–15 minutes. If the sauce begins to get too thick, add a little extra coconut milk or water. Season with a little salt and pepper, according to taste.

5 Serve garnished with chopped fresh basil and sprigs of fresh basil or cilantro.

VARIATION

Ground lamb makes a delicious alternative to beef. If you do use lamb, try substituting ground almonds for the peanuts and fresh mint for the basil.

Pork with Daikon

Pork and daikon are a perfect combination, especially with the added heat of the sweet chili sauce.

NUTRITIONAL INFORMATION

Calories 280	Sugars 1g	
Protein 25g	Fat 19g	
Carbohydrate 2g	Saturates 4g	

 🖐 🖐 🖐

 10 MINS   🕐 15 MINS

SERVES 4

I N G R E D I E N T S

4 tbsp vegetable oil

1 lb pork tenderloin

1 eggplant

8 oz daikon

2 cloves garlic, crushed

3 tbsp soy sauce

2 tbsp sweet chili sauce

boiled rice or noodles, to serve

1 Heat 2 tablespoons of the vegetable oil in a large preheated wok or skillet.

2 Using a sharp knife, thinly slice the pork into even-size pieces.

3 Add the slices of pork to the wok or skillet and stir-fry for about 5 minutes.

4 Using a sharp knife, trim and dice the eggplant. Peel and slice the daikon.

5 Add the remaining vegetable oil to the wok.

6 Add the diced eggplant to the wok or skillet together with the garlic and stir-fry for 5 minutes.

7 Add the daikon to the wok and stir-fry for about 2 minutes.

8 Stir the soy sauce and sweet chili sauce into the mixture in the wok and cook until heated through.

9 Transfer the pork and daikon to warm serving bowls and serve immediately with boiled rice or noodles.

COOK'S TIP

Daikon are long white vegetables common in Chinese cooking. Usually grated, it has a milder flavor than red radish. Ask for it in Oriental grocery stores.

Pork with Vegetables

This is a basic meat and veg recipe – the meat can be pork, chicken, beef, or lamb, and the vegetables can be varied according to the season.

NUTRITIONAL INFORMATION

Calories	227	Sugars	.........4g
Protein	........15g	Fat	..........16g
Carbohydrate	....7g	Saturates	.......3g

 25 MINS   10 MINS

SERVES 4

I N G R E D I E N T S

9 oz pork tenderloin

1 tsp sugar

1 tbsp light soy sauce

1 tsp rice wine or dry sherry

1 tsp cornstarch paste (see page 15)

1 small carrot

1 small green bell pepper, cored and seeded

about 6 oz Chinese cabbage

4 tbsp vegetable oil

1 scallion, cut into short sections

a few small slices of peeled gingerroot

1 tsp salt

2-3 tbsp Chinese Stock (see page 14) or water

a few drops of sesame oil

VARIATION

This dish can be made with other meats, as mentioned in the introduction. If using chicken strips, reduce the initial cooking time in the wok.

1 Thinly slice the pork tenderloin into small pieces and place in a shallow dish.

2 In a small bowl, mix together half the sugar and the soy sauce, the wine or sherry and cornstarch paste. Pour the mixture over the pork, stir well to coat the meat and leave in the refrigerator to marinate for 10-15 minutes.

3 Cut the carrot, green bell pepper, and Chinese cabbage into thin slices roughly the same length and width as the pork pieces.

4 Heat the oil in a preheated wok and stir-fry the pork for about 1 minute to seal in the flavor. Remove with a draining spoon and keep warm.

5 Add the carrot, bell pepper, Chinese cabbage, scallion, and ginger and stir-fry for about 2 minutes.

6 Add the salt and remaining sugar, followed by the pork and remaining soy sauce, and the Chinese stock or water. Blend well and stir for another 1-2 minutes until hot. Sprinkle the stir-fry with the sesame oil and serve immediately.

Sweet & Sour Pork

In this classic Chinese dish, tender pork pieces are fried and served in a crunchy sauce. This dish is perfect served with plain rice.

NUTRITIONAL INFORMATION

Calories 357   Sugars 25g
Protein . . . . .28g   Fat 14g
Carbohydrate . . .30g   Saturates 4g

 10 MINS   20 MINS

SERVES 4

INGREDIENTS

1 lb pork tenderloin

2 tbsp sunflower oil

8 oz zucchini

1 red onion, cut into thin wedges

2 cloves garlic, crushed

8 oz carrots, cut into thin sticks

1 red bell pepper, seeded and sliced

1 cup baby corn-on-the-cobs

1¼ cups button mushrooms, halved

1¼ cups fresh pineapple, cubed

1 cup bean sprouts

⅔ cup pineapple juice

1 tbsp cornstarch

2 tbsp soy sauce

3 tbsp tomato catsup

1 tbsp white wine vinegar

1 tbsp honey

1 Using a sharp knife, thinly slice the pork tenderloin into even-size pieces.

2 Heat the sunflower oil in a large preheated wok. Add the pork to the wok and stir-fry for 10 minutes, or until the pork is completely cooked through and beginning to turn crispy at the edges.

3 Meanwhile, cut the zucchini into thin sticks.

4 Add the onion, garlic, carrots, zucchini, bell pepper, corn-on-the-cobs, and mushrooms to the wok and stir-fry for a further 5 minutes.

5 Add the pineapple cubes and bean sprouts to the wok and stir-fry for 2 minutes.

6 Mix together the pineapple juice, cornstarch, soy sauce, tomato catsup, white wine vinegar, and honey.

7 Pour the sweet-and-sour mixture into the wok and cook over a high heat, tossing frequently, until the juices thicken. Transfer the sweet-and-sour pork to serving bowls and serve hot.

COOK'S TIP

If you prefer a crisper coating, toss the pork in a mixture of cornstarch and egg white and deep fry in the wok in step 2.

Spicy Pork & Rice

Pork is coated in a spicy mixture before being fried until crisp in this recipe and then stirred into a delicious egg rice for a very filling meal.

NUTRITIONAL INFORMATION

Calories 599	Sugars 11g	
Protein 30g	Fat 22g	
Carbohydrate ...76g	Saturates 7g	

10 MINS 35 MINS

SERVES 4

INGREDIENTS

1¼ cups long-grain white rice

2½ cups cold water

12 oz pork tenderloin

2 tsp Chinese five-spice powder

4 tbsp cornstarch

3 large eggs, beaten

2 tbsp brown crystal sugar

2 tbsp sunflower oil

1 onion

2 cloves garlic, crushed

¾ cup carrots, diced

1 red bell pepper, seeded and diced

¾ cup peas

2 tbsp butter

salt and pepper

using a sharp knife or meat cleaver. Set the pork strips aside until required.

3 Whisk together the Chinese five-spice powder, cornstarch, 1 egg, and the brown crystal sugar. Toss the pork in the mixture until coated.

4 Heat the sunflower oil in a large wok or skillet. Add the pork and cook over a high heat until the pork is cooked through and crispy. Remove the pork from the wok with a draining spoon and set aside until required.

5 Using a sharp knife, cut the onion into dice.

6 Add the onion, garlic, carrots, bell pepper, and peas to the wok and stir-fry for 5 minutes.

7 Return the pork to the wok together with the cooked rice and stir-fry for 5 minutes.

8 Heat the butter in a skillet. Add the remaining beaten eggs and cook until set. Turn out onto a clean board and slice thinly. Toss the strips of egg into the rice mixture and serve immediately.

1 Rinse the rice under cold running water. Place the rice in a large saucepan, and add the cold water and a pinch of salt. Bring to a boil, cover, then reduce the heat and leave to simmer for about 9 minutes, or until all of the liquid has been absorbed and the rice is tender.

2 Meanwhile, slice the pork tenderloin into very thin, even-sized pieces,

Spicy Pork Balls

These small meatballs are packed with flavor and cooked in a crunchy tomato sauce for a very quick dish.

NUTRITIONAL INFORMATION

Calories	299	Sugars	.........3g
Protein	........28g	Fat	..........15g
Carbohydrate	...14g	Saturates	.......4g

  10 MINS   40 MINS

SERVES 4

INGREDIENTS

1 lb ground pork

2 shallots, finely chopped

2 cloves garlic, crushed

1 tsp cumin seeds

½ tsp chili powder

½ cup wholewheat bread crumbs

1 egg, beaten

2 tbsp sunflower oil

2½ cups chopped tomatoes, flavored with chili

2 tbsp soy sauce

7-oz can water chestnuts, drained

3 tbsp chopped fresh cilantro

1 Place the ground pork in a large mixing bowl. Add the shallots, garlic, cumin seeds, chili powder, bread crumbs, and beaten egg and mix together well.

2 Form the mixture into balls between the palms of your hands.

3 Heat the oil in a large preheated wok. Add the pork balls and stir-fry, in batches, over a high heat for about 5 minutes or until sealed on all sides.

4 Add the tomatoes, soy sauce, and water chestnuts and bring to the boil. Return the pork balls to the wok, reduce the heat, and leave to simmer for 15 minutes.

5 Scatter with chopped fresh cilantro and serve hot.

COOK'S TIP

Add a few teaspoons of chili sauce to a can of chopped tomatoes, if you can't find the flavored variety.

Pork Ribs with Plum Sauce

Pork ribs are always very popular at grills, and you can flavor them with a number of spicy bastes.

NUTRITIONAL INFORMATION

Calories	590	Sugars	.........1g
Protein	........26g	Fat	.........51g
Carbohydrate	....3g	Saturates	......17g

 35 MINS   45 MINS

SERVES 4

I N G R E D I E N T S

2 lb pork spareribs

2 tbsp sunflower oil

1 tsp sesame oil

2 cloves garlic, crushed

1 inch piece gingerroot, grated

⅔ cup plum sauce

2 tbsp dry sherry

2 tbsp hoisin sauce

2 tbsp soy sauce

4–6 scallions, to garnish (optional)

1 To prepare the garnish, trim the scallions to about 3 inches long. Slice both ends into thin strips, leaving the onion intact in the center.

2 Put the scallions into a bowl of iced water for at least 30 minutes until the ends start to curl up. Leave them in the water and set aside until required.

3 If you buy the spareribs in a single piece, cut them into individual ribs. Bring a large pan of water to a boil and add the ribs. Cook for 5 minutes, then drain thoroughly.

4 Heat the oils in a pan, add the garlic and ginger, and cook gently for 1–2 minutes. Stir in the plum sauce, sherry, hoisin, and soy sauce, and heat through.

5 Brush the sauce over the pork ribs. Barbecue over hot coals for 5–10 minutes, then move to a cooler part of the barbecue for 15–20 minutes longer, basting with the remaining sauce. Garnish and serve hot.

COOK'S TIP

Parcooking the ribs in boiling water removes excess fat, which helps prevent the ribs from spitting during cooking. Do not be put off by the large quantity – there is only a little meat on each, but they are quite cheap to buy.

Pork Satay Stir-Fry

Satay sauce is easy to make and is one of the best known and loved sauces in Oriental cooking. It is perfect with beef, chicken, or pork.

NUTRITIONAL INFORMATION

Calories	506	Sugars	........11g
Protein	........31g	Fat	..........36g
Carbohydrate	...15g	Saturates	.......8g

10 MINS   15 MINS

SERVES 4

INGREDIENTS

5½ oz carrots

2 tbsp sunflower oil

12 oz pork tenderloin, thinly sliced

1 onion, sliced

2 cloves garlic, crushed

1 yellow bell pepper, seeded and sliced

2⅓ cups snow peas

1½ cups asparagus, chopped

chopped salted peanuts, to serve

SATAY SAUCE

6 tbsp crunchy peanut butter

6 tbsp coconut milk

1 tsp chili flakes

1 clove garlic, crushed

1 tsp tomato paste

COOK'S TIP

Cook the sauce just before serving as it tends to thicken very quickly and will not be spoonable if you cook it too far in advance.

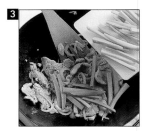

1 Using a sharp knife, slice the carrots into thin sticks.

2 Heat the oil in a large, preheated wok. Add the pork, onion, and garlic and stir-fry for 5 minutes or until the lamb is cooked through.

3 Add the carrots, bell pepper, snow peas, and asparagus to the wok and stir-fry for 5 minutes.

4 To make the satay sauce, place the peanut butter, coconut milk, chili flakes, garlic, and tomato paste in a small pan and heat gently, stirring, until well combined. Be careful not to let the sauce stick to the bottom of the pan.

5 Transfer the stir-fry to warm serving plates. Spoon the satay sauce over the stir-fry and scatter with chopped peanuts. Serve immediately.

Stir-Fried Pork & Cabbage

Rustle up this quick dish in a matter of moments. Assemble all your ingredients first, then everything is ready to hand as you start to stir-fry.

NUTRITIONAL INFORMATION

Calories 226	Sugars 2g
Protein 21g	Fat 12g
Carbohydrate 4g	Saturates 3g

5 MINS   10 MINS

SERVES 4

INGREDIENTS

13 oz pork tenderloin

8 scallions, trimmed

½ small white cabbage

½ cucumber

2 tsp finely grated fresh gingerroot

1 tbsp fish sauce or light soy sauce

2 tbsp dry sherry

2 tbsp water

2 tsp cornstarch

1 tbsp chopped fresh mint or cilantro

2 tbsp sesame oil

salt and pepper

TO GARNISH

sprigs of fresh mint or cilantro

1 chili flower (see Cook's Tip, right)

1 Slice the pork very thinly. Shred the scallions and cabbage, and cut the cucumber into matchsticks.

2 Mix together the ginger, fish sauce or soy sauce, sherry, water, cornstarch, and chopped mint or cilantro until blended.

3 Heat the sesame oil in a wok and add the pork. Stir-fry briskly over a high heat until browned, about 4–5 minutes.

4 Add the scallions, cabbage, and cucumber and stir-fry for a further 2 minutes. Add the cornstarch mixture and continue to cook for about 1 minute, until slightly thickened. Season to taste.

5 Transfer the stir-fry to a warmed dish and serve at once, garnished with sprigs of fresh mint or cilantro and a chili flower.

COOK'S TIP

To make chili flowers, hold the stem of the chili and cut down its length several times with a sharp knife. Place in a bowl of chilled water and chill so that the petals turn out. Remove the chili seeds when the petals have opened.

Sweet & Sour Pork

This dish is a popular choice in Western diets, and must be one of the best known of Chinese recipes.

NUTRITIONAL INFORMATION

Calories	471	Sugars	.......47g
Protein	........16g	Fat	..........13g
Carbohydrate	...77g	Saturates	.......2g

10 MINS   20 MINS

SERVES 4

I N G R E D I E N T S

⅔ cup vegetable oil, for deep-frying

8 oz pork tenderloin, cut into ½-inch cubes

1 onion, sliced

1 green bell pepper, seeded and sliced

1½ cups pineapple pieces

1 small carrot, cut into thin strips

1 oz canned bamboo shoots, drained, rinsed, and halved

rice or noodles, to serve

B A T T E R

1 cup all-purpose flour

1 tbsp cornstarch

1½ tsp baking powder

1 tbsp vegetable oil

S A U C E

⅔ cup light brown sugar

2 tbsp cornstarch

½ cup white wine vinegar

2 garlic cloves, crushed

4 tbsp tomato paste

6 tbsp pineapple juice

1 To make the batter, sift the all-purpose flour into a mixing bowl, together with the cornstarch and baking powder. Add the vegetable oil and stir in enough water to make a thick, smooth batter (about ¾ cup).

2 Pour the vegetable oil into a preheated wok and heat until almost smoking.

3 Dip the cubes of pork into the batter, and cook in the hot oil, in batches, until the pork is cooked through. Remove the pork from the wok with a draining spoon and drain on paper towels. Set aside and keep warm until required.

4 Drain all but 1 tablespoon of oil from the wok and return it to the heat. Add the onion, bell pepper, pineapple pieces, carrot, and bamboo shoots and stir-fry for 1–2 minutes. Remove from the wok with a draining spoon and set aside.

5 Mix all of the sauce ingredients together and pour into the wok. Bring to a boil, stirring until thickened and clear. Cook for 1 minute, then return the pork and vegetables to the wok. Cook for a further 1–2 minutes, then transfer to a serving plate and serve with rice or noodles.

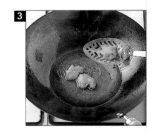

Roast Red Pork

Pork tenderloin is given a marvelous flavor and distinctive red color in this excellent recipe.

NUTRITIONAL INFORMATION

Calories	305	Sugars	4g
Protein	40g	Fat	13g
Carbohydrate	5g	Saturates	5g

12¼ HOURS   40 MINS

SERVES 4

INGREDIENTS

1 lb 10 oz pork tenderloin

1 tsp red food coloring

4 garlic cloves, crushed

1 tsp Chinese five-spice powder

1 tbsp light soy sauce

1 tbsp fish sauce

1 tbsp dry sherry

1 tbsp dark brown crystal sugar

1 tbsp sesame oil

1 tbsp finely grated fresh gingerroot

TO GARNISH

lettuce

scallions, finely sliced

1 Rinse the pork and trim off any fat. Place in a large, clear plastic food bag or freezer bag and add the red food coloring. Roll the pork around in the bag to coat it in the coloring.

2 Mix all the remaining ingredients together and add the mixture to the pork in the plastic bag. Secure the opening and chill overnight, or for at least 12 hours, turning the bag over occasionally.

3 Place the pork on a rack over a roasting pan. Cook in a preheated oven at 425°F for 15 minutes. Remove from the oven and baste with the remaining marinade.

4 Reduce the oven temperature to 350°F and roast the pork for a further 25 minutes, basting with any remaining marinade. Leave to cool for at least 10 minutes before slicing.

5 Slice thinly, arrange on a serving platter, garnish and serve.

COOK'S TIP

Putting the pork in a plastic bag helps to prevent your hands from turning red from the food coloring.

Lamb with Garlic Sauce

This dish contains Szechuan pepper, which is quite hot and may be replaced with black pepper, if preferred.

NUTRITIONAL INFORMATION

Calories 320	Sugars 2g
Protein 25g	Fat 21g
Carbohydrate 4g	Saturates 6g

 35 MINS   10 MINS

SERVES 4

INGREDIENTS

1 lb lamb tenderloin

2 tbsp dark soy sauce

2 tsp sesame oil

2 tbsp Chinese rice wine or dry sherry

½ tsp Szechuan pepper

4 tbsp vegetable oil

4 garlic cloves, crushed

2 oz water chestnuts, quartered

1 green bell pepper, seeded and sliced

1 tbsp wine vinegar

1 tbsp sesame oil

rice or noodles, to serve

1 Cut the lamb into 1-inch pieces and place in a shallow dish.

2 Mix together 1 tablespoon of the soy sauce, the sesame oil, Chinese rice wine or sherry, and Szechuan pepper. Pour the mixture over the lamb, turning to coat, and leave to marinate for 30 minutes.

3 Heat the vegetable oil in a preheated wok. Remove the lamb from the marinade and add to the wok, together with the garlic. Stir-fry for 2–3 minutes.

4 Add the water chestnuts and bell pepper to the wok and stir-fry for 1 minute.

5 Add the remaining soy sauce and the wine vinegar, mixing together well.

6 Add the sesame oil and cook, stirring constantly, for 1–2 minutes, or until the lamb is cooked through.

7 Transfer the lamb and garlic sauce to a warm serving dish and serve immediately with rice or noodles.

COOK'S TIP

Chinese chives, also known as garlic chives, make an appropriate garnish for this dish. Sesame oil is used as a flavoring, rather than for frying, as it burns readily, hence it is added at the end of cooking.

Hot Lamb

This is quite a spicy dish, using 2 chilies in the sauce. Halve the number of chilies to reduce the heat or seed the chilies before using, if desired.

NUTRITIONAL INFORMATION

Calories	323	Sugars	.........4g
Protein	........26g	Fat	..........22g
Carbohydrate	....5g	Saturates	.......7g

  25 MINS   15 MINS

SERVES 4

INGREDIENTS

1 lb lean, boneless lamb

2 tbsp hoisin sauce

1 tbsp dark soy sauce

1 garlic clove, crushed

2 tsp grated fresh gingerroot

2 tbsp vegetable oil

2 onions, sliced

1 fennel bulb, sliced

4 tbsp water

SAUCE

1 large fresh red chili, cut into thin strips

1 fresh green chili, cut into thin strips

2 tbsp rice wine vinegar

2 tsp light brown sugar

2 tbsp peanut oil

1 tsp sesame oil

VARIATION

Use beef, pork, or duck instead of the lamb and vary the vegetables, using leeks or celery instead of the onion and fennel.

1 Cut the lamb into 1-inch cubes and place in a glass dish.

2 Mix together the hoisin sauce, soy sauce, garlic, and ginger and pour over the lamb, turning to coat well. Leave to marinate for 20 minutes.

3 Heat the oil in a preheated wok and stir-fry the lamb for 1–2 minutes. Add the onions and fennel and cook for a further 2 minutes, or until they are just beginning to brown. Stir in the water, cover, and cook for 2–3 minutes.

4 To make the sauce, place all the ingredients in a pan and cook over a low heat for 3-4 minutes, stirring.

5 Transfer the lamb and onions to a serving dish, toss lightly in the sauce and serve immediately.

Lamb with Satay Sauce

This recipe demonstrates the classic serving of lamb satay – lamb marinated in chili and coconut and threaded onto wooden skewers.

NUTRITIONAL INFORMATION

Calories	.501	Sugars	.6g
Protein	.34g	Fat	.37g
Carbohydrate	.9g	Saturates	.10g

 35 MINS   25 MINS

SERVES 4

I N G R E D I E N T S

1 lb lamb loin tenderloin

1 tbsp mild curry paste

⅔ cup coconut milk

2 cloves garlic, crushed

½ tsp chili powder

½ tsp cumin

SATAY SAUCE

1 tbsp corn oil

1 onion, diced

6 tbsp crunchy peanut butter

1 tsp tomato paste

1 tsp fresh lime juice

1⅓ cup cold water

1 Using a sharp knife, thinly slice the lamb and place in a large dish.

2 Mix together the curry paste, coconut milk, garlic, chili powder, and cumin in a bowl. Pour over the lamb, toss well, cover and marinate for 30 minutes.

3 To make the satay sauce. Heat the oil in a large wok and stir-fry the onion for 5 minutes, then reduce the heat and cook for 5 minutes.

4 Stir in the peanut butter, tomato paste, lime juice, and water.

5 Thread the lamb onto wooden skewers, reserving the marinade.

6 Broil the lamb skewers under a hot broiler for 6–8 minutes, turning once.

7 Add the reserved marinade to the wok, bring to a boil, and cook for 5 minutes. Serve the lamb skewers with the satay sauce.

COOK'S TIP

Soak the wooden skewers in cold water for 30 minutes before broiling to prevent the skewers from burning.

Sesame Lamb Stir-Fry

This is a very simple, but delicious, dish in which lean pieces of lamb are cooked in sugar and soy sauce and then sprinkled with sesame seeds.

NUTRITIONAL INFORMATION

Calories	276	Sugars	.........4g
Protein	........25g	Fat	..........18g
Carbohydrate	....5g	Saturates	.......6g

5 MINS   10 MINS

SERVES 4

I N G R E D I E N T S

1 lb boneless lean lamb

2 tbsp peanut oil

2 leeks, sliced

1 carrot, cut into matchsticks

2 garlic cloves, crushed

⅓ cup lamb or vegetable stock

2 tsp light brown sugar

1 tbsp dark soy sauce

4½ tsp sesame seeds

1 Using a sharp knife, cut the lamb into thin strips.

2 Heat the peanut oil in a preheated wok or large skillet until it is really hot.

3 Add the lamb and stir-fry for 2–3 minutes. Remove the lamb from the wok with a draining spoon and set aside until required.

4 Add the leeks, carrot, and garlic to the wok or skillet and stir-fry in the remaining oil for 1–2 minutes.

5 Remove the vegetables from the wok with a draining spoon and set aside.

6 Drain any remaining oil from the wok. Place the lamb or vegetable stock,

light brown sugar, and dark soy sauce in the wok and add the lamb. Cook, stirring constantly to coat the lamb, for 2–3 minutes.

7 Sprinkle the sesame seeds over the top, turning the lamb to coat.

8 Spoon the leek, carrot, and garlic mixture onto a warm serving dish and top with the lamb. Serve immediately.

COOK'S TIP

Be careful not to burn the sugar in the wok when heating and coating the meat, otherwise the flavor of the dish will be spoiled.

Spareribs with Chili

For best results, chop the spareribs into small bite-size pieces after cooking so they are easy to eat.

NUTRITIONAL INFORMATION

Calories 497	Sugars 3g
Protein 13g	Fat 47g
Carbohydrate 4g	Saturates 11g

 60 MINS   20 MINS

SERVES 4

I N G R E D I E N T S

1 lb 2 oz pork spareribs

1 tsp sugar

1 tbsp light soy sauce

1 tsp rice wine or dry sherry

1 tsp cornstarch

2½ cups vegetable oil

1 garlic clove, finely chopped

1 scallion, cut into short sections

1 small hot chili pepper (green or red), thinly sliced

2 tbsp black bean sauce

⅔ cup Chinese stock (see page 14) or water

1 small onion, diced

1 medium green bell pepper, cored, seeded, and diced

COOK'S TIP

Be very careful when handling and cutting chili peppers because their juice can cause irritation of the skin. Be sure to wash your hands after handling, and keep them away from your face and eyes. The seeds of the chili are the hottest part – remove seeds if you want a milder dish.

1 Trim any excess fat from the ribs. Using a sharp knife or meat cleaver, chop each rib into 3-4 bite-sized piecess and place in a shallow dish.

2 Mix together the sugar, soy sauce, wine, and cornstarch and pour the mixture over the pork ribs. Leave to marinate for 35-45 minutes.

3 Heat the vegetable oil in a large heated wok or skillet.

4 Add the spareribs to the wok and deep-fry for 2-3 minutes until light brown. Remove with a draining spoon and drain on paper towels.

5 Pour off the oil, leaving about 1 tablespoon in the wok. Add the garlic, scallion, chili pepper, and black bean sauce and stir-fry for 30-40 seconds.

6 Add the spare ribs and blend well, then add the stock or water. Bring to a boil, then reduce the heat, cover, and braise for 8-10 minutes, stirring once or twice.

7 Add the onion and green bell pepper, increase the heat to high, and stir uncovered for about 2 minutes to reduce the sauce a little; serve hot.

Five-Spice Lamb

Chinese five-spice powder is a blend of cinnamon, fennel, star anise, ginger, and cloves, all finely ground together.

NUTRITIONAL INFORMATION

Calories 361	Sugars 3g	
Protein 35g	Fat 22g	
Carbohydrate 5g	Saturates 8g	

1¼ HOURS   10 MINS

SERVES 4

INGREDIENTS

1 lb 6 oz lean boneless lamb (leg or tenderloin)

2 tsp Chinese five-spice powder

3 tbsp sunflower oil

1 red bell pepper, cored, seeded, and thinly sliced

1 green bell pepper, cored, seeded, and thinly sliced

1 yellow or orange bell pepper, cored, seeded, and thinly sliced

4-6 scallions, thinly sliced diagonally

1¼ cups green or fine beans, cut into 1½-inch pieces

2 tbsp soy sauce

4 tbsp sherry

salt and pepper

Chinese noodles, to serve

TO GARNISH

strips of red and yellow bell pepper

fresh cilantro leaves

1 Cut the lamb into narrow strips, about 1½ inches long, across the grain. Place in a bowl, add the five-spice powder and ¼ teaspoon salt, mix well, and leave to marinate, covered, in a cool place for at least an hour and up to 24 hours.

2 Heat half the oil in the wok, swirling it around until really hot. Add the lamb and stir-fry briskly for 3-4 minutes until almost cooked through. Remove from the pan and set aside.

3 Add the remaining oil to the wok and when hot add the bell peppers and scallions. Stir-fry for 2-3 minutes, then add the beans and stir for a minute or so.

4 Add the soy sauce and sherry to the wok and when hot return the lamb and any juices to the wok. Stir-fry for 1-2 minutes until the lamb is really hot again and thoroughly coated in the sauce. Season to taste.

5 Serve the five-spice lamb with Chinese noodles, garnished with strips of red and green bell pepper and cilantro.

Fish & Seafood

China's many miles of coastline, rivers, and lakes offer an enormous variety of fresh- and saltwater fish and seafood. Among the most popular are carp, bass, bream, clams, crab,

crawfish, and shrimp. Dishes that include shark's fins, abalone, squid, and edible seaweed are also common. When buying fish and seafood for Chinese cooking, freshness is imperative to flavor, so be sure to buy it and use it as soon as possible, preferably the same day. Chinese chefs buy fish that are kept alive until just before cooking. Favorite cooking methods for fish are steaming and poaching in simmering water or broth.

Shrimp Fu-Yong

The classic ingredients of this popular dish are eggs, carrots, and shrimp. Add extra ingredients such as peas or crabmeat, if desired.

NUTRITIONAL INFORMATION

Calories 240	Sugars 1g	
Protein 22g	Fat 16g	
Carbohydrate 1g	Saturates 3g	

5 MINS   10 MINS

SERVES 4

INGREDIENTS

2 tbsp vegetable oil

1 carrot, grated

5 eggs, beaten

8 oz raw small shrimp, peeled

1 tbsp light soy sauce

pinch of Chinese five-spice powder

2 scallions, chopped

2 tsp sesame seeds

1 tsp sesame oil

COOK'S TIP

If only cooked shrimp are available, add them just before the end of cooking, but make sure they are fully incorporated into the fu yong. They require only heating through. Overcooking will make them chewy and tasteless.

1 Heat the vegetable oil in a preheated wok or skillet, swirling it around until the oil is really hot.

2 Add the grated carrot and stir-fry for 1–2 minutes.

3 Push the carrot to one side of the wok or skillet and add the beaten eggs. Cook, stirring gently, for 1–2 minutes.

4 Stir the shrimp, light soy sauce, and five-spice powder into the mixture in the wok. Stir-fry the mixture for 2–3 minutes, or until the shrimp change colour and the mixture is almost dry.

5 Turn the shrimp fu-yong out onto a warm plate and sprinkle the scallions, sesame seeds, and sesame oil on top. Serve immediately.

Chili Shrimp

Large shrimp are marinated in a chili mixture and stir-fried with cashews. Serve with a fluffy rice and braised vegetables.

NUTRITIONAL INFORMATION

Calories	435	Sugars	.........2g
Protein	........4.2g	Fat	23
Carbohydrate	...10g	Saturates	.......4g

2¼ HOURS   5 MINS

SERVES 4

I N G R E D I E N T S

5 tbsp soy sauce

5 tbsp dry sherry

3 dried red chilies, seeded and chopped

2 garlic cloves, crushed

2 tsp grated gingerroot

5 tbsp water

1 lb 6 oz shelled jumbo shrimp

1 large bunch scallions, chopped

⅔ cup salted cashew nuts

3 tbsp vegetable oil

2 tsp cornstarch

1 Mix the soy sauce, sherry, chilies, garlic, ginger, and water in a bowl.

2 Add the jumbo shrimp, scallions, and cashews and mix well. Cover tightly and leave to marinate for at least 2 hours, stirring occasionally.

3 Heat the oil in a large wok. Remove the shrimp, scallions, and cashews from the marinade with a draining spoon and add to the wok, reserving the marinade. Stir-fry over a high heat for 1-2 minutes.

4 Mix the reserved marinade with the cornstarch, add to the wok and stir-fry for about 30 seconds, until the marinade forms a slightly thickened shiny glaze over the shrimp mixture. Serve immediately.

COOK'S TIP

For an attractive presentation serve this dish on mixed wild rice and basmati rice. Start cooking the wild rice in boiling water. After 10 minutes, add the basmati rice or other rice and continue boiling until all grains are tender. Drain well and adjust the seasoning.

Fried Shrimp with Cashews

Cashew nuts are delicious as part of a stir-fry with almost any other ingredient. Use the unsalted variety in cooking.

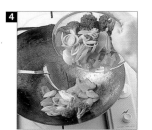

NUTRITIONAL INFORMATION

Calories	406	Sugar	.........3g
Protein	........31g	Fat	..........25g
Carbohydrate	...13g	Saturates	.......4g

5 MINS   5 MINS

SERVES 4

I N G R E D I E N T S

2 garlic cloves, crushed

1 tbsp cornstarch

pinch of superfine sugar

1 lb raw jumbo shrimp

4 tbsp vegetable oil

1 leek, sliced

4½ oz broccoli flowerets

1 orange bell pepper, seeded and diced

¾ cup unsalted cashew nuts

S A U C E

¾ cup fish stock

1 tbsp cornstarch

dash of chili sauce

2 tsp sesame oil

1 tbsp Chinese rice wine

1 Mix together the garlic, cornstarch, and sugar in a bowl.

2 Peel and devein the shrimp. Stir the shrimp into the mixture to coat thoroughly.

3 Heat the vegetable oil in a preheated wok and add the shrimp mixture. Stir-fry over a high heat for 20–30 seconds until the shrimp turn pink. Remove the shrimp from the wok with a draining spoon, drain on paper towels, and set aside until required.

4 Add the leek, broccoli, and bell pepper to the wok and stir-fry for 2 minutes.

5 To make the sauce, place the fish stock, cornstarch, chili sauce to taste, the sesame oil, and Chinese rice wine in a small bowl. Mix until thoroughly combined.

6 Add the sauce to the wok, together with the cashew nuts. Return the shrimp to the wok and cook for 1 minute to heat through.

7 Transfer the superfine stir-fry to a warm serving dish and serve immediately.

Seared Scallops

Scallops have a terrific, subtle flavor that is complemented in this dish by the buttery sauce.

NUTRITIONAL INFORMATION

Calories 272	Sugars 0g	
Protein 28g	Fat 17g	
Carbohydrate 2g	Saturates 8g	

 5 MINS   10 MINS

SERVES 4

I N G R E D I E N T S

1 lb fresh scallops, without roe, or the same amount of frozen scallops, defrosted thoroughly

6 scallions

2 tbsp vegetable oil

1 green chili, seeded and sliced

3 tbsp sweet soy sauce

1½ tbsp butter, cubed

1 Rinse the scallops thoroughly under cold running water, drain, and pat the scallops dry with paper towels.

2 Using a sharp knife, slice each scallop in half horizontally.

3 Using a sharp knife, trim and slice the scallions.

4 Heat the vegetable oil in a large preheated wok or heavy-based skillet, swirling the oil around the base of the wok until it is really hot.

5 Add the sliced green chili, scallions, and scallops to the wok and stir-fry over a high heat for 4–5 minutes, or until the scallops are just cooked through. If using frozen scallops, be sure not to overcook them as they will easily disintegrate.

6 Add the soy sauce and butter to the scallop stir-fry and heat through until the butter melts.

7 Transfer to warm serving bowls and serve hot.

COOK'S TIP

If you buy scallops on the shell, slide a knife underneath the membrane to loosen it and cut off the tough muscle that holds the scallop to the shell. Discard the black stomach sac and intestinal vein.

Scallop Fritters

Scallops, like most shellfish, require very little cooking, and this original dish is a perfect example of how to use shellfish to its full potential.

NUTRITIONAL INFORMATION

Calories 240   Sugars 1g
Protein . . . . .29g   Fat 9g
Carbohydrate . . . .11g   Saturates 1g

 5 MINS   30 MINS

SERVES 4

INGREDIENTS

3½ oz fine green beans

1 red chili

1 lb scallops, without roe

1 egg

3 scallions, sliced

½ cup rice flour

1 tbsp fish sauce

oil, for frying

salt

sweet chili dip, to serve

1 Using a sharp knife, trim the green beans and slice them very thinly.

2 Using a sharp knife, seed and very finely chop the red chili.

3 Bring a small saucepan of lightly salted water to the boil. Add the green beans to the pan and cook for 3–4 minutes, or until just softened.

4 Roughly chop the scallops and place them in a large bowl. Add the cooked beans to the scallops.

5 Mix the egg with the scallions, rice flour, fish sauce, and chili until well combined. Add to the scallops and mix well.

6 Heat about 1 inch of oil in a large preheated wok. Add a ladleful of the mixture to the wok and cook for 5 minutes until golden and set.

7 Remove the fritter from the wok and leave to drain on paper towels. Keep warm while cooking the remaining fritters mixture. Serve the fritters hot with a sweet chili dip.

VARIATION

You could use shrimp or shelled clams instead of the scallops, if you prefer.

Scallops in Ginger Sauce

Scallops are both attractive and delicious. Cooked with ginger and orange, this dish is perfect served with plain rice.

1 Heat the vegetable oil in a preheated wok or large skillet. Add the scallops and stir-fry for 1–2 minutes. Remove the scallops from the wok with a draining spoon, keep warm, and set aside until required.

2 Add the ginger and garlic to the wok and stir-fry for 30 seconds. Stir in the leeks and peas and cook, stirring, for a further 2 minutes.

3 Add the bamboo shoots and return the scallops to the wok. Stir gently to mix without breaking up the scallops.

4 Stir in the soy sauce, orange juice, and superfine sugar and cook for 1–2 minutes.

5 Transfer the stir-fry to a serving dish, garnish with the orange peel and serve immediately.

NUTRITIONAL INFORMATION

Calories . . . . .216 Sugars 4g
Protein . . . . .30g Fat 8g
Carbohydrate . . . .8g Saturates 1g

🧊 5 MINS 🕐 10 MINS

SERVES 4

INGREDIENTS

2 tbsp vegetable oil

1 lb scallops, cleaned and halved

1-inch piece fresh gingerroot, finely chopped

3 garlic cloves, crushed

2 leeks, shredded

¾ cup shelled peas

4½ oz canned bamboo shoots, drained and rinsed

2 tbsp light soy sauce

2 tbsp unsweetened orange juice

1 tsp superfine sugar

orange peel, to garnish

COOK'S TIP

The edible parts of a scallop are the round white muscle and the orange and white coral or roe. The frilly skirt surrounding the muscle – the gills and mantle – may be used for making shellfish stock. All other parts should be discarded.

Cantonese Shrimp

This superfine dish is very simple and is ideal for supper or lunch when time is short.

NUTRITIONAL INFORMATION

Calories 460   Sugar 3g
Protein . . . . .53g   Fat 24
Carbohydrate . . . .6g   Saturates 5g

 10 MINS   20 MINS

SERVES 4

I N G R E D I E N T S

5 tbsp vegetable oil

4 garlic cloves, crushed

1½ lb raw shrimp, shelled and deveined

2-inch piece fresh gingerroot , chopped

1¼ cups lean pork, diced

1 leek, sliced

3 eggs, beaten

shredded leek and red bell pepper matchsticks, to garnish

rice, to serve

S A U C E

2 tbsp Chinese rice wine or dry sherry

2 tbsp light soy sauce

2 tsp superfine sugar

⅔ cup fish stock

4½ tsp cornstarch

3 tbsp water

1 Heat 2 tablespoons of the vegetable oil in a preheated wok.

2 Add the garlic to the wok and stir-fry for 30 seconds.

3 Add the shrimp to the wok and stir-fry for 5 minutes, or until they

change color. Remove the shrimp from the wok or skillet with a draining spoon, set aside, and keep warm.

4 Add the remaining oil to the wok and heat, swirling the oil around the base of the wok until it is really hot.

5 Add the ginger, diced pork, and leek to the wok and stir-fry over a medium heat for 4-5 minutes, or until the pork is lightly colored and sealed.

6 To make the sauce, add the rice wine or sherry, soy sauce, superfine sugar, and fish stock to the wok and stir to blend.

7 In a small bowl, blend the cornstarch with the water to form a smooth paste and stir it into the wok. Cook, stirring, until the sauce thickens.

8 Return the shrimp to the wok and add the beaten eggs. Cook for 5–6 minutes, gently stirring occasionally, until the eggs set.

9 Transfer to a warm serving dish, garnish with shredded leek and bell pepper matchsticks and serve immediately with rice.

Mussels with Lemongrass

Give fresh mussels a Far-Eastern flavor by using some kaffir lime leaves, garlic, and lemongrass in the stock used for steaming them.

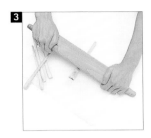

NUTRITIONAL INFORMATION

Calories 194	Sugar 0g	
Protein 33g	Fat 7g	
Carbohydrate 1g	Saturates 1g	

10 MINS   10 MINS

SERVES 4

INGREDIENTS

1 lb 10 oz live mussels

1 tbsp sesame oil

3 shallots, chopped finely

2 garlic cloves, chopped finely

1 stalk lemongrass

2 kaffir lime leaves

2 tbsp chopped fresh cilantro

finely grated peel of 1 lime

2 tbsp lime juice

1¼ cups hot vegetable stock

crusty bread, to serve

fresh cilantro, to garnish

1 Using a small sharp knife, scrape the beards off the mussels under cold running water. Scrub them well, discarding any that are damaged or remain open when tapped. Keep rinsing until there is no trace of sand.

2 Heat the sesame oil in a large saucepan and fry the shallots and garlic gently until softened, about 2 minutes.

3 Bruise the lemongrass, using a meat mallet or rolling pin, and add to the pan with the kaffir lime leaves, cilantro, lime peel and juice, mussels, and stock. Put the lid on the saucepan and cook over a medium heat for 3–5 minutes. Shake the pan from time to time.

4 Lift the mussels out into 4 warmed soup plates, discarding any that remain shut. Boil the remaining liquid rapidly to reduce slightly. Remove the lemongrass and lime leaves, then pour the liquid over the mussels.

5 Garnish with cilantro and lime wedges, and serve at once.

COOK'S TIP

Mussels are now farmed, so they should be available throughout the year.

Mussels in Black Bean Sauce

This dish looks so impressive, the combination of colors making it look almost too good to eat!

NUTRITIONAL INFORMATION

Calories ....174 Sugars 4g
Protein ....19g Fat 8g
Carbohydrate ....6g Saturates 1g

 5 MINS   10 MINS

SERVES 4

I N G R E D I E N T S

12 oz leeks

12 oz cooked green-lipped mussels (shelled)

1 tsp cumin seeds

2 tbsp vegetable oil

2 cloves garlic, crushed

1 red bell pepper, seeded and sliced

¾ cup canned bamboo shoots, drained

6 oz baby spinach

5¾ oz black bean sauce

1 Using a sharp knife, trim the leeks and shred them.

2 Place the cooked green-lipped mussels in a large bowl, sprinkle with the cumin seeds, and toss well to coat all over. Set aside until required.

COOK'S TIP

If the green-lipped mussels are not available they can be bought shelled in cans and jars from most supermarkets and gourmet food stores.

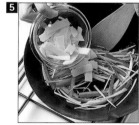

3 Heat the vegetable oil in a preheated wok, swirling the oil around the base of the wok until it is really hot.

4 Add the shredded leeks, garlic, and sliced red bell pepper to the wok and stir-fry for 5 minutes, or until the vegetables are tender.

5 Add the bamboo shoots, baby spinach leaves, and cooked green-lipped mussels to the wok and stir-fry for about 2 minutes.

6 Pour the black bean sauce over the ingredients in the wok, toss well to coat all the ingredients in the sauce, and leave to simmer for a few seconds, stirring occasionally.

7 Transfer the stir-fry to warm serving bowls and serve immediately.

Crab with Chinese Cabbage

The delicate flavor of Chinese cabbage and crabmeat are enhanced by the coconut milk in this recipe.

NUTRITIONAL INFORMATION

Calories 109   Sugars 1g
Protein . . . . .11g   Fat 6g
Carbohydrate . . . .2g   Saturates 1g

5 MINS   10 MINS

SERVES 4

INGREDIENTS

8 oz shiitake mushrooms

2 tbsp vegetable oil

2 cloves garlic, crushed

6 scallions, sliced

1 head Chinese cabbage, shredded

1 tbsp mild curry paste

6 tbsp coconut milk

7 oz can white crabmeat, drained

1 tsp chili flakes

1 Using a sharp knife, cut the mushrooms into slices.

2 Heat the vegetable oil in a large preheated wok or heavy-based skillet.

3 Add the mushrooms and garlic to the wok or skillet, and stir-fry for 3 minutes or until the mushrooms have softened.

4 Add the scallions and shredded Chinese cabbage to the wok and stir-fry until the leaves have wilted.

5 Mix together the mild curry paste and coconut milk in a small bowl.

6 Add the curry paste and coconut milk mixture to the wok, together with the crab meat and chili flakes. Mix together until well combined.

7 Heat the mixture in the wok until the juices start to bubble.

8 Transfer the crab and vegetable stir-fry to warm serving bowls and serve immediately.

COOK'S TIP

Shiitake mushrooms are now readily available in the fresh vegetable section of many large supermarkets.

Crab Claws with Chili

Crab claws are frequently used in Chinese cooking, and look sensational. They are perfect with this delicious chili sauce.

NUTRITIONAL INFORMATION

Calories	154	Sugar	.........3g
Protein	........16g	Fat	...........7g
Carbohydrate	....8g	Saturates	.......1g

 5 MINS   10 MINS

SERVES 4

INGREDIENTS

1 lb 9 oz crab claws

1 tbsp corn oil

2 cloves garlic, crushed

1 tbsp grated fresh gingerroot

3 red chilies, seeded and finely chopped

2 tbsp sweet chili sauce

3 tbsp tomato ketchup

1¼ cups cooled fish stock

1 tbsp cornstarch

salt and pepper

1 tbsp fresh chives, snipped

1 Gently crack the crab claws with a nut cracker. This process will allow the flavors of the chili, garlic, and ginger to fully penetrate the crabmeat.

2 Heat the corn oil in a large preheated wok.

3 Add the crab claws to the wok and stir-fry for about 5 minutes.

4 Add the garlic, ginger, and chilies to the wok and stir-fry for 1 minute, tossing the crab claws to coat all over.

5 Mix together the sweet chili sauce, tomato catsup, fish stock, and cornstarch in a small bowl. Add this mixture to the wok and cook, stirring occasionally, until the sauce starts to thicken.

6 Season the mixture in the wok with salt and pepper to taste.

7 Transfer the crab claws and chili sauce to warm serving dishes, garnish with snipped fresh chives, and serve.

COOK'S TIP

If crab claws are not easily available, use a whole crab cut into eight pieces.

Crabmeat Cakes

Make these tasty crabmeat cakes to serve as a snack or appetizer, or as an accompaniment to a main meal.

NUTRITIONAL INFORMATION

Calories	262	Sugars	.........4g
Protein	........13g	Fat	..........17g
Carbohydrate	...14g	Saturates	.......3g

🔥 20 MINS   🕐 55 MINS

SERVES 4

I N G R E D I E N T S

generous 1 cup long-grain rice

1 tbsp sesame oil

1 small onion, chopped finely

1 large garlic clove, crushed

2 tbsp chopped fresh coriander

7 oz canned crabmeat, drained

1 tbsp fish sauce or light soy sauce

1 cup coconut milk

2 eggs

4 tbsp vegetable oil

salt and pepper

sliced scallions, to garnish

1 Cook the rice in plenty of boiling, lightly salted water until just tender, about 12 minutes. Rinse with cold water and drain well.

2 Heat the sesame oil in a small skillet and fry the onion and garlic gently for about 5 minutes, until softened and golden brown.

3 Combine the rice, onion, garlic, coriander, crabmeat, fish sauce or soy sauce, and coconut milk. Season. Beat the eggs and add to the mixture. Divide the mixture between 8 greased ramekins or heatproof teacups and place them in a

baking dish or roasting pan with enough warm water to come halfway up their sides. Place in a preheated oven at 350°F for 25 minutes, until set. Leave to cool.

4 Turn the crab cakes out of the ramekins. Heat the oil in a wok or skillet and fry the crab cakes in the oil until golden brown. Drain on paper towels, garnish, and serve.

COOK'S TIP

If you want, prepare these crab cakes up to the point where they have been baked. Cool them, then cover and chill, ready for frying when needed.

Baked Crab with Ginger

In Chinese restaurants, only live crabs are used, but cooked ones can be used at home successfully.

NUTRITIONAL INFORMATION

Calories 261	Sugars 0.5g
Protein 18g	Fat 17g
Carbohydrate 5g	Saturates 2g

25 MINS   10 MINS

SERVES 4

I N G R E D I E N T S

1 large or 2 medium crabs, weighing about 1 lb 10 oz in total

2 tbsp Chinese rice wine or dry sherry

1 egg, lightly beaten

1 tbsp cornstarch

3-4 tbsp vegetable oil

1 tbsp finely chopped gingerroot

3-4 scallions, cut into sections

2 tbsp light soy sauce

1 tsp sugar

⅓ cup Chinese Stock (see page 14) or water

½ tsp sesame oil

coriander leaves, to garnish

1 Cut the crab in half from the under-belly. Break off the claws and crack them with the back of a cleaver or a large kitchen knife.

2 Discard the legs and crack the shell, breaking it into several pieces. Discard the feathery gills and the stomach sac. Place the crabmeat in a bowl.

3 Mix together the wine or sherry, egg, and cornstarch. Pour the mixture over the crab and leave to marinate for 10-15 minutes.

4 Heat the vegetable oil in a preheated wok and stir-fry the crab with the chopped ginger and scallions for 2-3 minutes.

5 Add the soy sauce, sugar, and Chinese stock or water, blend well and bring to a boil. Cover and cook for 3-4 minutes, then remove the lid, sprinkle with sesame oil and serve, garnished with fresh cilantro leaves.

COOK'S TIP

Crabs are almost always sold cooked. The crab should feel heavy for its size, and when it is shaken, there should not be a sound of water inside. A good medium-sized crab should yield about lb 2 oz meat, enough for 3-4 people.

Fried Squid Flowers

The addition of green bell pepper and black bean sauce to the squid makes a colorful and delicious dish from the Cantonese school.

NUTRITIONAL INFORMATION

Calories 172	Sugars 1g	
Protein 13g	Fat 13g	
Carbohydrate 2g	Saturates 1g	

10 MINS   5 MINS

SERVES 4

INGREDIENTS

12-14 oz prepared and cleaned squid (see Cook's Tip, below)

1 medium green bell pepper, cored and seeded

3-4 tbsp vegetable oil

1 garlic clove, finely chopped

¼ tsp finely chopped gingerroot

2 tsp finely chopped scallions

½ tsp salt

2 tbsp crushed black bean sauce

1 tsp Chinese rice wine or dry sherry

a few drops sesame oil

boiled rice, to serve

1 If ready-prepared squid is not available, prepare as instructed in the Cook's Tip, below.

2 Open up the squid and, using a meat cleaver or sharp knife, score the inside of the flesh in a crisscross pattern.

3 Cut the squid into pieces about the size of an oblong postage stamp.

4 Blanch the squid pieces in a bowl of boiling water for a few seconds. Remove and drain; dry on paper towels.

5 Cut the bell pepper into small triangular pieces. Heat the oil in a heated wok or large skillet and stir-fry the bell pepper for about 1 minute.

6 Add the garlic, ginger, scallion, salt, and squid. Continue stirring for another minute.

7 Finally add the black bean sauce and Chinese rice wine or dry sherry, and blend well.

8 Transfer the squid flowers to a serving dish, sprinkle with sesame oil, and serve with boiled rice.

COOK'S TIP

Clean the squid by first cutting off the head. Cut off the tentacles and reserve. Remove the small soft bone at the base of the tentacles and the transparent backbone, as well as the ink bag. Peel off the thin skin, then wash and dry well.

Squid with Black Bean Sauce

Squid really is wonderful if quickly cooked as in this recipe, and contrary to popular belief, it is not tough and rubbery unless it is overcooked.

NUTRITIONAL INFORMATION

Calories 180	Sugars 2g
Protein 19g	Fat 7g
Carbohydrate . . .10g	Saturates 1g

5 MINS   20 MINS

SERVES 4

I N G R E D I E N T S

1 lb squid rings

2 tbsp all-purpose flour

½ tsp salt

1 green bell pepper

2 tbsp peanut oil

1 red onion, sliced

5¾ oz black bean sauce

1 Rinse the squid rings under cold running water and pat dry thoroughly with paper towels.

2 Place the all-purpose flour and salt in a bowl and mix together. Add the squid rings and toss until they are evenly coated.

3 Using a sharp knife, seed the bell pepper. Slice the bell pepper into thin strips.

4 Heat the peanut oil in a large preheated wok or heavy-based skillet, swirling the oil around the base of the wok until it is really hot.

5 Add the bell pepper slices and red onion to the wok or skillet and stir-fry for about 2 minutes, or until the vegetables are just softening.

6 Add the squid rings to the wok or skillet and cook for a further 5 minutes, or until the squid is cooked through. Be careful not to overcook the squid.

7 Add the black bean sauce to the wok and heat through until the juices are bubbling. Transfer the squid stir-fry to warm serving bowls and serve immediately.

COOK'S TIP

Serve this recipe with fried rice or noodles tossed in soy sauce, if you wish.

Octopus & Squid with Chili

Buy cleaned squid tubes for this dish; if they are not available,
see page 173 for directions on preparing squid.

NUTRITIONAL INFORMATION

Calories	.319	Sugars	.2g
Protein	.40g	Fat	.13g
Carbohydrate	.4g	Saturates	.1g

8½ HOURS   10 MINS

SERVES 6

INGREDIENTS

⅔ cup rice vinegar

¼ cup dry sherry

2 red chilies, chopped

1 tsp sugar

4 tbsp oil

12 baby octopus

12 small squid tubes, cleaned

2 scallions, sliced

1 garlic clove, crushed

1-inch piece gingerroot, grated

4 tbsp sweet chili sauce

salt

1 Combine the vinegar, dry sherry, red chilies, sugar, 2 tbsp of the oil, and a pinch of salt in a large bowl.

2 Wash each octopus under cold running water and drain. Lay each on its side on a chopping board. Find the neck and cut through. The beak of the octopus should be left in the head; if it is not, make a cut nearer the tentacles and check again. Discard the head and beak, and put the tentacles, which should all be in one piece, into the vinegar mixture.

3 Put the squid tubes into the vinegar mixture and turn to coat well. Cover and chill for 8 hours or overnight.

4 Heat the remaining oil in a wok and stir-fry the scallions, garlic, and ginger for 1 minute over a very hot barbecue. Remove from the heat and add the chili sauce; set aside.

5 Drain the fish from the marinade. Cut the pointed bottom end off each squid tube, so the tubes are an even width. Open out the squid so that it is flat. Score the squid to create a lattice pattern.

6 Cook the octopus and squid over the hottest part of the barbecue for 4–5 minutes, turning them constantly. The octopus tentacles will curl up, and are cooked when the flesh is no longer translucent. The squid tubes will curl back on themselves, revealing the lattice cuts.

7 When cooked, toss them into the pan with the chili sauce to coat completely and serve immediately.

Seafood Medley

Use any combination of fish and seafood in this delicious dish of coated fish served in a wine sauce.

NUTRITIONAL INFORMATION

Calories ....168 Sugars 2g

Protein ....29g Fat 3g

Carbohydrate ....4g Saturates 1g

5 MINS   15 MINS

SERVES 4

INGREDIENTS

2 tbsp dry white wine

1 egg white, lightly beaten

½ tsp Chinese five-spice powder

1 tsp cornstarch

10½ oz raw shrimp, peeled and deveined

4½ oz prepared squid, cut into rings

4½ oz white fish fillets, cut into strips

vegetable oil, for deep-frying

1 green bell pepper, seeded and
   cut into thin strips

1 carrot, cut into thin strips

4 baby corn-on-the-cobs, halved
   lengthways

1 Mix the wine, egg white, five-spice powder, and cornstarch in a large bowl. Add the shrimp, squid rings, and fish fillets and stir to coat evenly. Remove the fish and seafood with a draining spoon, reserving any leftover cornstarch mixture.

2 Heat the oil in a preheated wok and deep-fry the shrimp, squid, and fish for 2–3 minutes. Remove from the wok with a draining spoon and set aside.

3 Pour off all but 1 tablespoon of oil from the wok and return to the heat. Add the bell pepper, carrot, and corn cobs and stir-fry for 4–5 minutes.

4 Return the seafood to the wok with any remaining cornstarch mixture. Heat through, stirring, and serve.

COOK'S TIP

If you want, open up the squid rings and using a sharp knife, score a lattice pattern on the flesh to make them look attractive.

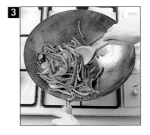

Gingered Angler Fish

This dish is a real treat and is perfect for special occasions. Angler fish has a tender flavor that is ideal with asparagus, chili, and ginger.

NUTRITIONAL INFORMATION

Calories	133	Sugars	.........0g
Protein	........21g	Fat	...........5g
Carbohydrate	....1g	Saturates	.......1g

5 MINS

10 MINS

SERVES 4

INGREDIENTS

1 lb angler fish

1 tbsp freshly grated gingerroot

2 tbsp sweet chili sauce

1 tbsp corn oil

1 cup asparagus

3 scallions, sliced

1 tsp sesame oil

1 Using a sharp knife, slice the angler fish into thin flat rounds. Set aside until required.

2 Mix together the freshly grated gingerroot and the sweet chili sauce in a small bowl until thoroughly blended. Brush the ginger and chili sauce mixture over the angler fish pieces, using a pastry brush.

3 Heat the corn oil in a large preheated wok or heavy-based skillet.

4 Add the angler fish pieces, asparagus, and scallions to the wok or skillet and cook for about 5 minutes, stirring gently so the fish pieces do not break up.

5 Remove the wok or skillet from the heat, drizzle the sesame oil over the stir-fry, and toss well to combine.

6 Transfer the stir-fried gingered angler fish to warm serving plates and serve immediately.

COOK'S TIP

Angler fish is quite expensive, but it is well worth using as it has a wonderful flavor and texture. At a push you could use cubes of chunky cod fillet instead.

Szechuan White Fish

Szechuan pepper is hot and should be used sparingly to avoid making the dish unbearably spicy.

NUTRITIONAL INFORMATION

Calories . . . . . . .225 Sugars 3g
Protein . . . . .20g Fat 8g
Carbohydrate . . .17g Saturates 1g

5 MINS   20 MINS

SERVES 4

INGREDIENTS

12 oz white fish fillets

1 small egg, beaten

3 tbsp all-purpose flour

4 tbsp dry white wine

3 tbsp light soy sauce

vegetable oil, for frying

1 garlic clove, cut into slivers

½-inch piece fresh gingerroot, finely
    chopped

1 onion, finely chopped

1 celery stick, chopped

1 fresh red chili, chopped

3 scallions, chopped

1 tsp rice wine vinegar

½ tsp ground Szechuan pepper

¾ cup fish stock

1 tsp superfine sugar

1 tsp cornstarch

2 tsp water

1 Cut the fish into 1½-inch cubes. Beat together the egg, flour, wine, and 1 tablespoon of soy sauce to make a batter. Dip the cubes of fish into the batter to coat well.

2 Heat the oil in a wok, reduce the heat slightly, and cook the fish, in batches, for 2–3 minutes, until golden brown. Remove with a draining spoon, drain on paper towels, set aside, and keep warm.

3 Pour all but 1 tablespoon of oil from the wok and return to the heat. Add the garlic, ginger, onion, celery, chili, and scallions and stir-fry for 1–2 minutes. Stir in the remaining soy sauce and the vinegar.

4 Add the Szechuan pepper, fish stock, and superfine sugar to the wok. Mix the cornstarch with the water to form a smooth paste and stir it into the stock. Bring to a boil and cook, stirring, for 1 minute, until the sauce thickens.

5 Return the fish cubes to the wok and cook for 1–2 minutes. Serve immediately.

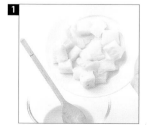

Salmon with Pineapple

Presentation plays a major part in Chinese cooking and this dish demonstrates this perfectly with the wonderful combination of colors.

NUTRITIONAL INFORMATION

Calories	347	Sugars	12g
Protein	24g	Fat	20g
Carbohydrate	16g	Saturates	3g

10 MINS   15 MINS

SERVES 4

INGREDIENTS

2 tbsp sunflower oil

1 red onion, sliced

1 orange bell pepper, seeded and sliced

1 green bell pepper, seeded and sliced

1 cup baby corn-on-the-cobs

1 lb salmon fillet, skin removed

1 tbsp paprika

1½ cups canned cubed pineapple, drained

1 cup bean sprouts

2 tbsp tomato catsup

2 tbsp soy sauce

2 tbsp medium sherry

1 tsp cornstarch

1 Cut each baby corn in half. Heat the oil in a large preheated wok. Add the onion, bell peppers, and baby corn cobs to the wok and stir-fry for 5 minutes.

2 Rinse the salmon fillet under cold running water and pat dry with paper towels.

3 Cut the salmon flesh into thin strips and place in a large bowl. Sprinkle with the paprika and toss well to coat.

4 Add the salmon to the wok together with the pineapple and stir-fry for 2–3 minutes, or until the fish is tender.

5 Add the beansprouts to the wok and toss well.

6 Mix together the tomato catsup, soy sauce, sherry, and cornstarch. Add to the wok and cook until the juices thicken. Serve immediately.

VARIATION

Use trout fillets instead of the salmon as an alternative, if you prefer.

Sesame Salmon with Cream

Salmon fillet holds its shape when tossed in sesame seeds and stir-fried. It is served in a creamy sauce of diced zucchini.

NUTRITIONAL INFORMATION

Calories	550	Sugars	.........1g
Protein	........35g	Fat	..........45g
Carbohydrate	....2g	Saturates	......12g

5 MINS   10 MINS

SERVES 4

INGREDIENTS

1 lb 6 oz-1 lb 10 oz salmon or pink trout fillets

2 tbsp light soy sauce

3 tbsp sesame seeds

3 tbsp sunflower oil

4 scallions, thinly sliced diagonally

2 large zucchini, diced, or 5-inch piece cucumber, diced

grated peel of ½ lemon

1 tbsp lemon juice

½ tsp turmeric

6 tbsp fish stock or water

3 tbsp heavy cream or fromage blanc

salt and pepper

curly endive, to garnish

1 Skin the fish and cut into strips about 1½ x ¾ inches. Pat dry on paper towels. Season lightly, then brush with soy sauce and sprinkle with sesame seeds.

2 Heat 2 tablespoons of oil in the wok. Add the pieces of fish and stir-fry for 3-4 minutes until lightly browned all over. Remove with a pancake turner, drain on paper towels, and keep warm.

3 Heat the remaining oil in the wok and add the scallions and zucchini or cucumber and stir-fry for 1-2 minutes. Add the lemon peel and juice, turmeric, stock, and seasoning, and bring to a boil for 1 minute. Add the cream or fromage blanc.

4 Return the fish pieces to the wok and toss gently in the sauce until they are really hot. Garnish and serve.

COOK'S TIP

Lay the fillet skin-side down. Insert a sharp, flexible knife at one end between the flesh and the skin. Hold the skin tightly at the end and push the knife along, keeping the knife blade as flat as possible against the skin.

Stir-Fried Salmon with Leeks

Salmon is marinated in a deliciously rich, sweet sauce, stir-fried, and served on a bed of crispy leeks.

NUTRITIONAL INFORMATION

Calories 360   Sugars 9g
Protein ....24g   Fat 25
Carbohydrate ....11g   Saturates 4g

35 MINS   15 MINS

SERVES 4

I N G R E D I E N T S

1 lb salmon fillet, skinned

2 tbsp sweet soy sauce

2 tbsp tomato ketchup

1 tsp rice wine vinegar

1 tbsp brown crystal sugar

1 clove garlic, crushed

4 tbsp corn oil

3 cups leeks, thinly shredded

finely chopped red chilies, to garnish

1 Using a sharp knife, cut the salmon into slices. Place the slices of salmon in a shallow nonmetallic dish.

2 Mix together the soy sauce, tomato catsup, rice wine vinegar, sugar, and garlic.

3 Pour the mixture over the salmon, toss well, and leave to marinate for about 30 minutes.

4 Meanwhile, heat 3 tablespoons of the corn oil in a large heated wok.

5 Add the leeks to the wok and stir-fry over a medium-high heat for about 10 minutes, or until the leeks become crispy and tender.

6 Using a draining spoon, carefully remove the leeks from the wok and transfer to warmed serving plates.

7 Add the remaining oil to the wok. Add the salmon and the marinade to the wok and cook for 2 minutes.

8 Remove the salmon from the wok and spoon over the leeks, garnish with finely chopped red chilies, and serve immediately.

VARIATION

You can use a tenderloin of beef instead of the salmon, if you prefer.

Fish with Saffron Sauce

White fish cooked in a bamboo steamer over the wok and served with a light creamy saffron sauce with a real bite to it.

NUTRITIONAL INFORMATION

Calories	254	Sugars	.......0.5g
Protein	........30g	Fat	..........14g
Carbohydrate	....2g	Saturates	.......5g

 5 MINS   30 MINS

SERVES 4

I N G R E D I E N T S

1 lb 6 oz–1 lb 10 oz white fish fillets (cod, haddock, whiting, and so on)

pinch of Chinese five-spice powder

4 sprigs fresh thyme

large pinch saffron threads

1 cup boiling fish or vegetable stock

2 tbsp sunflower oil

1½ cups button mushrooms, thinly sliced

grated peel of ½ lemon

1 tbsp lemon juice

½ tsp freshly chopped thyme or ¼ tsp dried thyme, plus extra to garnish

½ bunch watercress, chopped

1½ tsp cornstarch

3 tbsp single or heavy cream

salt and pepper

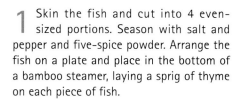

1 Skin the fish and cut into 4 even-sized portions. Season with salt and pepper and five-spice powder. Arrange the fish on a plate and place in the bottom of a bamboo steamer, laying a sprig of thyme on each piece of fish.

2 Stand a low metal trivet in a wok and add water to come almost to the top of it. Bring to a boil, stand the bamboo steamer on the trivet, and cover with the bamboo lid and then the lid of the wok or a piece of foil. Simmer for 20 minutes until the fish is tender, adding more boiling water to the wok if necessary. Meanwhile, soak the saffron threads in the boiling stock.

3 When the fish is tender, remove and keep warm. Empty the wok and wipe dry. Heat the oil in the wok and stir-fry the mushrooms for about 2 minutes. Add the saffron stock, lemon peel, and juice and chopped thyme and bring to a boil. Add the watercress and simmer for 1–2 minutes.

4 Blend the cornstarch with the cream, add a little of the sauce from the wok, then return to the wok and heat gently until thickened. Serve the fish surrounded by the sauce and garnish.

Braised Fish Fillets

Any white fish, such as sole or flounder, is ideal for this delicious dish.

NUTRITIONAL INFORMATION

Calories 107	Sugars 2g
Protein 17g	Fat 2g
Carbohydrate 6g	Saturates 0.3g

 45 MINS   10 MINS

SERVES 4

I N G R E D I E N T S

3-4 small Chinese dried mushrooms

10½-12 oz fish fillets

1 tsp salt

½ egg white, lightly beaten

1 tsp cornstarch paste (see page 15)

2½ cups vegetable oil

1 tsp finely chopped gingerroot

2 scallions, finely chopped

1 garlic clove, finely chopped

½ small green bell pepper, seeded and cut into small cubes

½ small carrot, thinly sliced

½ cup canned sliced bamboo shoots, rinsed and drained

½ tsp sugar

1 tbsp light soy sauce

1 tsp rice wine or dry sherry

1 tbsp chili bean sauce

2-3 tbsp Chinese stock (see page 14) or water

a few drops of sesame oil

1 Soak the dried mushrooms in a bowl of warm water for 30 minutes. Drain thoroughly on paper towels, reserving the soaking water for stock or soup. Squeeze the mushrooms to extract all of the moisture, cut off and discard any hard stems, and slice thinly.

2 Cut the fish into bite-sized pieces, then place in a shallow dish and mix with a pinch of salt, the egg white, and cornstarch paste, turning the fish to coat well.

3 Heat the oil in a preheated wok. Add the fish pieces to the wok and deep-fry for about 1 minute. Remove the fish pieces with a draining spoon and leave to drain on paper towels.

4 Pour off the excess oil, leaving about 1 tablespoon in the wok. Add the ginger, scallions, and garlic to flavor the oil for a few seconds, then add the bell pepper, carrots, and bamboo shoots and stir-fry for about 1 minute.

5 Add the sugar, soy sauce, wine, chili bean sauce, stock, or water, and the remaining salt and bring to a boil. Add the fish pieces, stirring to coat with the sauce, and braise for 1 minute. Sprinkle with sesame oil and serve.

Fish with Coconut & Basil

Fish curries are sensational and this is no exception. Red curry paste and coconut are fantastic flavors with the fried fish.

NUTRITIONAL INFORMATION

Calories ....209 Sugars 10g
Protein ....21g Fat 8g
Carbohydrate ...15g Saturates 1g

 5 MINS   15 MINS

SERVES 4

INGREDIENTS

2 tbsp vegetable oil

1 lb skinless cod fillet

¼ cup seasoned flour

1 clove garlic, crushed

2 tbsp red curry paste

1 tbsp fish sauce

1¼ cups coconut milk

6 oz cherry tomatoes, halved

20 fresh basil leaves

fragrant rice, to serve

1 Heat the vegetable oil in a large heated wok.

2 Using a sharp knife, cut the fish into large cubes, removing any bones with a pair of clean tweezers.

3 Place the seasoned flour in a bowl. Add the fish and mix until coated.

4 Add the coated fish to the wok and stir-fry over a high heat for 3–4 minutes, or until the fish just begins to brown at the edges.

5 In a small bowl, mix together the garlic, curry paste, fish sauce and coconut milk. Pour the mixture over the fish and bring to a boil.

6 Add the tomatoes to the mixture in the wok and leave to simmer for 5 minutes.

7 Roughly chop or tear the fresh basil leaves. Add the basil to the wok, stir carefully to combine, taking care not to break up the cubes of fish.

8 Transfer to serving plates and serve hot with fragrant rice.

COOK'S TIP

Take care not to overcook the dish once the tomatoes are added, otherwise they will break down and the skins will come away.

Fish & Ginger Stir-Fry

This delicious and spicy recipe is really quick to prepare, ideal for midweek family meals or light weekend lunches.

NUTRITIONAL INFORMATION

Calories 280	Sugars 2g
Protein 31g	Fat 10g
Carbohydrate . . .17g	Saturates 2g

🕐 5 MINS   🕐 15 MINS

SERVES 4

INGREDIENTS

4 tbsp cornstarch

½ tsp ground ginger

1½ lb firm white fish fillets, skinned and cubed

3 tbsp peanut oil

1-inch fresh gingerroot, grated

1 leek, thinly sliced

1 tbsp white wine vinegar

2 tbsp Chinese rice wine or dry sherry

3 tbsp dark soy sauce

1 tsp superfine sugar

2 tbsp lemon juice

finely shredded leek, to garnish

1 Mix the cornstarch and ground ginger in a bowl.

2 Add the cubes of fish, in batches, to the cornstarch mixture, turning to coat the fish thoroughly in the mixture.

3 Heat the peanut oil in a preheated wok or large, heavy-based skillet, swirling the oil around the base of the wok until it is really hot.

4 Add the grated fresh ginger and sliced leek to the wok or skillet and stir-fry for 1 minute.

5 Add the coated fish to the wok and cook for a further 5 minutes until browned, stirring to prevent the fish from sticking to the base of the wok.

6 Add the remaining ingredients and cook over a low heat for 3–4 minutes, until the fish is cooked through.

7 Transfer the fish and ginger stir-fry to a serving dish and serve immediately.

VARIATION

Use any firm white fish that will hold its shape, such as cod, haddock, or monkfish.

Steamed Stuffed Snapper

Red mullet can be used instead of the snapper, although they are a little more difficult to stuff because of their size; use one mullet per person.

NUTRITIONAL INFORMATION

Calories	406	Sugar	.........4g
Protein	........68g	Fat	...........9g
Carbohydrate	....9g	Saturates	.......0g

20 MINS   10 MINS

SERVES 4

I N G R E D I E N T S

3 lb whole snapper, cleaned and scaled

6 oz spinach

orange slices and shredded scallion, to garnish

S T U F F I N G

2 cups cooked long-grain rice

1 tsp grated fresh ginger root

2 scallions, finely chopped

2 tsp light soy sauce

1 tsp sesame oil

½ tsp ground star anise

1 orange, segmented and chopped

1 Rinse the fish inside and out under cold running water and pat dry with paper towels.

2 Blanch the spinach for 40 seconds, rinse in cold water and drain well, pressing out as much moisture as possible.

3 Arrange the spinach on a heatproof plate and place the fish on top.

4 To make the stuffing, mix together the cooked rice, grated ginger, scallions, soy sauce, sesame oil, star anise, and orange in a bowl.

5 Spoon the stuffing into the body cavity of the fish, pressing it in well with a spoon.

6 Cover the plate and cook in a steamer for 10 minutes, or until the fish is cooked through.

7 Transfer the fish to a warmed serving dish, garnish with orange slices, and shredded scallion and serve.

COOK'S TIP

The name snapper covers a family of tropical and subtropical fish that vary in color. They may be red, orange, pink, gray, or blue-green. Some are striped or spotted, and they range in size from about 6 inches to 3 ft.

Tuna & Vegetable Stir-Fry

Fresh tuna is a dark, meaty fish and is now widely available at fresh fish counters. It lends itself perfectly to the rich flavors in this recipe.

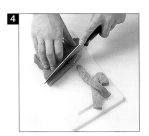

NUTRITIONAL INFORMATION

Calories ....245 Sugars 11g
Protein ....30g Fat 7g
Carbohydrate ...14g Saturates 1g

10 MINS   10 MINS

SERVES 4

INGREDIENTS

8 oz carrots

1 onion

1¾ cups baby corn-on-the-cobs

2 tbsp corn oil

2½ cups snow peas

1 lb fresh tuna

2 tbsp fish sauce

1 tbsp palm sugar

finely grated peel and juice of 1 orange

2 tbsp sherry

1 tsp cornstarch

rice or noodles, to serve

1 Using a sharp knife, cut the carrots into thin sticks, slice the onion, and halve the baby corn-on-the-cobs.

2 Heat the corn oil in a large preheated wok or skillet.

3 Add the onion, carrots, snow peas, and baby corn-on-the-cobs to the wok or skillet and stir-fry for 5 minutes.

4 Using a sharp knife, thinly slice the fresh tuna.

5 Add the tuna slices to the wok or skillet and stir-fry for about 2–3 minutes, or until the tuna turns opaque.

6 Mix together the fish sauce, palm sugar, orange peel, and juice, sherry and cornstarch.

7 Pour the mixture over the tuna and vegetables and cook for 2 minutes, or until the juices thicken. Serve the stir-fry with rice or noodles.

VARIATION

Try using swordfish steaks instead of the tuna. Swordfish steaks are similar in texture to tuna.

Mullet with Ginger

Ginger is used widely in Chinese cooking for its strong, pungent flavor. Although fresh ginger is best, ground ginger can be used instead.

NUTRITIONAL INFORMATION

Calories	195	Sugars	.........6g
Protein	........31g	Fat	...........3g
Carbohydrate	....9g	Saturates	.......0g

🥗 10 MINS   🕐 15 MINS

SERVES 4

I N G R E D I E N T S

1 whole mullet, cleaned and scaled

2 scallions, chopped

1 tsp grated fresh gingerroot

½ cup garlic wine vinegar

½ cup light soy sauce

3 tsp superfine sugar

dash of chili sauce

½ cup fish stock

1 green bell pepper, seeded and thinly sliced

1 large tomato, skinned, seeded, and cut into thin strips

salt and pepper

sliced tomato, to garnish

1 Rinse the fish inside and out and pat dry with paper towels.

2 Make 3 diagonal slits in the flesh on each side of the fish. Season the fish with salt and pepper inside and out, according to taste.

3 Place the fish on a flameproof gratin dish and scatter the chopped scallions and grated ginger over the top. Cover and steam for 10 minutes, or until the fish is cooked through.

4 Meanwhile, place the garlic wine vinegar, light soy sauce, superfine sugar, chili sauce, fish stock, bell pepper, and tomato in a saucepan and bring to a boil, stirring occasionally.

5 Cook the sauce over a high heat until the sauce has slightly reduced and thickened.

6 Remove the fish from the steamer and transfer to a warm serving dish. Pour the sauce over the fish, garnish with tomato slices, and serve immediately.

VARIATION

Use fillets of fish for this recipe if preferred, and reduce the cooking time to 5–7 minutes.

Trout with Pineapple

Pineapple is widely used in Chinese cooking. The tartness of fresh pineapple complements fish particularly well.

NUTRITIONAL INFORMATION

Calories	243	Sugars	.........4g
Protein	........30g	Fat	...........11g
Carbohydrate	....6g	Saturates	.......2g

   5 MINS 15 MINS

SERVES 4

INGREDIENTS

4 trout fillets, skinned

2 tbsp vegetable oil

2 garlic cloves, cut into slivers

4 slices fresh pineapple, peeled and diced

1 celery stick, sliced

1 tbsp light soy sauce

¼ cup fresh or unsweetened pineapple juice

⅔ cup fish stock

1 tsp cornstarch

2 tsp water

shredded celery leaves and fresh red chili slices, to garnish

1 Cut the trout fillets into strips. Heat 1 tablespoon of the vegetable oil in a preheated wok until almost smoking. Reduce the heat slightly, add the fish, and sauté for 2 minutes. Remove from the wok and set aside.

2 Add the remaining oil to the wok, reduce the heat and add the garlic, diced pineapple, and celery. Stir-fry for 1–2 minutes.

3 Add the soy sauce, pineapple juice, and fish stock to the wok. Bring to a boil and cook, stirring, for 2–3 minutes, or until the sauce has reduced.

4 Blend the cornstarch with the water to form a paste and stir it into the wok. Bring the sauce to a boil and cook, stirring constantly, until the sauce thickens and clears.

5 Return the fish to the wok, and cook, stirring gently, until heated through. Transfer to a warmed serving dish and serve, garnished with shredded celery leaves and red chili slices.

VARIATION

Use canned pineapple instead of fresh pineapple if you wish, choosing slices in unsweetened, natural juice in preference to a syrup.

Noodles

Noodles are a symbol of longevity in China and are always served at birthday and New Year celebrations. It is considered bad luck to cut noodles into shorter periods because the Chinese believe the longer the noodle are the longer and happier your life will be. Noodles are available in several varieties, both fresh and dried, made from

wheat, buckwheat, or rice flours, or you can even make your own if you have time! Nodles come in fine threads, strings, or flat ribbons, and can be bought from supermarkets or oriental food stores. Like rice, noodles are very versatile and can be boiled, fried, added to soups, or served plain. Noodles are precooked as part of the manufacturing process so most only need soaking in hot water to rehydrate them.

Chow Mein

This is a basic recipe for Chow Mein. Additional ingredients such as chicken or pork can be added, you if liked.

NUTRITIONAL INFORMATION

Calories 716	Sugars 2g
Protein 4g	Fat 12g
Carbohydrate . . .14g	Saturates 1g

 5 MINS 15 MINS

SERVES 4

I N G R E D I E N T S

9½ oz egg noodles

3-4 tbsp vegetable oil

1 small onion, finely shredded

4½ oz fresh beansprouts

1 scallion,
   finely shredded

2 tbsp light soy sauce

a few drops of sesame oil

salt

1 Bring a wok or saucepan of salted water to a boil.

2 Add the egg noodles to the saucepan or wok and cook according to the directions on the package (usually no more than 4-5 minutes).

COOK'S TIP

Noodles, a symbol of longevity, are made from wheat or rice flour, water, and egg. Handmade noodles are made by an elaborate process of kneading, pulling, and twisting the dough, and it takes years to learn the art.

3 Drain the noodles well and rinse in cold water; drain thoroughly again, then transfer to a large mixing bowl and toss with a little vegetable oil.

4 Heat the remaining vegetable oil in a preheated wok or large skillet until really hot.

5 Add the shredded onion to the wok and stir-fry for about 30-40 seconds.

6 Add the beansprouts and drained noodles to the wok, stir and toss for 1 more minute.

7 Add the shredded scallion and light soy sauce and blend well.

8 Transfer the noodles to a warm serving dish, sprinkle with the sesame oil and serve immediately.

Curried Shrimp Noodles

Athough these noodles are almost a meal in themselves, if served as an accompaniment, they are ideal with plain vegetable or fish dishes.

NUTRITIONAL INFORMATION

Calories 246	Sugars 1g
Protein 17g	Fat 14g
Carbohydrate ...14g	Saturates 2g

5 MINS   15 MINS

SERVES 4

I N G R E D I E N T S

8 oz rice noodles

4 tbsp vegetable oil

1 onion, sliced

2 cooked ham slices, shredded

2 tbsp Chinese curry powder

⅔ cups fish stock

8 oz peeled, raw shrimp

2 garlic cloves, minced

6 scallions, chopped

1 tbsp light soy sauce

2 tbsp hoisin sauce

1 tbsp dry sherry

2 tsp lime juice

fresh snipped chives, to garnish

COOK'S TIP

Hoisin sauce is made from soy beans, sugar, flour, vinegar, salt, garlic, chili, and sesame seed oil. Sold in cans or jars, it will keep in the refrigerator for several months.

  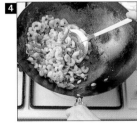

1 Cook the noodles in a pan of boiling water for 3-4 minutes. Drain well, rinse under cold water, and drain again.

2 Heat 2 tablespoons of the oil in a wok. Add the onion and ham and stir-fry for 1 minute. Add the curry powder and stir-fry for a further 30 seconds.

3 Stir the noodles and fish stock into the wok and cook for 2-3 minutes.

Remove the noodles from the wok and keep warm.

4 Heat the remaining oil in the wok. Add the shrimp, garlic and scallions and stir-fry for about 1 minute.

5 Stir in the remaining ingredients. Pour the mixture over the noodles, toss to mix and garnish with fresh chives.

Chili Pork Noodles

This is a spicy dish, with a delicious peanut flavor. Increase or reduce the amount of chili to your liking.

NUTRITIONAL INFORMATION

Calories 421   Sugars 3g
Protein . . . . .27g   Fat 26g
Carbohydrate . . .20g   Saturates 6g

 35 MINS   10 MINS

SERVES 4

INGREDIENTS

12 oz ground pork

1 tbsp light soy sauce

1 tbsp dry sherry

12 oz egg noodles

2 tsp sesame oil

2 tbsp vegetable oil

2 garlic cloves, minced

2 tsp grated gingerroot

2 fresh red chilies, sliced

1 red bell pepper, seeded and finely sliced

¼ cup unsalted peanuts

3 tbsp peanut butter

3 tbsp dark soy sauce

dash of chili oil

1¼ cups pork stock

1 Mix together the pork, light soy sauce, and dry sherry in a large bowl. Cover and leave to marinate for 30 minutes.

2 Meanwhile, cook the noodles in a saucepan of boiling water, for 4 minutes. Drain well, rinse in cold water and drain again. Toss the noodles in the sesame oil.

3 Heat the vegetable oil in a preheated wok and stir-fry the garlic, ginger, chilies, and bell pepper for 30 seconds.

4 Add the pork to the mixture in the wok, together with the marinade. Continue cooking for about 1 minute until the pork is sealed.

5 Add the peanuts, peanut butter, soy sauce, chili oil, and stock and cook for 2-3 minutes.

6 Toss the noodles in the mixture and serve at once.

VARIATION

Ground chicken or lamb would also be excellent in this recipe instead of the pork.

Chicken on Crispy Noodles

Blanched noodles are fried in the wok until crisp and brown, and then topped with a shredded chicken sauce for a delightfully tasty dish.

NUTRITIONAL INFORMATION

Calories 376	Sugars 2g
Protein 15g	Fat 27g
Carbohydrate ...17g	Saturates 4g

  35 MINS 25 MINS

SERVES 4

I N G R E D I E N T S

8 oz skinless, boneless chicken breasts, shredded

1 egg white

5 tsp cornstarch

8 oz thin egg noodles

1⅔ cups vegetable oil

2½ cups chicken stock

2 tbsp dry sherry

2 tbsp oyster sauce

1 tbsp light soy sauce

1 tbsp hoisin sauce

1 red bell pepper, seeded and very thinly sliced

2 tbsp water

3 scallions, chopped

1 Mix together the chicken, egg white and 2 teaspoons of the cornstarch in a bowl, leave to stand for at least 30 minutes.

2 Blanch the noodles in boiling water for 2 minutes, then drain thoroughly.

3 Heat the vegetable oil in a preheated wok. Add the noodles, spreading them to cover the base of the wok. Cook over a low heat for about 5 minutes, until the noodles are browned on the underside.

Flip the noodles over and brown on the other side. Remove from the wok when crisp and browned, place on a serving plate, and keep warm. Drain the oil from the wok.

4 Add 1¼ cups of the chicken stock to the wok. Remove from the heat and add the chicken, stirring well so that it does not stick. Return to the heat and cook for 2 minutes. Drain, discarding the stock.

5 Wipe the wok with paper towels and return to the heat. Add the sherry, sauces, bell pepper and the remaining stock and bring to a boil. Blend the remaining cornstarch with the water and stir it into the mixture.

6 Return the chicken to the wok and cook over a low heat for 2 minutes. Place the chicken on top of the noodles and sprinkle with scallions.

Hot & Crispy Noodles

These crispy noodles will add a delicious crunch to your Chinese meal. They can be served as a side dish or as an appetizer for people to share.

NUTRITIONAL INFORMATION

Calories	.104	Sugars	.0.3g
Protein	.2g	Fat	.6g
Carbohydrate	.11g	Saturates	.1g

 5 MINS   15 MINS

SERVES 4

INGREDIENTS

9 oz rice noodles

oil, for deep-frying

2 garlic cloves, chopped finely

8 scallions, trimmed and chopped finely

1 small red or green chili, seeded and finely chopped

2 tbsp fish sauce

2 tbsp light soy sauce

2 tbsp lime or lemon juice

2 tbsp molasses sugar

TO GARNISH

scallions, shredded

cucumber, sliced thinly

fresh chilies

1 Break the noodles into smaller pieces with your hands. Heat the oil for deep-frying in a wok or large skillet and fry small batches of the noodles until pale golden brown and puffed up. Lift the noodles out with a draining spoon and leave to drain on paper towels.

2 When all of the noodles are cooked, pour off the oil, leaving 3 tbsp in the wok. Add the garlic, scallions and chili, and stir-fry for 2 minutes.

3 Mix together the fish sauce, soy sauce, lime or lemon juice, and sugar. Add to the wok or skillet and cook for 2 minutes, until the sugar has dissolved. Tip all the noodles back into the wok and toss lightly to coat with the sauce mixture.

4 Serve the noodles garnished with shredded scallions, thinly sliced cucumber, and chilies.

VARIATION

Stir-fry some uncooked peeled shrimp or chopped raw chicken with the scallions and garlic in step 2. Cook for an extra 3–4 minutes to make sure they are thoroughly cooked.

Curried Rice Noodles

Rice noodles or vermicelli are also known as rice sticks. The ideal meat to use in this dish is pork.

NUTRITIONAL INFORMATION

Calories	223	Sugars	.........2g
Protein	........15g	Fat	..........13g
Carbohydrate	....11g	Saturates	.......2g

 15 MINS   15 MINS

SERVES 4

I N G R E D I E N T S

7 oz rice vermicelli

4½ oz cooked chicken or pork

2 oz peeled shrimp, defrosted if frozen

4 tbsp vegetable oil

1 medium onion, thinly shredded

4¼ oz fresh mung beansprouts

1 tsp salt

1 tbsp mild curry powder

2 tbsp light soy sauce

2 scallions,
    thinly shredded

1-2 small fresh green or red chili peppers,
    seeded and thinly shredded

1 Soak the rice vermicelli in boiling water for about 8-10 minutes, then rinse in cold water and drain well, set aside until required.

2 Using a sharp knife or meat cleaver, thinly slice the cooked meat.

3 Dry the shrimp on absorbent paper towels.

4 Heat the vegetable oil in a preheated wok or large skillet.

5 Add the shredded onion to the wok or pan and stir-fry until opaque. Add the beansprouts and stir-fry for 1 minute.

6 Add the drained noodles with the meat and shrimp, and continue stirring for another minute.

7 Mix together the salt, curry powder, and soy sauce in a little bowl.

8 Blend the sauce mixture into the wok, followed by the scallions and chili peppers. Stir-fry for one more minute, then serve immediately.

COOK'S TIP

Rice noodles are very delicate noodles made from rice flour. They become soft and pliable after being soaked for about 15 minutes. If you wish to store them after they have been soaked, toss them in sesame, oil then place them in a container in the refrigerator.

Satay Noodles

Rice noodles and vegetables are tossed in a crunchy peanut and chili sauce for a quick satay-flavored recipe.

NUTRITIONAL INFORMATION

Calories	281	Sugars	.........7g
Protein	.........9g	Fat	..........20g
Carbohydrate	...18g	Saturates	.......4g

 5 MINS   20 MINS

SERVES 4

INGREDIENTS

9½ oz rice sticks (wide, flat rice noodles)

3 tbsp peanut oil

2 garlic cloves, minced

2 shallots, sliced

8 oz green beans, sliced

3¾ oz cherry tomatoes, halved

1 tsp chili flakes

4 tbsp crunchy peanut butter

⅔ cup coconut milk

1 tbsp tomato paste

sliced scallions,
   to garnish

1 Place the rice sticks (wide, flat rice noodles) in a large bowl and pour enough boiling water over to cover. Leave to stand for 10 minutes.

2 Heat the peanut oil in a large preheated wok or heavy-based skillet.

3 Add the minced garlic and sliced shallots to the wok or skillet and stir-fry for 1 minute.

4 Drain the rice sticks (wide, flat rice noodles) thoroughly. Add the green beans and drained noodles to the wok or skillet and stir-fry for about 5 minutes.

5 Add the cherry tomatoes to the wok and mix well.

6 Mix together the chili flakes, peanut butter, coconut milk, and tomato paste.

7 Pour the chili mixture over the noodles, toss well until all the ingredients are thoroughly combined and heat through.

8 Transfer the satay noodles to warm serving dishes and garnish with scallion slices and serve immediately.

Oyster Sauce Noodles

Chicken and noodles are cooked and then tossed in an oyster sauce and egg mixture in this delicious recipe.

NUTRITIONAL INFORMATION

Calories 278	Sugars 2g
Protein 30g	Fat 12g
Carbohydrate ...13g	Saturates 3g

🍲 5 MINS   🕐 25 MINS

SERVES 4

I N G R E D I E N T S

9 oz egg noodles

1 lb chicken thighs

2 tbsp peanut oil

3½ oz carrots, sliced

3 tbsp oyster sauce

2 eggs

3 tbsp cold water

1 Place the egg noodles in a large bowl or dish. Pour enough boiling water over the noodles to cover and leave to stand for 10 minutes.

2 Meanwhile, remove the skin from the chicken thighs. Cut the chicken flesh into small pieces, using a sharp knife.

VARIATION

Flavor the eggs with soy sauce or hoisin sauce as an alternative to the oyster sauce, if you prefer.

3 Heat the peanut oil in a large preheated wok or skillet, swirling the oil around the base of the wok until it is really hot.

4 Add the pieces of chicken and the carrot slices to the wok and stir-fry for about 5 minutes.

5 Drain the noodles thoroughly. Add the noodles to the wok and stir-fry for a further 2–3 minutes, or until the noodles are heated through.

6 Beat together the oyster sauce, eggs and 3 tablespoons of cold water. Drizzle the mixture over the noodles and stir-fry for a further 2–3 minutes or until the eggs set.

7 Transfer the mixture in the wok to warm serving bowls and serve hot.

Quick Chicken Noodles

Chicken and fresh vegetables are flavored with ginger and Chinese five-spice powder in this speedy stir-fry.

NUTRITIONAL INFORMATION

Calories 266	Sugars 4g	
Protein 25g	Fat 13g	
Carbohydrate ...12g	Saturates 2g	

  10 MINS   15 MINS

SERVES 4

I N G R E D I E N T S

6 oz Chinese thread egg noodles

2 tbsp sesame or vegetable oil

¼ cup peanuts

1 bunch scallions, sliced

1 green bell pepper, seeded and cut into thin strips

1 large carrot, cut into matchsticks

4½ oz cauliflower broken into small florets

12 oz skinless, boneless chicken, cut into strips

9 oz mushrooms, sliced

1 tsp finely grated gingerroot

1 tsp Chinese five-spice powder

1 tbsp chopped fresh cilantro

1 tbsp light soy sauce

salt and pepper

fresh chives, to garnish

Stir-fry over a high heat for 4–5 minutes.

1 Put the noodles in a large bowl and cover with boiling water, leave to soak for 6 minutes.

2 Heat the oil in a wok and stir-fry the peanuts for 1 minute until browned. Remove from the wok and leave to drain.

3 Add the scallions, bell pepper, carrot, cauliflower, and chicken to the pan.

4 Drain the noodles thoroughly and add to the wok. Add the mushrooms and stir-fry for 2 minutes. Add the ginger, five-spice, and cilantro; stir-fry for 1 minute.

5 Season with soy sauce and salt and pepper. Sprinkle with the peanuts, garnish and serve.

VARIATION

Instead of gingerroot, ½ teaspoon ground ginger can be used.

Vary the vegetables according to what is in season. Make the most of bargains bought from your greengrocer or market.

Twice-Cooked Lamb

Here lamb is first boiled and then fried with soy sauce, oyster sauce and spinach and finally tossed with noodles for a richly flavored dish.

NUTRITIONAL INFORMATION

Calories . . . . .315 Sugars 5g
Protein . . . . .27g Fat 16g
Carbohydrate . . .16g Saturates 6g

5 MINS   30 MINS

SERVES 4

I N G R E D I E N T S

9 oz packet egg noodles

1 lb lamb loin tenderloin, thinly sliced

2 tbsp soy sauce

2 tbsp sunflower oil

2 garlic cloves, minced

1 tbsp superfine sugar

2 tbsp oyster sauce

6 oz baby spinach

1 Place the egg noodles in a large bowl and cover with boiling water, leave to soak for about 10 minutes.

2 Bring a large saucepan of water to a boil. Add the lamb and cook for 5 minutes. Drain thoroughly.

3 Place the slices of lamb in a bowl and mix with the soy sauce and 1 tablespoon of the sunflower oil.

4 Heat the remaining sunflower oil in a large preheated wok, swirling the oil around until it is really hot.

5 Add the marinated lamb and minced garlic to the wok and stir-fry for about 5 minutes, or until the meat is just beginning to brown.

6 Add the superfine sugar and oyster sauce to the wok and stir well to combine.

7 Drain the noodles thoroughly. Add the noodles to the wok and stir-fry for a further 5 minutes.

8 Add the spinach to the wok and cook for 1 minute or until the leaves just wilt. Transfer the lamb and noodles to serving bowls and serve hot.

COOK'S TIP

If using dried noodles, follow the directions on the package because they require less soaking.

Crispy Noodles & Tofu

This dish requires a certain amount of care and attention to get the crispy noodles properly cooked, but it is well worth the effort.

NUTRITIONAL INFORMATION

Calories 242	Sugars 2g
Protein 13g	Fat 17g
Carbohydrate ...10g	Saturates 3g

🦪 🦪 🦪

🧊 35 MINS   🕐 25 MINS

SERVES 4

I N G R E D I E N T S

6 oz thread egg noodles

2½ cups sunflower oil, for deep-frying

2 tsp grated lemon peel

1 tbsp light soy sauce

1 tbsp rice vinegar

1 tbsp lemon juice

1½ tbsp sugar

1 cup marinated bean curd, diced

2 garlic cloves, minced

1 red chili, sliced finely

1 red bell pepper, diced

4 eggs, beaten

red chili flower, to garnish

temperature with a few strands of noodles, they should swell to many times their size, but if they do not, wait until the oil is hot enough; otherwise they will be tough and stringy, not puffy and light.

4 Cook the noodles in batches. As soon as they turn a pale gold color, scoop them out, and drain on plenty of absorbent paper towels. Leave to cool.

5 Reserve 2 tablespoons of the oil and drain off the rest. Heat the reserved oil in the wok or skillet.

6 Add the marinated bean curd to the wok or skillet and cook quickly over a high heat to seal.

7 Add the minced garlic cloves, sliced red chili and diced red bell pepper to the wok, stir-fry for 1–2 minutes.

8 Add the reserved vinegar mixture to the wok, stir to mix well, and add the beaten eggs, stirring until they are set.

9 Serve the bean curd mixture with the crispy fried noodles, garnished with a red chili flower.

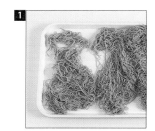

1 Blanch the egg noodles briefly in hot water to which a little of the oil has been added. Drain the noodles and spread out to dry for at least 30 minutes. Cut into threads about 3 inches long.

2 Combine the lemon peel, light soy sauce, rice vinegar, lemon juice, and sugar in a small bowl, set the mixture aside until required.

3 Heat the sunflower oil in a wok or large, heavy skillet, and test the

Yellow Bean Noodles

Cellophane or thread noodles are excellent reheated, unlike other noodles which must be served as soon as they are ready.

NUTRITIONAL INFORMATION

Calories	.212	Sugars	.0.5g
Protein	.28g	Fat	.7g
Carbohydrate	.10g	Saturates	.2g

 5 MINS   30 MINS

SERVES 4

INGREDIENTS

6 oz cellophane noodles

1 tbsp peanut oil

1 leek, sliced

2 garlic cloves, minced

1 lb ground chicken

1 cup chicken stock

1 tsp chili sauce

2 tbsp yellow bean sauce

4 tbsp light soy sauce

1 tsp sesame oil

chopped chives, to garnish

1 Place the cellophane noodles in a bowl, pour boiling water over and soak for 15 minutes.

2 Drain the noodles thoroughly and cut into short pieces with a pair of kitchen scissors.

3 Heat the oil in a wok or skillet and stir-fry the leek and garlic for 30 seconds.

4 Add the chicken to the wok and stir-fry for 4-5 minutes until the chicken is completely cooked through.

5 Add the chicken stock, chili sauce, yellow bean sauce and soy sauce to the wok and cook for 3-4 minutes.

6 Add the drained noodles and sesame oil to the wok and cook, tossing to mix well, for 4-5 minutes.

7 Spoon the mixture into warm serving bowls, sprinkle with chopped chives and serve immediately.

COOK'S TIP

Cellophane noodles are available from many supermarkets and all Chinese grocery stores.

Garlic Pork & Noodles

This is a wonderful one-pot dish of stir-fried pork tenderloin with shrimp and noodles that is made in minutes.

NUTRITIONAL INFORMATION

Calories	424	Sugars	.........1g
Protein	........33g	Fat	..........27g
Carbohydrate	...13g	Saturates	.......5g

 5 MINS   15 MINS

SERVES 4

INGREDIENTS

9 oz packet medium egg noodles

3 tbsp vegetable oil

2 garlic cloves, minced

12 oz pork tenderloin, cut into strips

⅓ cup dried shrimp, or
    4½ oz peeled shrimp

1 bunch scallions, finely chopped

¾ cup chopped roasted and shelled
    unsalted peanuts

3 tbsp fish sauce

1½ tsp palm or demerara sugar

1-2 small red chilies, seeded and finely
    chopped (to taste)

3 tbsp lime juice

3 tbsp chopped fresh cilantro

1 Place the noodles in a large pan of boiling water, then immediately remove from the heat. Cover and leave to stand for 6 minutes, stirring once halfway through the time. After 6 minutes the noodles will be perfectly cooked. Alternatively, follow the directions on the package. Drain and keep warm.

2 Heat the oil in a wok, add the garlic, and pork and stir-fry until the pork strips are browned, about 2-3 minutes.

3 Add the dried shrimp or shelled shrimp, scallions, peanuts, fish sauce, jaggery or demerara sugar, chilies to taste, and lime juice. Stir-fry for a further 1 minute.

4 Add the cooked noodles and chopped fresh cilantro and stir-fry until heated through, about 1 minute. Serve the stir-fry immediately.

COOK'S TIP

Fish sauce is made from pressed, salted fish and is widely available in supermarkets and oriental stores. It is very salty, so no extra salt should be added.

Chicken Chow Mein

This classic dish requires no introduction as it is already a favorite among most Chinese.

NUTRITIONAL INFORMATION

Calories	230	Sugars	2g
Protein	19g	Fat	11g
Carbohydrate	14g	Saturates	2g

 5 MINS   20 MINS

SERVES 4

INGREDIENTS

9 oz packet medium egg
  noodles

2 tbsp sunflower oil

9½ oz cooked chicken breasts, shredded

1 garlic clove, finely chopped

1 red bell pepper, seeded and thinly sliced

3½ oz shiitake mushrooms, sliced

6 scallions, sliced

1 cup beansprouts

3 tbsp soy sauce

1 tbsp sesame oil

VARIATION

You can make the chow mein with a selection of vegetables for a vegetarian dish, if you prefer.

1 Place the egg noodles in a large bowl or dish and break them up slightly. Pour enough boiling water over to cover the noodles and leave to stand.

2 Heat the sunflower oil in a large preheated wok. Add the shredded chicken, finely chopped garlic, bell pepper slices, mushrooms, scallions and beansprouts to the wok and stir-fry for about 5 minutes.

3 Drain the noodles thoroughly. Add the noodles to the wok, toss well and stir-fry for a further 5 minutes.

4 Drizzle the soy sauce and sesame oil over the chow mein and toss until well combined.

5 Transfer the chicken chow mein to warm serving bowls and serve immediately.

Speedy Peanut Stir-Fry

Thread egg noodles are the ideal accompaniment to this quick dish because they can be cooked quickly and easily while the stir-fry sizzles.

NUTRITIONAL INFORMATION

Calories	563	Sugars	.........7g
Protein	........45g	Fat	..........33g
Carbohydrate	...22g	Saturates	.......7g

5 MINS　　　15 MINS

SERVES 4

I N G R E D I E N T S

2 cups zucchini

1⅓ cups baby-corn-on-the-cob

9 oz thread egg noodles

2 tbsp corn oil

1 tbsp sesame oil

8 boneless chicken thighs or 4 breasts, sliced thinly

3¾ cups button mushrooms

1½ cups mung beansprouts

4 tbsp smooth peanut butter

2 tbsp soy sauce

2 tbsp lime or lemon juice

½ cup roasted peanuts

salt and pepper

cilantro, to garnish

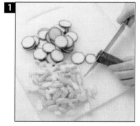

1 Using a sharp knife, trim and thinly slice the zucchini and baby-corn-on-the-cob, set the vegetables aside until required.

2 Cook the noodles in lightly salted boiling water for 3–4 minutes.

3 Meanwhile, heat the corn oil and sesame oil in a large wok or skillet and fry the chicken over a fairly high heat for 1 minute.

4 Add the zucchini, corn, and mushrooms and stir-fry for 5 minutes.

5 Add the beansprouts, peanut butter, soy sauce, lime or lemon juice and pepper, then cook for a further 2 minutes.

6 Drain the noodles thoroughly. Scatter with the roasted peanuts and serve with the zucchini and mushroom mixture. Garnish and serve.

COOK'S TIP

Try serving this stir-fry with rice sticks. These are broad, pale, translucent ribbon noodles made from ground rice.

Noodles in Soup

Noodles in soup are far more popular than fried noodles in China. You can use different ingredients for the dressing according to taste.

NUTRITIONAL INFORMATION

Calories 231	Sugars 1g
Protein 18g	Fat 11g
Carbohydrate . . .16g	Saturates 2g

10 MINS   15 MINS

SERVES 4

I N G R E D I E N T S

9 oz chicken breast, pork tenderloin, or any other cooked meat

3-4 Chinese dried mushrooms, soaked

4½ oz canned sliced bamboo shoots, rinsed and drained

4½ oz spinach leaves, lettuce hearts, or Chinese cabbage, shredded

2 scallions, finely shredded

9 oz egg noodles

2½ cups Chinese Stock (see page 14)

2 tbsp light soy sauce

2 tbsp vegetable oil

1 tsp salt

½ tsp sugar

2 tsp Chinese rice wine or dry sherry

a few drops sesame oil

1 tsp red chili oil (optional)

COOK'S TIP

Noodle soup is wonderfully satisfying and is ideal to serve on cold winter days.

1 Using a sharp knife or meat cleaver, cut the meat into thin shreds.

2 Squeeze dry the soaked Chinese mushrooms and discard the hard stalk.

3 Thinly shred the mushrooms, bamboo shoots, spinach leaves, and scallions.

4 Cook the noodles in boiling water according to the directions on the package, then drain and rinse under cold water. Place the noodles in a bowl.

5 Bring the Chinese stock to a boil, add about 1 tablespoon soy sauce and pour over the noodles. Keep warm.

6 Heat the vegetable oil in a preheated wok, add about half of the scallions, the meat, and the vegetables (mushrooms, bamboo shoots, and greens). Stir-fry for about 2-3 minutes. Add all the seasonings and stir until well combined.

7 Pour the mixture in the wok over the noodles, garnish with the remaining scallions, and serve immediately.

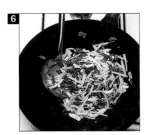

Chicken Noodles

Rice noodles are used in this recipe. They are available from supermarkets or Chinese grocery stores.

NUTRITIONAL INFORMATION

Calories	169	Sugars	.........2g
Protein	........14g	Fat	...........7g
Carbohydrate	...12g	Saturates	.......2g

 5 MINS   15 MINS

SERVES 4

I N G R E D I E N T S

8 oz rice noodles

2 tbsp peanut oil

8 oz skinless, boneless chicken breast, sliced

2 garlic cloves, minced

1 tsp grated gingerroot

1 tsp Chinese curry powder

1 red bell pepper, seeded and thinly sliced

2¾ oz snow peas, shredded

1 tbsp light soy sauce

2 tsp Chinese rice wine

2 tbsp chicken stock

1 tsp sesame oil

1 tbsp chopped fresh cilantro

1 Soak the rice noodles for 4 minutes in warm water, drain thoroughly, and set aside until required.

2 Heat the peanut oil in a preheated wok or large heavy-based skillet and stir-fry the chicken slices for 2-3 minutes.

3 Add the garlic, ginger, and Chinese curry powder and stir-fry for 30 seconds. Add the red bell pepper and snow peas and stir-fry for 2-3 minutes.

4 Add the noodles, soy sauce, Chinese rice wine, and chicken stock to the wok and mix well, stirring occasionally, for 1 minute.

5 Sprinkle the sesame oil and chopped cilantro over the noodles. Transfer to serving plates and serve.

VARIATION

You can use pork or duck in this recipe instead of the chicken, if you prefer.

Noodles with Cod & Mango

Fish and fruit are tossed with a trio of bell peppers in this spicy dish served with noodles for a quick, healthy meal.

NUTRITIONAL INFORMATION

Calories	274	Sugars	........11g
Protein	........25g	Fat	...........8g
Carbohydrate	...26g	Saturates	.......1g

 10 MINS · 25 MINS

SERVES 4

I N G R E D I E N T S

9 oz packet egg noodles

1 lb skinless cod fillet

1 tbsp paprika

2 tbsp sunflower oil

1 red onion, sliced

1 orange bell pepper, seeded and sliced

1 green bell pepper, seeded and sliced

3½ oz baby corn-on-the-cobs, halved

1 mango, sliced

1 cup beansprouts

2 tbsp tomato catsup

2 tbsp soy sauce

2 tbsp medium sherry

1 tsp cornstarch

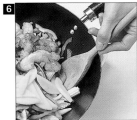

1 Place the egg noodles in a large bowl and cover with boiling water. Leave to stand for about 10 minutes.

2 Rinse the cod fillet and pat dry with paper towels. Cut the cod flesh into thin strips.

3 Place the cod strips in a large bowl. Add the paprika and toss well to coat the fish.

4 Heat the sunflower oil in a large preheated wok.

5 Add the onion, bell peppers, and baby corn-on-the-cobs to the wok and stir-fry for about 5 minutes.

6 Add the cod to the wok together with the sliced mango and stir-fry for a further 2–3 minutes, or until the fish is tender.

7 Add the beansprouts to the wok and toss well to combine.

8 Mix together the tomato ketchup, soy sauce , sherry, and cornstarch. Add the mixture to the wok and cook, stirring occasionally, until the juices thicken.

9 Drain the noodles thoroughly and transfer to warm serving bowls. Transfer the cod and mango stir-fry to separate serving bowls and serve immediately.

Chili Shrimp Noodles

Cellophane or glass noodles are made from mung beans. They are sold dried, so they need soaking before use.

NUTRITIONAL INFORMATION

Calories 152	Sugars 2g
Protein 11g	Fat 8g
Carbohydrate ...10g	Saturates 1g

25 MINS · 10 MINS

SERVES 4

I N G R E D I E N T S

2 tbsp light soy sauce

1 tbsp lime or lemon juice

1 tbsp fish sauce

4½ oz firm bean curd, cut into chunks

4½ oz cellophane noodles

2 tbsp sesame oil

4 shallots, sliced finely

2 garlic cloves, minced

1 small red chili, seeded and chopped finely

2 celery sticks, sliced finely

2 carrots, sliced finely

⅔ cup cooked, peeled shrimp

1 cup beansprouts

T O   G A R N I S H

celery leaves

fresh chilies

1 Mix together the light soy sauce, lime or lemon juice, and fish sauce in a small bowl. Add the bean curd cubes and toss them until coated in the mixture. Cover and set aside for 15 minutes.

2 Put the noodles into a large bowl and cover with warm water. Leave them to soak for about 5 minutes, and then drain them well.

3 Heat the sesame oil in a wok or large skillet. Add the shallots, garlic, and red chili, and stir-fry for 1 minute.

4 Add the sliced celery and carrots to the wok or pan and stir-fry for a further 2–3 minutes.

5 Tip the drained noodles into the wok or skillet and cook, stirring, for 2 minutes, then add the shrimp, beansprouts, and bean curd, with the soy sauce mixture. Cook over a medium high heat for 2–3 minutes until heated through.

6 Transfer the mixture in the wok to a serving dish and garnish with celery leaves and chilies.

Egg Noodles with Beef

Quick and easy, this mouth-watering Chinese-style noodle dish is cooked in minutes.

NUTRITIONAL INFORMATION

Calories	329	Sugars	.........3g
Protein	........23g	Fat	..........16g
Carbohydrate	...20g	Saturates	.......4g

10 MINS   15 MINS

SERVES 4

I N G R E D I E N T S

10 oz egg noodles

3 tbsp walnut oil

1-inch piece gingerroot, cut into thin strips

5 scallions, finely shredded

2 garlic cloves, finely chopped

1 red bell pepper, cored, seeded, and
 thinly sliced

1½ cups button mushrooms, thinly sliced

12 oz beef tenderloin, cut into thin strips

1 tbsp cornstarch

5 tbsp dry sherry

3 tbsp soy sauce

1 tsp light brown sugar

2¼ cups beansprouts

1 tbsp sesame oil

salt and pepper

scallion strips, to garnish

1 Bring a large saucepan of water to a boil. Add the egg noodles and cook according to the directions on the package. Drain the noodles, rinse under cold running water, drain thoroughly again, and set aside.

2 Heat the walnut oil in a heated wok until it is really hot.

3 Add the grated gingerroot, shredded scallions, and chopped garlic and stir-fry for 45 seconds.

4 Add the red bell pepper, button mushrooms, and tenderloin and stir-fry for 4 minutes. Season to taste with salt and pepper.

5 Mix together the cornstarch, dry sherry, and soy sauce in a small jug to form a paste, and pour into the wok. Sprinkle over the brown sugar and stir-fry all of the ingredients for a further 2 minutes.

6 Add the beansprouts, drained noodles, and sesame oil to the wok. Stir and toss together for 1 minute.

7 Transfer the stir-fry to warm serving dishes, garnish with strips of scallion, and serve.

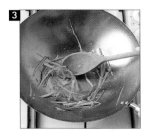

Beef with Crispy Noodles

Crispy noodles are terrific and may also be served on their own as a side dish, sprinkled with sugar and salt.

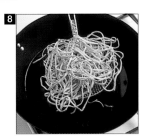

NUTRITIONAL INFORMATION

Calories	244	Sugars	.........9g
Protein	........20g	Fat	..........10g
Carbohydrate	...19g	Saturates	.......2g

 5 MINS   30 MINS

SERVES 4

I N G R E D I E N T S

8 oz medium egg noodles

12 oz beef tenderloin

2 tbsp sunflower oil

1 tsp ground ginger

1 clove garlic, minced

1 red chili, seeded and very finely chopped

1 cup carrots, cut into thin sticks

6 scallions, sliced

2 tbsp lime marmalade

2 tbsp soy sauce

vegetable oil, for frying

1 Place the noodles in a large dish or bowl. Pour enough boiling water over to cover the noodles and leave to stand for about 10 minutes while you stir-fry the rest of the ingredients.

2 Using a sharp knife, thinly slice the beef tenderloin.

3 Heat the sunflower oil in a large preheated wok or skillet.

4 Add the beef and ground ginger to the wok or skillet and stir-fry for about 5 minutes.

5 Add the minced garlic, chopped red chili, carrots, and scallions to the wok and stir-fry for a further 2–3 minutes.

6 Add the lime marmalade and soy sauce to the wok and allow to bubble for 2 minutes. Remove the chili beef and ginger mixture, set aside, and keep warm.

7 Heat the oil for frying in the wok or skillet.

8 Drain the noodles thoroughly and pat dry with paper towels. Carefully lower the noodles into the hot oil and cook for 2–3 minutes or until crispy. Drain the noodles on paper towels.

9 Divide the noodles between 4 warm serving plates and top with the chili beef and ginger mixture. Serve immediately.

Mushroom & Pork Noodles

This dish benefits from the use of oyster mushrooms. If these are unavailable, plain gray mushrooms will suffice.

NUTRITIONAL INFORMATION

Calories	286	Sugars	.........3g
Protein	........23g	Fat	..........13g
Carbohydrate	...21g	Saturates	.......3g

10 MINS   20 MINS

SERVES 4

I N G R E D I E N T S

1 lb thin egg noodles

2 tbsp peanut oil

12 oz pork tenderloin, sliced

2 garlic cloves, minced

1 onion, cut into 8 pieces

8 oz oyster mushrooms

4 tomatoes, skinned, seeded and thinly sliced

2 tbsp light soy sauce

¼ cup pork stock

1 tbsp chopped fresh cilantro

1 Cook the noodles in a saucepan of boiling water for 2-3 minutes. Drain well, rinse under cold running water, and drain thoroughly again.

2 Heat 1 tablespoon of the oil in a preheated wok or skillet.

3 Add the noodles to the wok or skillet and stir-fry for about 2 minutes.

4 Using a draining spoon, remove the noodles from the wok, drain well, and set aside until required.

5 Heat the remaining peanut oil in the wok. Add the pork slices and stir-fry for 4-5 minutes.

6 Stir in the minced garlic and chopped onion and stir-fry for a further 2-3 minutes.

7 Add the oyster mushrooms, tomatoes, light soy sauce, pork stock, and drained noodles. Stir well and cook for 1-2 minutes.

8 Sprinkle with chopped cilantro and serve immediately.

COOK'S TIP

For crisper noodles, add 2 tablespoons of oil to the wok and fry the noodles for 5-6 minutes, spreading them thinly in the wok and turning half-way through cooking.

Sesame Hot Noodles

Plain egg noodles are tossed in a dressing made with sesame oil, soy sauce, peanut butter, cilantro, lime, chili, and sesame seeds.

NUTRITIONAL INFORMATION

Calories	300	Sugars	.........1g
Protein	.........7g	Fat	..........21g
Carbohydrate	...21g	Saturates	.......3g

5 MINS   10 MINS

SERVES 4

INGREDIENTS

2 x 9 oz packets medium egg noodles

3 tbsp sunflower oil

2 tbsp sesame oil

1 garlic clove, minced

1 tbsp smooth peanut butter

1 small green chili, seeded and very finely chopped

3 tbsp toasted sesame seeds

4 tbsp light soy sauce

½ tbsp lime juice

salt and pepper

4 tbsp chopped fresh cilantro

1 Place the noodles in a large pan of boiling water, then immediately remove from the heat. Cover and leave to stand for 6 minutes, stirring once halfway through the time. At the end of 6 minutes the noodles will be perfectly cooked. Alternatively, cook the noodles following the package directions.

2 Meanwhile, make the dressing. Mix together the sunflower oil, sesame oil, minced garlic, and peanut butter in a mixing bowl until smooth.

3 Add the chopped green chili, sesame seeds, and light soy sauce to the other dressing ingredients. Add the lime juice, according to taste, and mix well. Season with salt and pepper.

4 Drain the noodles thoroughly then place in a heated serving bowl.

5 Add the dressing and chopped fresh cilantro to the noodles and toss well to mix. Serve hot as a main meal accompaniment.

COOK'S TIP

If you are cooking the noodles ahead of time, toss the cooked, drained noodles in 2 teaspoons of sesame oil, then turn into a bowl. Cover and keep warm until required.

Seafood Chow Mein

Use whatever seafood is available for this delicious noodle dish – mussels or crab are also suitable.

NUTRITIONAL INFORMATION

Calories 281	Sugars 1g
Protein 15g	Fat 18g
Carbohydrate . . .16g	Saturates 2g

🄖 🄖 🄖

🕙 15 MINS   ⏱ 15 MINS

SERVES 4

I N G R E D I E N T S

3 oz squid, cleaned

3-4 fresh scallops

3 oz raw shrimp, shelled

½ egg white, lightly beaten

1 tbsp cornstarch paste (see page 15)

9½ oz egg noodles

5-6 tbsp vegetable oil

2 tbsp light soy sauce

2 oz snowpeas

½ tsp salt

½ tsp sugar

1 tsp Chinese rice wine

2 scallions, finely shredded

a few drops of sesame oil

1 Open up the squid and score the inside in a criss-cross pattern, then cut into pieces about the size of a postage stamp. Soak the squid in a bowl of boiling water until all the pieces curl up. Rinse in cold water and drain.

2 Cut each scallop into 3-4 slices. Cut the shrimp in half lengthways if large. Mix the scallops and shrimp with the egg white and cornstarch paste.

3 Cook the noodles in boiling water according to the package directions, drain, and rinse under cold water. Drain well, then toss with about 1 tablespoon of oil.

4 Heat 3 tablespoons of oil in a preheated wok. Add the noodles and 1 tablespoon of the soy sauce and stir-fry for 2-3 minutes. Remove to a large serving dish.

5 Heat the remaining oil in the wok and add the snowpeas and seafood. Stir-fry for about 2 minutes, then add the salt, sugar, wine, remaining soy sauce, and about half the scallions. Blend well and add a little stock or water if necessary. Pour the seafood mixture on top of the noodles and sprinkle with sesame oil. Garnish with the remaining scallions and serve.

COOK'S TIP

Chinese rice wine, made from glutinous rice, is also known as yellow wine because of its golden amber color. If it is unavailable, a good dry or medium sherry is an acceptable substitute.

Special Noodles

This dish combines meat, vegetables, shrimp, and noodles in a curried coconut sauce. Serve as a main meal or as an accompaniment.

NUTRITIONAL INFORMATION

Calories	409	Sugars	........12g
Protein	........24g	Fat	..........23g
Carbohydrate	...28g	Saturates	.......8g

5 MINS   25 MINS

SERVES 4

I N G R E D I E N T S

9 oz thin rice noodles

4 tbsp peanut oil

2 cloves garlic, minced

2 red chilies, seeded and very finely chopped

1 tsp grated fresh gingerroot

2 tbsp Madras curry paste

2 tbsp rice-wine vinegar

1 tbsp superfine sugar

1½ cup cooked ham, finely shredded

1¼ cups canned water chestnuts, sliced

1½ cups mushrooms, sliced

¾ cup peas

1 red bell pepper, seeded and thinly sliced

3½ oz peeled shrimp

2 large eggs

4 tbsp coconut milk

¼ cup shredded coconut

2 tbsp chopped fresh cilantro

1 Place the rice noodles in a large bowl, cover with boiling water, and leave to soak for about 10 minutes. Drain the noodles thoroughly, then toss with 2 tablespoons of peanut oil.

2 Heat the remaining peanut oil in a large preheated wok until the oil is really hot.

3 Add the garlic, chilies, ginger, curry paste, rice wine vinegar, and superfine sugar to the wok and stir-fry for 1 minute.

4 Add the ham, water chestnuts, mushrooms, peas, and red bell pepper to the wok and stir-fry for 5 minutes.

5 Add the noodles and shrimp to the wok and stir-fry for 2 minutes.

6 In a small bowl, beat together the eggs and coconut milk. Drizzle over the mixture in the wok and stir-fry until the egg sets.

7 Add the shredded coconut and chopped fresh cilantro to the wok and toss to combine. Transfer the noodles to warm serving dishes and serve immediately.

Homemade Noodles

These noodles are simple to make; you do not need a pasta-making machine because they are rolled out by hand.

NUTRITIONAL INFORMATION

Calories	294	Sugars	........3g
Protein	.........7g	Fat	.........15g
Carbohydrate	...35g	Saturates	.......2g

20 MINS   15 MINS

SERVES 2–4

I N G R E D I E N T S

N O O D L E S

1 cup all-purpose flour

2 tbsp cornstarch

½ tsp salt

½ cup boiling water

5 tbsp vegetable oil

S T I R - F R Y

1 zucchini, cut into thin sticks

1 celery stick, cut into thin sticks

1 carrot, cut into thin sticks

1½ cups open-cap mushrooms, sliced

1 cup broccoli flowerets and stalks, peeled and thinly sliced

1 leek, sliced

2 cups beansprouts

1 tbsp soy sauce

2 tsp rice wine vinegar

½ tsp sugar

1 To prepare the noodles, sift the flour, cornstarch, and salt into a bowl. Make a well in the center and pour in the boiling water and 1 teaspoon of oil. Mix quickly to make a soft dough, cover, and leave for 5–6 minutes.

2 Make the noodles by breaking off small pieces of dough and rolling into balls. Roll each ball across a very lightly oiled work counter with the palm of your hand to form thin noodles. Do not worry if some of the noodles break into shorter lengths. Set the noodles aside.

3 Heat 3 tablespoons of oil in a wok. Add the noodles in batches and fry over a high heat for 1 minute. Reduce the heat and cook for a further 2 minutes. Remove, drain on paper towels, and set aside.

4 Heat the remaining oil in the pan. Add the zucchini, celery, and carrot, and stir-fry for 1 minute. Add the mushrooms, broccoli, and leek, and stir-fry for a further minute. Stir in the remaining ingredients and mix well until thoroughly heated.

5 Add the noodles and cook over a high heat, tossing to mix the ingredients. Serve immediately.

Noodles with Shrimp

This is a simple dish using egg noodles and large shrimp, which give the dish a wonderful flavor, texture, and color.

NUTRITIONAL INFORMATION

Calories 142	Sugars 0.4g	
Protein 11g	Fat 7g	
Carbohydrate 11g	Saturates 1g	

 5 MINS   10 MINS

SERVES 4

INGREDIENTS

8 oz thin egg noodles

2 tbsp peanut oil

1 garlic clove, minced

½ tsp ground star anise

1 bunch scallions, cut into 2-inch pieces

24 raw jumbo shrimp, peeled with tails intact

2 tbsp light soy sauce

2 tsp lime juice

lime wedges, to garnish

1 Blanch the noodles in a saucepan of boiling water for about 2 minutes.

2 Drain the noodles well, rinse under cold water, and drain thoroughly again. Keep warm and set aside until required.

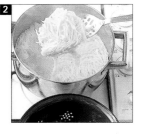

3 Heat the peanut oil in a preheated wok or large skillet until almost smoking.

4 Add the minced garlic and ground star anise to the wok and stir-fry for 30 seconds.

5 Add the scallions and jumbo shrimp to the wok and stir-fry for 2-3 minutes.

6 Stir in the light soy sauce, lime juice, and noodles and mix well.

7 Cook the mixture in the wok for about 1 minute until thoroughly heated through and all the ingredients are thoroughly incorporated.

8 Spoon the noodle and shrimp mixture into a warm serving dish. Transfer to serving bowls, garnish with lime wedges, and serve immediately.

COOK'S TIP

If fresh egg noodles are available, these require very little cooking: simply place in boiling water for about 3 minutes, drain, and toss in oil. Noodles can be boiled and eaten plain, or stir-fried with meat and vegetables for a light meal or snack.

Chilled Noodles & Peppers

This is a convenient dish to serve when you are arriving home just before family or friends. Quick to prepare and assemble, it is ready in minutes.

NUTRITIONAL INFORMATION

Calories 260	Sugars 4g
Protein 4g	Fat 21g
Carbohydrate ...15g	Saturates 4g

 5 MINS   15 MINS

SERVES 4–6

I N G R E D I E N T S

9 oz ribbon noodles, or Chinese egg noodles

1 tbsp sesame oil

1 red bell pepper

1 yellow bell pepper

1 green bell pepper

6 scallions, cut into matchstick strips

salt

D R E S S I N G

5 tbsp sesame oil

2 tbsp light soy sauce

1 tbsp sesame seed paste

4-5 drops hot pepper sauce

1 Preheat the broiler to medium. Cook the noodles in a large pan of boiling, salted water until they are almost tender. Drain them in a colander, run cold water through them, and drain thoroughly. Tip the noodles into a bowl, stir in the sesame oil, cover, and chill.

2 Cook the bell peppers under the broiler, turning them frequently, until they are blackened. Plunge into cold water, then skin them. Cut in half, remove the core and seeds, and cut into thick strips. Set aside in a covered container.

3 To make the dressing, mix together the sesame oil, light soy sauce, sesame seed paste, and hot pepper sauce until well combined.

4 Pour the dressing on the noodles, reserving 1 tablespoon, and toss well. Turn the noodles into a serving dish, arrange the grilled bell peppers over the noodles and spoon over the reserved dressing. Scatter on the scallion strips.

COOK'S TIP

If you have time, another way of skinning bell peppers is to first broil them, then place in a plastic bag, seal, and leave for about 20 minutes. The skin will then peel off easily.

Pork Chow Mein

This is a basic recipe – the meat and/or vegetables can be varied as much as you like.

NUTRITIONAL INFORMATION

Calories 239   Sugars 1g
Protein . . . . .17g   Fat 14g
Carbohydrate . . .12g   Saturates 2g

15 MINS   15 MINS

SERVES 4

I N G R E D I E N T S

9 oz egg noodles

4-5 tbsp vegetable oil

9 oz pork tenderloin, cooked

4½ oz green beans

2 tbsp light soy sauce

1 tsp salt

½ tsp sugar

1 tbsp Chinese rice wine or dry sherry

2 scallions, finely shredded

a few drops sesame oil

chili sauce, to serve (optional)

1 Cook the noodles in boiling water according to the directions on the package, drain, and rinse under cold water. Drain again then toss with 1 tablespoon of the oil.

2 Slice the pork into thin shreds and top and tail the beans.

3 Heat 3 tablespoons of oil in a preheated wok until hot. Add the noodles and stir-fry for 2-3 minutes with 1 tablespoon soy sauce, then transfer to a serving dish. Keep warm.

4 Heat the remaining oil and stir-fry the beans and meat for 2 minutes. Add the salt, sugar, wine or sherry, the

remaining soy sauce, and about half the scallions to the wok.

5 Stir the mixture in the wok, adding a little stock if necessary, then pour on top of the noodles. Sprinkle with sesame oil and the remaining scallions.

6 Serve the chow mein hot or cold with chili sauce, if desired.

COOK'S TIP

Chow Mein literally means "stir-fried noodles" and is highly popular in the West as well as in China. Almost any ingredient can be added, such as fish, meat, poultry, or vegetables. It is very popular for lunch and makes a tasty salad served cold.

Fried Vegetable Noodles

In this recipe, noodles are first boiled and then deep-fried for a crisply textured dish, and tossed with fried vegetables.

NUTRITIONAL INFORMATION

Calories ....229 Sugars 4g
Protein ....5g Fat 15g
Carbohydrate ...20g Saturates 2g

🥟 5 MINS   🕐 25 MINS

SERVES 4

I N G R E D I E N T S

3 cups dried egg noodles

2 tbsp peanut oil

2 garlic cloves, minced

½ tsp ground star anise

1 carrot, cut into matchsticks

1 green bell pepper, cut into matchsticks

1 onion, quartered and sliced

4½ oz broccoli flowerets

2¾ oz bamboo shoots

1 celery stick, sliced

1 tbsp light soy sauce

⅔ cup vegetable stock

vegetable oil, for deep-frying

1 tsp cornstarch

2 tsp water

1 Cook the noodles in a saucepan of boiling water for 1-2 minutes. Drain well and rinse under cold running water. Leave the noodles to drain thoroughly in a colander until required.

2 Heat the peanut oil in a preheated wok until smoking. Reduce the heat, add the minced garlic and ground star anise, and stir-fry for 30 seconds. Add the remaining vegetables and stir-fry for 1-2 minutes.

3 Add the soy sauce and vegetable stock to the wok and cook over a low heat for 5 minutes.

4 Heat the oil for deep-frying in a separate wok to 350°F or until a cube of bread browns in 30 seconds.

5 Using a fork, twist the drained noodles and form them into rounds. Deep-fry them in batches until crisp, turning once. Leave to drain on absorbent paper towels.

6 Blend the cornstarch with the water to form a paste and stir into the vegetables. Bring to a boil, stirring until the sauce is thickened and clear.

7 Arrange the noodles on a warm serving plate, spoon the vegetables on top, and serve immediately.

Lamb with Noodles

Lamb is quick fried, coated in a soy sauce, and served on a bed of transparent noodles for a richly flavored dish.

NUTRITIONAL INFORMATION

Calories 285	Sugars 1g
Protein 27g	Fat 16g
Carbohydrate . . .10g	Saturates 6g

 5 MINS 15 MINS

SERVES 4

INGREDIENTS

5½ oz cellophane noodles

2 tbsp peanut oil

1 lb lean, boneless lamb, thinly sliced

2 garlic cloves, minced

2 leeks, sliced

3 tbsp dark soy sauce

1 cup lamb stock

dash of chili sauce

red chili strips, to garnish

1 Bring a large saucepan of water to a boil. Add the cellophane noodles and cook for 1 minute. Drain the noodles well, place in a sieve, rinse under cold running water, and drain thoroughly again. Set aside until required.

2 Heat the peanut oil in a preheated wok or skillet, swirling the oil around until it is really hot.

3 Add the lamb to the wok or skillet and stir-fry for about 2 minutes.

4 Add the minced garlic and sliced leeks to the wok and stir-fry for 2 minutes.

5 Stir in the dark soy sauce, lamb stock, and chili sauce and cook for 3-4 minutes, stirring frequently, until the meat is cooked through.

6 Add the drained cellophane noodles to the wok or skillet and cook for about 1 minute, stirring, until heated through.

7 Transfer the lamb and cellophane noodles to serving plates, garnish with red chili strips, and serve.

COOK'S TIP

Transparent noodles are available in Chinese supermarkets. Use egg noodles instead if transparent noodles are unavailable, and cook them according to the instructions on the packet.

Chicken & Noodle One-Pot

Flavorsome chicken and vegetables are cooked with Chinese egg noodles in a coconut sauce. Serve in deep soup bowls.

NUTRITIONAL INFORMATION

Calories	256	Sugars 7g
Protein	........30g	Fat 8g
Carbohydrate	...18g	Saturates 2g

5 MINS   20 MINS

SERVES 4

INGREDIENTS

1 tbsp sunflower oil

1 onion, sliced

1 garlic clove, minced

1 inch gingerroot, peeled and grated

1 bunch scallions, sliced diagonally

3½ cups chicken breast, skinned and cut into bite-sized pieces

2 tbsp mild curry paste

2 cups coconut milk

1¼ cups chicken stock

9 oz Chinese egg noodles

2 tsp lime juice

salt and pepper

basil sprigs, to garnish

1 Heat the sunflower oil in a wok or large, heavy-based skillet.

2 Add the onion, garlic, ginger, and scallions to the wok and stir-fry for 2 minutes until softened.

3 Add the chicken and curry paste and stir-fry for 4 minutes, or until the vegetables and chicken are golden brown. Stir in the coconut milk, stock, and salt and pepper to taste, and mix well.

4 Bring to a boil, break the noodles into large pieces, if necessary, add to the pan, cover, and simmer for about 6-8 minutes until the noodles are just tender, stirring occasionally.

5 Add the lime juice and adjust the seasoning, if necessary.

6 Serve the chicken and noodle one-pot at once in deep soup bowls, garnished with basil sprigs.

COOK'S TIP

If you enjoy hot flavors, substitute the mild curry paste in the above recipe with hot curry paste (found in most food stores) but reduce the quantity to 1 tablespoon.

Noodles with Chili & Shrimp

This is a simple dish to prepare and is packed with flavor, making it an ideal choice for special occasions.

NUTRITIONAL INFORMATION

Calories	259	Sugars	.........9g
Protein	........28g	Fat	...........8g
Carbohydrate	...20g	Saturates	.......1g

   10 MINS   5 MINS

SERVES 4

I N G R E D I E N T S

9 oz thin glass noodles

2 tbsp sunflower oil

1 onion, sliced

2 red chilies, seeded and very finely chopped

4 lime leaves, thinly shredded

1 tbsp fresh cilantro

2 tbsp palm sugar or superfine sugar

2 tbsp fish sauce

1 lb raw jumbo shrimp, peeled

1 Place the noodles in a large bowl. Pour enough boiling water over to cover the noodles and leave to stand for 5 minutes. Drain thoroughly and set aside until required.

COOK'S TIP

If you cannot buy raw jumbo shrimp, use cooked shrimp instead and cook them with the noodles for 1 minute only, just to heat through.

2 Heat the sunflower oil in a large heated wok or skillet until it is really hot.

3 Add the onion, red chilies, and lime leaves to the wok and stir-fry for 1 minute.

4 Add the cilantro, palm or superfine sugar, fish sauce, and shrimp. Stir-fry for 2 minutes or until the shrimp turn pink.

5 Add the drained noodles to the wok, toss to mix well, and stir-fry for 1–2 minutes or until heated through.

6 Transfer the noodles and shrimp to warm serving bowls and serve immediately.

Sweet & Sour Noodles

This delicious dish combines sweet-and-sour flavors with the addition of egg, rice noodles, jumbo shrimp, and vegetables for a real treat.

NUTRITIONAL INFORMATION

Calories	352	Sugars	........14g
Protein	........23g	Fat	..........17g
Carbohydrate	...29g	Saturates	.......3g

10 MINS   10 MINS

SERVES 4

INGREDIENTS

3 tbsp fish sauce

2 tbsp distilled white vinegar

2 tbsp superfine or palm sugar

2 tbsp tomato paste

2 tbsp sunflower oil

3 cloves garlic, minced

12 oz rice noodles, soaked in boiling water for 5 minutes

8 scallions, sliced

1 cup carrot, grated

1¼ cups beansprouts

2 eggs, beaten

8 oz peeled jumbo shrimp

½ cup chopped peanuts

1 tsp chili flakes, to garnish

1 Mix together the fish sauce, vinegar, sugar, and tomato paste.

2 Heat the sunflower oil in a large preheated wok.

3 Add the garlic to the wok and stir-fry for 30 seconds.

4 Drain the noodles thoroughly and add them to the wok together with the fish sauce and tomato paste mixture. Mix well to combine.

5 Add the scallions, carrot, and beansprouts to the wok and stir-fry for 2–3 minutes.

6 Move the contents of the wok to one side, add the beaten eggs to the empty part of the wok, and cook until the egg sets. Add the noodles, jumbo shrimp, and peanuts to the wok and mix well. Transfer to warm serving dishes and garnish with chili flakes. Serve hot.

COOK'S TIP

Chili flakes may be found in the spice section of large supermarkets.

Rice

Together with noodles, rice forms the central part of a Chinese meal, particularly in southern China. In the north, the staple foods tend to be more wheat-based. For an everyday meal, plain rice is served with one or two dishes and a soup. Rice can be boiled and then steamed, or it can be fried with other ingredients such as eggs, shrimp, meat,

and vegetables and then flavored with soy sauce. The most common type of rice used in Chinese cooking is short-grain, or glutinous rice, which become slightly sticky when cooked and is therefore ideal for eating with chopsticks. This chapter includes some delicious rice dishes that can be eaten on their own or as an accompaniment. Fried rice is a particular favorite in Western restaurants so several variations are included here.

Egg Fried Rice

In this classic Chinese dish, boiled rice is fried with peas, scallions, and egg and flavored with soy sauce.

NUTRITIONAL INFORMATION

Calories	203	Sugars	1g
Protein	9g	Fat	11g
Carbohydrate	19g	Saturates	2g

🍚 20 MINS   🕐 10 MINS

SERVES 4

I N G R E D I E N T S

⅔ cup long-grain rice

3 eggs, beaten

2 tbsp vegetable oil

2 garlic cloves, crushed

4 scallions, chopped

1 cup cooked peas

1 tbsp light soy sauce

pinch of salt

shredded scallion, to garnish

1 Cook the rice in a pan of boiling water for 10-12 minutes, until almost cooked, but not soft. Drain well, rinse under cold water, and drain again.

2 Place the beaten eggs in a saucepan and cook over a gentle heat, stirring until softly scrambled.

3 Heat the vegetable oil in a preheated wok or large skillet, swirling the oil around the base of the wok until it is really hot.

4 Add the crushed garlic, scallions, and peas and sauté, stirring occasionally, for 1-2 minutes. Stir the rice into the wok, mixing to combine.

5 Add the eggs, light soy sauce, and a pinch of salt to the wok or skillet and stir to mix the egg in thoroughly.

6 Transfer the egg fried rice to serving dishes and serve garnished with the shredded scallion.

COOK'S TIP

The rice is rinsed under cold water to wash out the starch and prevent it from sticking together.

Chili Fried Rice

Not so much a side dish as a meal in itself, this delicious fried rice can be served on its own or as an accompaniment to many Chinese dishes.

NUTRITIONAL INFORMATION

Calories	290	Sugars	2g
Protein	11g	Fat	14g
Carbohydrate	26g	Saturates	2g

20 MINS   15 MINS

SERVES 4

INGREDIENTS

generous 1 cup long-grain rice

4 tbsp vegetable oil

2 garlic cloves, chopped finely

1 small red chili, seeded and chopped finely

8 scallions, trimmed and sliced finely

1 tbsp red curry paste or 2 tsp chili sauce

1 red bell pepper, cored, seeded, and chopped

¾ cup green beans, chopped

1½ cups cooked peeled shrimp or chopped cooked chicken

2 tbsp fish sauce

TO GARNISH

cucumber slices

shredded scallion

COOK'S TIP

Cook the rice the day before if you can remember – it will give an even better result. Alternatively, use rice left over from another dish to make this recipe.

1 Cook the rice in plenty of boiling, lightly salted water until tender, about 12 minutes. Drain, rinse with cold water, and drain thoroughly.

2 Heat the vegetable oil in a wok or large skillet until the oil is really hot.

3 Add the garlic to the wok and fry gently for 2 minutes until golden.

4 Add the chili and scallions and cook, stirring, for 3–4 minutes.

5 Add the red curry paste or chili sauce to the wok or skillet and fry for 1 minute, then add the red bell pepper and green beans. Stir-fry briskly for 2 minutes.

6 Tip the cooked rice into the wok or skillet and add the shrimp or chicken and the fish sauce. Stir-fry over a medium-high heat for about 4–5 minutes, until the rice is hot.

7 Transfer the chili fried rice to warm serving dishes, garnish with cucumber slices and shredded scallion and serve.

Fragrant Coconut Rice

This fragrant, sweet rice is delicious served with meat, vegetable, or fish dishes as part of a Chinese menu.

NUTRITIONAL INFORMATION

Calories 306	Sugars 2g
Protein 5g	Fat 6g
Carbohydrate . . .61g	Saturates 4g

 5 MINS   15 MINS

SERVES 4

INGREDIENTS

9½ oz long-grain white rice

2½ cups water

½ tsp salt

⅓ cup coconut milk

¼ cup shredded coconut

1 Rinse the rice thoroughly under cold running water until the water runs completely clear.

2 Drain the rice thoroughly in a strainer set over a large bowl. This is to remove some of the starch and to prevent the grains from sticking together.

3 Place the rice in a wok with 2½ cups water.

4 Add the salt and coconut milk to the wok and bring to the boil.

5 Cover the wok with a lid or foil, curved into a domed shape and resting on the sides of the wok. Reduce the heat and leave to simmer for 10 minutes.

6 Remove the lid from the wok and fluff up the rice with a fork – all of the liquid should be absorbed and the rice grains should be tender. If not, add more water and continue to simmer for a few more minutes until all the liquid has been absorbed.

7 Spoon the rice into a warm serving bowl and scatter with the shredded coconut. Serve immediately.

COOK'S TIP

Coconut milk is not the liquid found inside coconuts – that is called coconut water. Coconut milk is made from the white coconut flesh soaked in water and milk and then squeezed to extract all of the flavor. You can make your own or buy it in cans.

Sweet Chili Pork Fried Rice

This is a variation of egg-fried rice which can be served as an accompaniment to a main meal dish.

NUTRITIONAL INFORMATION

Calories	366	Sugars	5g
Protein	29g	Fat	16g
Carbohydrate	28g	Saturates	4g

🍲 25 MINS   🕐 20 MINS

SERVES 4

INGREDIENTS

1 lb pork tenderloin

2 tbsp sunflower oil

2 tbsp sweet chili sauce, plus extra
  to serve

1 onion, sliced

1¼ cups carrots, cut into thin sticks

1½ cup zucchini, cut into sticks

1 cup canned bamboo shoots, drained

4¾ cups cooked long-grain rice

1 egg, beaten

1 tbsp chopped fresh parsley

1. Using a sharp knife, cut the pork tenderloin into thin slices.

2. Heat the sunflower oil in a large heated wok or skillet.

3. Add the pork to the wok and stir-fry for 5 minutes.

4. Add the chili sauce to the wok and allow to bubble, stirring, for 2–3 minutes or until syrupy.

5. Add the onion, carrots, zucchini, and bamboo shoots to the wok and stir-fry for a further 3 minutes.

6. Add the cooked rice and stir-fry for 2–3 minutes or until the rice is heated through.

7. Drizzle the beaten egg over the top of the fried rice and cook, tossing the ingredients in the wok with two spoons, until the egg sets.

8. Scatter with chopped fresh parsley and serve immediately, with extra sweet chili sauce, if desired.

COOK'S TIP

For a really quick dish, add frozen mixed vegetables to the rice instead of the freshly prepared vegetables.

Special Fried Rice

This dish is a popular choice in Chinese restaurants. Ham and shrimp are mixed with vegetables in a soy-flavored rice.

NUTRITIONAL INFORMATION

Calories	301	Sugars	1g
Protein	26g	Fat	13g
Carbohydrate	21g	Saturates	3g

5 MINS   30 MINS

SERVES 4

INGREDIENTS

¾ cup long-grain rice

2 tbsp vegetable oil

2 eggs, beaten

2 garlic cloves, crushed

1 tsp grated fresh gingerroot

3 scallions, sliced

¾ cup cooked peas

⅔ cup beansprouts

1⅓ cups shredded ham

5½ oz peeled, cooked shrimp

2 tbsp light soy sauce

1 Cook the rice in a saucepan of boiling water for about 15 minutes. Drain well, rinse under cold water, and drain thoroughly again.

2 Heat 1 tablespoon of the vegetable oil in a preheated wok.

3 Add the beaten eggs and a further 1 teaspoon of oil. Tilt the wok so that the egg covers the base to make a thin pancake.

4 Cook until lightly browned on the underside, then flip the pancake over and cook on the other side for 1 minute. Remove from the wok and leave to cool.

5 Heat the remaining oil in the wok and stir-fry the garlic and ginger for 30 seconds. Add the scallions, peas, beansprouts, ham, and shrimp. Stir-fry for 2 minutes.

6 Stir in the soy sauce and rice and cook for a further 2 minutes. Transfer the rice to serving dishes. Roll up the pancake, slice it very thinly, and use to garnish the rice. Serve immediately.

COOK'S TIP

As this recipe contains meat and fish, it is ideal served with simpler vegetable dishes.

Chicken & Rice Casserole

This is a quick-cooking, spicy casserole of rice, chicken, vegetables, and chili in a soy- and ginger-flavored broth.

NUTRITIONAL INFORMATION

Calories	502	Sugars	2g
Protein	55g	Fat	9g
Carbohydrate	52g	Saturates	3g

35 MINS   50 MINS

SERVES 4

INGREDIENTS

¾ cup long-grain rice

1 tbsp dry sherry

2 tbsp light soy sauce

2 tbsp dark soy sauce

2 tsp dark brown sugar

1 tsp salt

1 tsp sesame oil

6 cups skinless, boneless chicken meat, diced

3¾ cups chicken stock

2 open-cap mushrooms, sliced

½ cup water chestnuts, halved

½ cup broccoli flowerets

1 yellow bell pepper, sliced

4 tsp grated fresh gingerroot

whole chives, to garnish

VARIATION

This dish works equally well with beef or pork. Chinese dried mushrooms may be used instead of the open-cap mushrooms, if rehydrated before adding to the dish.

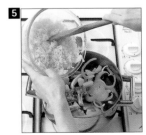

1 Cook the rice in a saucepan of boiling water for about 15 minutes. Drain well, rinse under cold water, and drain again thoroughly.

2 Mix together the sherry, soy sauces, sugar, salt, and sesame oil.

3 Stir the chicken into the soy mixture, turning to coat the chicken well. Leave to marinate for about 30 minutes.

4 Bring the stock to a boil in a saucepan or preheated wok. Add the chicken with the marinade, mushrooms, water chestnuts, broccoli, bell pepper, and ginger.

5 Stir in the rice, reduce the heat, cover and cook for 25-30 minutes until the chicken and vegetables are cooked through. Transfer to serving plates, garnish with chives and serve.

Fried Rice with Shrimp

Use either peeled shrimp or jumbo shrimp for this rice dish.

NUTRITIONAL INFORMATION

Calories	599	Sugars	0g
Protein	26g	Fat	16g
Carbohydrate	94g	Saturates	3g

5 MINS   35 MINS

SERVES 4

INGREDIENTS

1½ cups long-grain rice

2 eggs

4 tsp cold water

salt and pepper

3 tbsp sunflower oil

4 scallions, thinly sliced diagonally

1 garlic clove, crushed

4½ oz closed-cap or button mushrooms, thinly sliced

2 tbsp oyster or anchovy sauce

1¾ cups water chestnuts, drained and sliced

9 oz peeled shrimp, defrosted if frozen

½ bunch watercress, roughly chopped

watercress sprigs, to garnish (optional)

1 Cook the rice in boiling salted water, following the directions given on page 244 and keep warm.

2 Beat each egg separately with 2 teaspoons of cold water and salt and pepper.

3 Heat 2 teaspoons of sunflower oil in a wok or large skillet, swirling it around until really hot. Pour in the first egg, swirl it around, and leave to cook undisturbed until set. Remove to a plate or board and repeat with the second egg. Cut the omelets into 1-inch squares.

4 Heat the remaining oil in the wok and when really hot add the scallions and garlic and stir-fry for 1 minute. Add the mushrooms and continue to cook for a further 2 minutes.

5 Stir in the oyster or anchovy sauce and seasoning, and add the water chestnuts and shrimp; stir-fry for 2 minutes.

6 Stir in the cooked rice and stir-fry for 1 minute, then add the watercress and omelet squares and stir-fry for a further 1–2 minutes until piping hot. Serve at once garnished with sprigs of watercress, if liked.

Coconut Rice with Lentils

Rice and green lentils are cooked with coconut, lemongrass and curry leaves. It will serve 2 people as a main course or 4 as a side dish.

NUTRITIONAL INFORMATION

Calories	511	Sugars	3g
Protein	12g	Fat	24g
Carbohydrate	67g	Saturates	15g

5 MINS   50 MINS

SERVES 4

I N G R E D I E N T S

⅓ cup green lentils

generous 1 cup long-grain rice

2 tbsp vegetable oil

1 onion, sliced

2 garlic cloves, crushed

3 curry leaves

1 stalk lemongrass, chopped (if unavailable, use grated peel of ½ lemon)

1 green chili, seeded and chopped

½ tsp cumin seeds

1½ tsp salt

⅓ cup creamed coconut

2½ cups hot water

2 tbsp chopped fresh cilantro

TO GARNISH

shredded radishes

shredded cucumber

1 Wash the lentils and place in a saucepan. Cover with cold water, bring to a boil, and boil rapidly for 10 minutes.

2 Wash the rice thoroughly and drain well. Set aside until required.

3 Heat the vegetable oil in a large saucepan which has a tight-fitting lid and fry the onion for 3–4 minutes. Add the garlic, curry leaves, lemongrass, chili, cumin seeds, and salt, and stir well.

4 Drain the lentils and rinse. Add to the onion and spices with the rice and mix well.

5 Add the creamed coconut to the hot water and stir until dissolved. Stir the coconut liquid into the rice mixture and bring to a boil. Turn down the heat to low, put the lid on tightly, and leave to cook undisturbed for 15 minutes.

6 Without removing the lid, remove the pan from the heat and leave to rest for 10 minutes to allow the rice and lentils to finish cooking in their own steam.

7 Stir in the cilantro and remove the curry leaves. Serve garnished with the radishes and cucumber.

Vegetable Fried Rice

This dish can be served as part of a substantial meal for a number of people or as a vegetarian meal in itself for four.

NUTRITIONAL INFORMATION

Calories	175	Sugars 3g
Protein	3g	Fat 10g
Carbohydrate 20g		Saturates 2g

10 MINS   20 MINS

SERVES 4

INGREDIENTS

⅔ cup long-grain white rice

3 tbsp peanut oil

2 garlic cloves, crushed

½ tsp Chinese five-spice powder

⅓ cup green beans

1 green bell pepper, seeded and chopped

4 baby corn cobs, sliced

1 oz bamboo shoots, chopped

3 tomatoes, skinned, seeded, and chopped

½ cup cooked peas

1 tsp sesame oil

1 Bring a large saucepan of water to a boil.

2 Add the long-grain white rice to the saucepan and cook for about 15 minutes. Drain the rice well, rinse under cold running water, and drain thoroughly again.

3 Heat the peanut oil in a preheated wok or large skillet. Add the garlic and Chinese five-spice and stir-fry for 30 seconds.

4 Add the green beans, chopped green bell pepper, and sliced corn cobs and stir-fry the ingredients in the wok for 2 minutes.

5 Stir the bamboo shoots, tomatoes, peas, and rice into the mixture in the wok and stir-fry for 1 further minute.

6 Sprinkle with sesame oil and transfer to serving dishes Serve immediately.

VARIATION

Use a selection of vegetables of your choice in this recipe, cutting them to a similar size to insure they cook in the same amount of time.

Steamed Rice in Lotus Leaves

The fragrance of the leaves penetrates the rice, giving it a unique taste. Lotus leaves can be bought from specialist Chinese grocery stores.

NUTRITIONAL INFORMATION

Calories	163	Sugars 0.1g	
Protein	5g	Fat	6g
Carbohydrate	2.1g	Saturates	1g

1 HOUR   40 MINS

SERVES 4

INGREDIENTS

2 lotus leaves

4 Chinese dried mushrooms (if unavailable, use thinly sliced open-cap mushrooms)

generous ¾ cup long-grain rice

1 cinnamon stick

6 cardamom pods

4 cloves

1 tsp salt

2 eggs

1 tbsp vegetable oil

2 scallions, chopped

1 tbsp soy sauce

2 tbsp sherry

1 tsp sugar

1 tsp sesame oil

1 Unfold the lotus leaves carefully and cut along the fold to divide each leaf in half. Lay on a large baking sheet and pour over enough hot water to cover; soak for about 30 minutes until softened.

2 Place the dried mushrooms in a small bowl and cover with warm water. Leave to soak for 20–25 minutes.

3 Cook the rice in a saucepan of boiling water with the cinnamon stick, cardamom pods, cloves, and salt for about 10 minutes – the rice should be partially cooked. Drain thoroughly and remove the cinnamon stick; place the rice in a bowl

4 Beat the eggs lightly. Heat the oil in a wok and cook the eggs quickly, stirring until set. Remove and set aside.

5 Drain the mushrooms, squeezing out the excess water. Remove the tough centers and chop the mushrooms. Stir into the rice with the cooked egg, scallions, soy sauce, sherry, sugar, and sesame oil.

6 Drain the lotus leaves and divide the rice into four portions. Place a portion in the center of each leaf and fold up to form a packet. Place in a steamer, cover, and steam over simmering water for 20 minutes. To serve, cut the tops of the lotus leaves open to expose the rice inside.

Curried Rice with Pork

This rice dish is flavored with vegetables and pork, soy sauce, and curry spices with strips of omelet added as a topping.

NUTRITIONAL INFORMATION

Calories	436	Sugars	2g
Protein	30g	Fat	20g
Carbohydrate	37g	Saturates	5g

 10 MINS   35 MINS

SERVES 4

INGREDIENTS

1½ cups long-grain rice

12 oz-1 lb 2 oz pork tenderloin or lean pork slices

3 tomatoes, peeled, quartered, and seeded

2 eggs

4 tsp water

3 tbsp sunflower oil

1 onion, thinly sliced

1-2 garlic cloves, crushed

1 tsp medium or mild curry powder

½ tsp ground coriander

¼ tsp medium chili powder or 1 tsp bottled sweet chili sauce

2 tbsp soy sauce

4½ oz frozen peas, defrosted

salt and pepper

1 Cook the rice in boiling, salted water, following the directions given on page 244 and keep warm until required.

2 Meanwhile, cut the pork into narrow strips across the grain, discarding any fat. Slice the tomatoes.

3 Beat each egg separately with 2 teaspoons cold water and salt and pepper. Heat 2 teaspoons of oil in the wok until really hot. Pour in the first egg, swirl it around and cook undisturbed until set. Transfer to a plate or board and repeat with the second egg. Cut the omelets into strips about ½ inch wide.

4 Heat the remaining oil in the wok and when really hot add the onion and garlic and stir-fry for 1-2 minutes. Add the pork and continue to stir-fry for about 3 minutes, or until almost cooked.

5 Add the curry powder, coriander, chili powder or chili sauce, and soy sauce to the wok and cook for a further minute, stirring constantly.

6 Stir in the rice, tomatoes, and peas and stir-fry for about 2 minutes until piping hot. Adjust the seasoning to taste and turn into a heated serving dish. Arrange the strips of omelet on top and serve at once.

Crab Congee

This is a typical Chinese breakfast dish, although it is probably best served as a lunch or supper dish at a Western table!

NUTRITIONAL INFORMATION

Calories	327	Sugars 0.1g	
Protein	18g	Fat	7g
Carbohydrate	50g	Saturates	2g

 5 MINS   🕐 1¼ HOURS

SERVES 4

I N G R E D I E N T S

1 cup short-grain rice

1½ quarts fish stock

½ tsp salt

3½ oz Chinese sausage, thinly sliced

8 oz white crabmeat

6 scallions, sliced

2 tbsp chopped fresh cilantro

freshly ground black pepper,
   to serve

1 Place the short-grain rice in a large heated wok or skillet.

2 Add the fish stock to the wok or skillet and bring to a boil.

3 Reduce the heat, then simmer gently for 1 hour, stirring the mixture from time to time.

4 Add the salt, sliced Chinese sausage, white crabmeat, sliced scallions, and chopped fresh cilantro to the wok and heat through for about 5 minutes.

5 Add a little more water to the wok if the congee "porridge" is too thick, stirring well.

6 Transfer the crab congee to warm serving bowls, sprinkle with freshly ground black pepper, and serve immediately.

COOK'S TIP

Always buy the freshest possible crabmeat; fresh is best, although frozen or canned will work for this recipe. In the West, crabs are almost always sold cooked. The crab should feel heavy for its size, and when it is shaken, there should not be any sound of water inside.

Crab Fried Rice

Canned crabmeat is used in this recipe for convenience, but fresh white crabmeat can be used – quite deliciously – in its place.

NUTRITIONAL INFORMATION

Calories	225	Sugars	1g
Protein	12g	Fat	11g
Carbohydrate	20g	Saturates	2g

5 MINS 25 MINS

SERVES 4

INGREDIENTS

⅔ cup long-grain rice

2 tbsp peanut oil

4½ oz canned white crabmeat, drained

1 leek, sliced

⅔ cup beansprouts

2 eggs, beaten

1 tbsp light soy sauce

2 tsp lime juice

1 tsp sesame oil

salt

sliced lime, to garnish

1 Cook the rice in a saucepan of boiling salted water for 15 minutes. Drain well, rinse under cold running water, and drain again thoroughly.

2 Heat the peanut oil in a preheated wok until it is really hot.

3 Add the crabmeat, leek, and beansprouts to the wok and stir-fry for 2-3 minutes. Remove the mixture from the wok with a draining spoon and set aside until required.

4 Add the eggs to the wok and cook, stirring occasionally, for 2-3 minutes, until they begin to set.

5 Stir the rice and the crabmeat, leek, and bean sprout mixture into the eggs in the wok.

6 Add the soy sauce and lime juice to the mixture in the wok. Cook for 1 minute, stirring to combine, and sprinkle with the sesame oil.

7 Transfer the crab-fried rice to a serving dish, garnish with the sliced lime, and serve immediately.

VARIATION

Cooked lobster may be used instead of the crab for a really special dish.

Curried Rice with Bean Curd

Cooked rice is combined with marinated bean curd, vegetables, and peanuts to make this deliciously rich curry.

NUTRITIONAL INFORMATION

Calories	598	Sugars	2g	
Protein	16g	Fat	25	
Carbohydrate	81g	Saturates	4g	

15 MINS   15 MINS

SERVES 4

INGREDIENTS

1 tsp coriander seeds

1 tsp cumin seeds

1 tsp ground cinnamon

1 tsp cloves

1 whole star anise

1 tsp cardamom pods

1 tsp white peppercorns

1 tbsp oil

6 shallots, chopped very roughly

6 garlic cloves, chopped very roughly

2-inch piece lemongrass, sliced

4 fresh red chilies, seeded and chopped

grated peel of 1 lime

1 tsp salt

3 tbsp sunflower oil

1 cup marinated bean curd, cut into 1-inch cubes

1 cup green beans, cut into 1-inch pieces

6 cups cooked rice (1½ cups raw weight)

3 shallots, diced finely and deep-fried

1 scallion, chopped finely

2 tbsp chopped roast peanuts

1 tbsp lime juice

1 To make the curry paste, grind together the seeds and spices in a mortar and pestle or spice grinder.

2 Heat the sunflower oil in a preheated wok until it is really hot. Add the shallots, garlic, and lemongrass and cook over a low heat until soft, about 5 minutes. Add the chilies and grind together with the dry spices. Stir in the lime peel and salt.

3 To make the curry, heat the oil in a wok or large, heavy skillet. Cook the bean curd over a high heat for 2 minutes to seal. Stir in the curry paste and beans. Add the rice and stir over a high heat for about 3 minutes.

4 Transfer to a warmed serving dish. Sprinkle with the deep-fried shallots, scallion, and peanuts. Squeeze the lime juice over.

Chatuchak Fried Rice

An excellent way to use up leftover rice. Put the in the freezer as soon as it is cool, and it will be ready to reheat at any time.

NUTRITIONAL INFORMATION

Calories	241	Sugars	5g	
Protein	7g	Fat	5g	
Carbohydrate	46g	Saturates		1g

 25 MINS   15 MINS

SERVES 4

INGREDIENTS

1 tbsp sunflower oil

3 shallots, chopped finely

2 garlic cloves, crushed

1 red chili, seeded and chopped finely

1-inch piece gingerroot, shredded finely

½ green bell pepper, seeded and
   sliced finely

2-3 baby eggplants, quartered

3 oz sugar snap peas or snow peas,
   trimmed and blanched

6 baby corn-on-the-cobs, halved
   lengthways and blanched

1 tomato, cut into 8 pieces

1½ cups beansprouts

3 cups cooked jasmine rice

2 tbsp tomato ketchup

2 tbsp light soy sauce

TO GARNISH

fresh cilantro leaves

lime wedges

1 Heat the sunflower oil in a wok or large, heavy skillet over a high heat.

2 Add the shallots, garlic, chili, and ginger to the wok or skillet. Stir until the shallots have softened.

3 Add the green bell pepper and baby eggplants and stir well.

4 Add the sugar snap peas or snow peas, baby corn-on-the-cobs, tomato, and beansprouts. Stir-fry for 3 minutes.

5 Add the cooked jasmine rice to the wok, and lift and stir with two spoons for 4–5 minutes, until no more steam is released.

6 Stir the tomato catsup and soy sauce into the mixture in the wok.

7 Serve the Chatuchak fried rice immediately, garnished with cilantro leaves and lime wedges to squeeze over.

Fried Rice in Pineapple

This looks very impressive on a party buffet. Mix the remaining pineapple flesh with papaya and mango for an exotic fruit salad.

NUTRITIONAL INFORMATION

Calories	197	Sugars	8g
Protein	5g	Fat	8g
Carbohydrate	29g	Saturates	1g

 20 MINS   10 MINS

SERVES 4

INGREDIENTS

1 large pineapple

1 tbsp sunflower oil

1 garlic clove, crushed

1 small onion, diced

½ celery stick, sliced

1 tsp coriander seeds, ground

1 tsp cumin seeds, ground

1½ cups button mushrooms, sliced

1⅓ cups cooked rice

2 tbsp light soy sauce

½ tsp sugar

½ tsp salt

¼ cup cashew nuts

TO GARNISH

1 scallion, sliced finely

fresh cilantro leaves

mint sprig

1 Using a sharp knife, halve the pineapple lengthways, and cut out the flesh to make 2 boat-shaped shells.

2 Cut the flesh into cubes and reserve 1 cup to use in this recipe. (Any remaining pineapple cubes can be served separately.)

3 Heat the sunflower oil in a wok or large, heavy skillet.

4 Cook the garlic, onion, and celery over a high heat, stirring constantly, for 2 minutes. Stir in the coriander and cumin seeds, and the mushrooms.

5 Add the reserved pineapple cubes and cooked rice to the wok or skillet and stir well.

6 Stir in the soy sauce, sugar, salt, and cashew nuts.

7 Using 2 spoons, lift and stir the rice for about 4 minutes until it is thoroughly heated.

8 Spoon the rice mixture into the pineapple boats. Garnish with sliced scallion, cilantro leaves, and a mint sprig.

Chinese Chicken Rice

This is a really colorful main meal or side dish that tastes just as good as it looks.

NUTRITIONAL INFORMATION

Calories	324	Sugars	4g	
Protein	24g	Fat	10g	
Carbohydrate	37g	Saturates	2g	

5 MINS   25 MINS

SERVES 4

INGREDIENTS

1¾ cups long-grain white rice

1 tsp turmeric

2 tbsp sunflower oil

2½ cups skinless, boneless chicken breasts or thighs, sliced

1 red bell pepper, seeded and sliced

1 green bell pepper, seeded and sliced

1 green chili, seeded and finely chopped

1 medium carrot, coarsely grated

1½ cups beansprouts

6 scallions, sliced, plus extra to garnish

2 tbsp soy sauce

salt

1 Place the rice and turmeric in a large saucepan of lightly salted water and cook until the grains of rice are just tender, about 10 minutes. Drain the rice thoroughly and press out any excess water with paper towels.

2 Heat the sunflower oil in a large preheated wok or skillet.

3 Add the strips of chicken to the wok or skillet and stir-fry over a high heat until the chicken is just beginning to turn a golden color.

4 Add the sliced bell peppers and green chili to the wok and stir-fry for 2–3 minutes.

5 Add the cooked rice to the wok, a little at a time, tossing well after each addition until well combined and the grains of rice are separated.

6 Add the carrot, beansprouts, and scallions to the wok and stir-fry for a further 2 minutes.

7 Drizzle with the soy sauce and toss to combine.

8 Transfer the Chinese chicken rice to a warm serving dish, garnish with extra scallions, if wished, and serve at once.

Fruity Coconut Rice

A pale yellow rice flavored with coconut and spices to serve as an accompaniment – or as a main dish with added diced chicken or pork.

NUTRITIONAL INFORMATION

Calories	578	Sugars	17g
Protein	8g	Fat	31g
Carbohydrate	71g	Saturates	15g

5 MINS   35 MINS

SERVES 4

INGREDIENTS

3 oz creamed coconut

3 cups boiling water

1 tbsp sunflower oil (or olive oil for a strong flavor)

1 onion, thinly sliced or chopped

generous 1 cup long-grain rice

¼ tsp turmeric

6 whole cloves

1 cinnamon stick

½ tsp salt

½ cup raisins or sultanas

½ cup walnut or pecan halves, roughly chopped

2 tbsp pumpkin seeds (optional)

1 Blend the creamed coconut with half the boiling water until smooth, then stir in the remainder until well blended.

2 Heat the oil in a preheated wok, add the onion, and stir-fry gently for 3-4 minutes until the onion begins to soften.

3 Rinse the rice thoroughly under cold running water, drain well, and add to the wok with the turmeric. Cook for 1-2 minutes, stirring all the time.

4 Add the coconut milk, cloves, cinnamon stick, and salt and bring to a boil. Cover and simmer very gently for 10 minutes.

5 Add the raisins, nuts, and pumpkin seeds, if using, and mix well. Cover the wok again and continue to cook for a further 5-8 minutes, or until all the liquid has been absorbed and the rice is tender. Remove from the heat and leave to stand, still tightly covered, for 5 minutes. Remove the cinnamon stick and serve.

COOK'S TIP

Add 2 cups cooked chicken or pork cut into dice or thin slivers with the raisins to turn this into a main dish. The addition of coconut milk makes the cooked rice slightly sticky.

Green-Fried Rice

Spinach is used in this recipe to give the rice a wonderful green coloring. Tossed with the carrot strips, it is a really appealing dish.

NUTRITIONAL INFORMATION

Calories	139	Sugars	2g
Protein	3g	Fat	7g
Carbohydrate	18g	Saturates	1g

 5 MINS   20 MINS

SERVES 4

I N G R E D I E N T S

⅔ cup long-grain rice

2 tbsp vegetable oil

2 garlic cloves, crushed

1 tsp grated fresh gingerroot

1 carrot, cut into matchsticks

1 zucchini, diced

8 oz baby spinach

2 tsp light soy sauce

2 tsp light brown sugar

1 Cook the rice in a saucepan of boiling water for about 15 minutes. Drain the rice well, rinse under cold running water and then rinse the rice thoroughly again. Set aside until required.

2 Heat the vegetable oil in a preheated wok or large, heavy-based skillet.

3 Add the crushed garlic and grated fresh gingerroot to the wok or skillet and stir-fry for about 30 seconds.

4 Add the carrot matchsticks and diced zucchini to the mixture in the wok and stir-fry for about 2 minutes, so the vegetables still retain their crunch.

5 Add the baby spinach and stir-fry for 1 minute, until wilted.

6 Add the rice, soy sauce, and sugar to the wok and mix together well.

7 Transfer the green-fried rice to serving dishes and serve immediately.

COOK'S TIP

Light soy sauce has more flavor than the sweeter, dark soy sauce, which gives the food a rich, reddish color.

Chinese Vegetable Rice

This rice can either be served as a meal in itself or as an accompaniment to other vegetable recipes.

NUTRITIONAL INFORMATION

Calories	228	Sugars	5g	
Protein	5g	Fat	7g	
Carbohydrate	37g	Saturates		1g

5 MINS   25 MINS

SERVES 4

INGREDIENTS

1¾ cups long-grain white rice

1 tsp turmeric

2 tbsp sunflower oil

1½ cups zucchini, sliced

1 red bell pepper, seeded and sliced

1 green bell pepper, seeded and sliced

1 green chili, seeded and finely chopped

1 medium carrot, coarsley grated

1½ cups beansprouts

6 scallions, sliced, plus extra to garnish (optional)

2 tbsp soy sauce

salt

1 Place the rice and turmeric in a pan of lightly salted water and bring to a boil. Reduce the heat and leave to simmer until the rice is just tender. Drain the rice thoroughly and press out any excess water with a sheet of paper towels. Set aside until required.

2 Heat the sunflower oil in a large preheated wok.

3 Add the zucchini to the wok and stir-fry for about 2 minutes.

4 Add the bell peppers and chili to the wok and stir-fry for 2–3 minutes.

5 Add the cooked rice to the mixture in the wok, a little at a time, tossing well after each addition.

6 Add the carrots, beansprouts, and scallions to the wok and stir-fry for a further 2 minutes.

7 Drizzle with soy sauce and serve at once, garnished with extra scallions, if desired.

COOK'S TIP

For real luxury, add a few saffron strands infused in boiling water instead of the turmeric.

Hot & Spicy Chicken Rice

Chicken is cooked with rice and vegetables and flavored with red curry paste, ginger, coriander, and lime for a deliciously spicy dish.

NUTRITIONAL INFORMATION

Calories	350	Sugars 2g	
Protein	26g	Fat	16g
Carbohydrate	27g	Saturates	3g

10 MINS   30 MINS

SERVES 4

INGREDIENTS

generous 1 cup white long-grain rice

4 tbsp vegetable oil

2 garlic cloves, chopped finely

6 shallots, sliced finely

1 red bell pepper, seeded and diced

1 cup green beans, cut into 1-inch pieces

1 tbsp red curry paste

2½ cups cooked skinless, boneless chicken, chopped

½ tsp ground coriander seeds

1 tsp finely grated fresh gingerroot

2 tbsp fish sauce

finely grated peel of 1 lime

3 tbsp lime juice

1 tbsp chopped fresh cilantro

salt and pepper

TO GARNISH

lime wedges

sprigs of fresh cilantro

1 Cook the rice in plenty of boiling, lightly salted water for 12–15 minutes until tender. Drain, rinse in cold water, and drain thoroughly.

2 Heat the vegetable oil in a large preheated wok or skillet.

3 Add the garlic and shallots to the wok or skillet and fry gently for 2–3 minutes until golden.

4 Add the bell pepper and green beans and stir-fry for 2 minutes. Add the red curry paste and stir-fry for 1 minute.

5 Add the cooked rice to the wok or skillet, then add the cooked chicken, ground coriander seeds, ginger, fish sauce, lime peel and juice, and fresh cilantro.

6 Stir-fry the mixture in the wok over a medium-high heat for about 4–5 minutes until the rice and chicken are thoroughly reheated. Season to taste.

7 Transfer the chicken and rice mixture to a warm serving dish, garnish with lime wedges and fresh cilantro, and serve immediately.

Green Rice

The rice used in this recipe gets its color from the cilantro and mint that infuses the rice, giving it a distinctive aroma.

NUTRITIONAL INFORMATION

Calories	582	Sugars	11g
Protein	15g	Fat	12g
Carbohydrate	110g	Saturates	4g

45 MINS   20 MINS

SERVES 4

I N G R E D I E N T S

2 tbsp olive oil

2¼ cups basmati rice, soaked for 1 hour, washed and drained

3 cups coconut milk

1 tsp salt

1 bay leaf

2 tbsp chopped fresh cilantro

2 tbsp chopped fresh mint

2 green chilies, seeded and chopped finely

1 Heat the olive oil in a saucepan.

2 Add the basmati rice to the saucepan and stir with a wooden spatula until the rice becomes translucent.

3 Add the coconut milk, salt, and bay leaf. Bring to a boil and cook until all the liquid is absorbed.

4 Lower the heat as much as possible, cover the saucepan tightly and cook for 10 minutes.

5 Remove the bay leaf and stir in the cilantro, mint, and chopped green chilies. Fork through the rice gently and serve.

COOK'S TIP

Two segments of fresh lime make an attractive garnish for this dish and complement the cilantro perfectly.

Rice with Five-Spice Chicken

This dish has a wonderful color from the turmeric and a great spicy flavor, making it very appealing all around.

NUTRITIONAL INFORMATION

Calories	412	Sugars	1g
Protein	23g	Fat	13g
Carbohydrate	53g	Saturates	2g

5 MINS   20 MINS

SERVES 4

INGREDIENTS

1 tbsp Chinese five-spice powder

2 tbsp cornstarch

2½ cups boneless, skinless chicken breasts, cubed

3 tbsp peanut oil

1 onion, diced

1 cup long-grain white rice

½ tsp turmeric

2½ cups chicken stock

2 tbsp snipped fresh chives

1 Place the Chinese five-spice powder and cornstarch in a large bowl. Add the chicken pieces and toss to coat all over.

COOK'S TIP

Be careful when using turmeric because it can stain the hands and clothes a distinctive shade of yellow.

2 Heat 2 tablespoons of the peanut oil in a large preheated wok. Add the chicken pieces to the wok and stir-fry for 5 minutes. Using a draining spoon, remove the chicken and set aside.

3 Add the remaining peanut oil to the wok.

4 Add the onion to the wok and stir-fry for 1 minute.

5 Add the rice, turmeric, and chicken stock to the wok and gently bring to a boil.

6 Return the chicken pieces to the wok, reduce the heat, and leave to simmer for 10 minutes, or until the liquid has been absorbed and the rice is tender.

7 Add the snipped fresh chives, stir to mix, and serve hot.

Rice with Crab & Mussels

Shellfish makes an ideal partner for rice. Mussels and crab add flavor and texture to this spicy dish.

NUTRITIONAL INFORMATION

Calories	336	Sugars 4g	
Protein	32g	Fat	10g
Carbohydrate	33g	Saturates	1g

20 MINS   10 MINS

SERVES 4

INGREDIENTS

1½ cups long-grain rice

6 oz white crabmeat, fresh, canned or frozen (defrosted if frozen), or 8 crab sticks, defrosted if frozen

2 tbsp sesame or sunflower oil

1 inch piece ginger root, grated

4 scallions, thinly sliced diagonally

1 cup snow peas, cut into 2-3 pieces

½ tsp turmeric

1 tsp ground cumin

2 x 7 oz jars mussels, well drained, or 12 oz frozen mussels, defrosted

15 oz canned beansprouts, well drained

salt and pepper

1 Cook the rice in boiling salted water, following the instructions given on page 244.

2 Extract the crabmeat, if using fresh crab (see right). Flake the crabmeat or cut the crab sticks into 3 or 4 pieces.

3 Heat the oil in a preheated wok and stir-fry the ginger and scallions for a minute or so. Add the snow peas and continue to cook for a further minute.

Sprinkle the turmeric, cumin, and seasoning over the vegetables and mix well.

4 Add the crabmeat and mussels and stir-fry for 1 minute. Stir in the cooked rice and beansprouts and stir-fry for 2 minutes or until hot and well mixed.

5 Adjust the seasoning to taste and serve immediately.

COOK'S TIP

To prepare fresh crab, twist off the claws and legs, crack with a heavy knife and pick out the meat with a skewer. Discard the gills and pull out the under shell; discard the stomach sac. Pull the soft meat from the shell. Cut open the body section and prise out the meat with a skewer.

Egg Fu-Yung with Rice

In this dish, cooked rice is mixed with scrambled eggs and Chinese vegetables. It is a great way of using up leftover cooked rice.

NUTRITIONAL INFORMATION

Calories	258	Sugars 1g
Protein	8g	Fat 16g
Carbohydrate	21g	Saturates 3g

30 MINS   25 MINS

SERVES 4

INGREDIENTS

generous ¾ cup long-grain rice

2 Chinese dried mushrooms
(if unavailable, use thinly sliced
open-cap mushrooms)

3 eggs, beaten

3 tbsp vegetable oil

4 scallions, sliced

½ green bell pepper, chopped

⅓ cup canned bamboo shoots

⅓ cup canned water chestnuts, sliced

2 cups beansprouts

2 tbsp light soy sauce

2 tbsp dry sherry

2 tsp sesame oil

salt and pepper

1 Cook the rice in lightly salted boiling water according to the package directions.

2 Place the Chinese dried mushrooms in a small bowl, cover with warm water, and leave to soak for about 20–25 minutes.

3 Mix the beaten eggs with a little salt. Heat 1 tablespoon of the oil in a preheated wok or large skillet. Add the eggs and stir until just set; remove and set aside.

4 Drain the mushrooms and squeeze out the excess water. Remove the tough centers and chop the mushrooms.

5 Heat the remaining oil in a clean wok or skillet. Add the mushrooms, scallions, and green bell pepper, and stir-fry for 2 minutes. Add the bamboo shoots, water chestnuts, and beansprouts, and stir-fry for 1 minute.

6 Drain the rice thoroughly and add to the pan with the remaining ingredients. Mix well, heating the rice thoroughly. Season to taste with salt and pepper. Stir in the reserved eggs and serve.

COOK'S TIP

To wash beansprouts, place them in a bowl of cold water and swirl with your hand. Remove any long tail ends, then rinse and drain thoroughly.

Stir-Fried Rice with Sausage

This is a very quick rice dish as it uses cooked rice. It is therefore ideal when time is short or for a speedy lunch-time dish.

NUTRITIONAL INFORMATION

Calories	383	Sugars	9g
Protein	19g	Fat	17g
Carbohydrate	42g	Saturates	4g

5 MINS   20 MINS

SERVES 4

INGREDIENTS

12 oz Chinese sausage

2 tbsp sunflower oil

2 tbsp soy sauce

1 onion, sliced

1 cup carrots, cut into thin sticks

1¼ cups peas

¾ cup canned pineapple cubes, drained

4¾ cups cooked long-grain rice

1 egg, beaten

1 tbsp chopped fresh parsley

1 Using a sharp knife, thinly slice the Chinese sausage.

2 Heat the sunflower oil in a large preheated wok. Add the sausage to the wok and stir-fry for 5 minutes.

3 Stir in the soy sauce and allow to bubble for about 2–3 minutes, or until syrupy.

4 Add the onion, carrots, peas, and pineapple to the wok and stir-fry for a further 3 minutes.

5 Add the cooked rice to the wok and stir-fry the mixture for about 2–3 minutes, or until the rice is completely heated through.

6 Drizzle the beaten egg over the top of the rice and cook, tossing the ingredients in the wok, until the egg sets.

7 Transfer the stir-fried rice to a large, warm serving bowl and scatter with plenty of chopped fresh parsley. Serve immediately.

COOK'S TIP

Cook extra rice and freeze it in prepration for some of the other rice dishes included in this book to save time, enabling a meal to be prepared in minutes. Be sure to cool any leftover cooked rice quickly before freezing to avoid food poisoning.

Index